UPSIDE D

Upside Down

DAVID PYTCHES

KINGSWAY PUBLICATIONS
EASTBOURNE

ISBN 978–1–84291–345–1

01 02 03 04 05 06 Printing/Year 10 09 08 07

KINGSWAY COMMUNICATIONS LTD
Lottbridge Drove, Eastbourne BN23 6NT, England.
Email: books@kingsway.co.uk

Printed in the USA

Contents

Dedication

This book is dedicated to Richard and Prue Bedwell. They joined us on the staff at St Andrew's, Chorley-wood, where they continued to serve faithfully and fruitfully for the next 15 years. They were with us from the first visit of John Wimber and his team in 1981 – a visit that unexpectedly launched St Andrew's into a whole new pro-gramme of equipping the saints for the work of the min-istry, which led into the New Wine and Soul Survivor conferences.

When Mary and I began to get requests to travel further afield both in the UK and overseas (requests that have sur-prisingly continued to this day), I could never have coped if Richard had not undertaken to oversee these for me. Cor-respondence, accommodation, programmes, timetables, transport, tickets, books and literature – you name it, he just got on with it in his usual thorough and efficient way.

They were also ready to drive us anywhere in just about anything, to share in leading workshops and to cope with a whole lot of backstage arrangements – right down to ensur-ing cups of cold water on the platform and lozenges for the throat, and prayer for those who requested it.

They were utterly dedicated to the Lord and to the

programme, absolutely dependable and loyal, always ready to sacrifice and serve, and really good friends into the bargain. Richard and Prue, after 25 years of working and holidaying together, we salute you for all you do, not only for us but for so many, many others, and we thank God for all your help and encouragement.

May God continue to bless you both.

Acknowledgements

I want to thank Simon Ponsonby, Bob Hubbard, Prue Bedwell and Charlotte Cocksworth, who have read all or parts of this book, kindly helping in differing ways with suggestions, corrections and encouragement. And especially Peggy Knight, who has helped me so much with her eagle eye and encyclopaedic knowledge, and for her 'editing'. May she forgive me for all the sneaky insertions that may have been slipped in after all her patient, constructive and dedicated work. I thank my son-in-law John Wright also for suggesting the title.

Finally, I am hugely grateful to Carolyn Owen at Kingsway and Bryony Benier, for their patient editing and for tidying up the final manuscript.

We have made every effort to acknowledge the source of any reproduced material in this book and apologise for any we have not been able to trace. We would be grateful if those who may have been troubled by such omissions would make contact with the publishers, and we will endeavour to make a full acknowledgement in any future edition.

We are most grateful to CWR, the publishers of Selwyn Hughes' *My Story*, for their kind permission to use some very pertinent quotes.

Introduction

The focus of this book is on the stunning teaching of Jesus that prefaced his first detailed sermon. His words were addressed to the leaders of the future church that he was building as an agency for extending the good news of his kingdom. Some have called the Beatitudes 'blessed attitudes'. Such attitudes create great character. To many they contrast paradoxically with the accommodating attitudes of the world surrounding us.

Most teachers comment on the implications of these Beatitudes in a more cerebral mode (which approach we must never undervalue), whereas the manner here is more visceral. This may mean that occasionally a connection is made with a revealing personal illustration which does not always convey a clearly logical sequence. The intention is to help those who struggle with a very rational approach; those who would find it easier to reflect on common life situations. Hopefully the appeal here is more for those who prefer word pictures rather than word processes, parables rather than paraphrases, practices rather than theories – engaging the heart more than the head.

In most books illustrations are used to clarify the teaching. Here the illustrations themselves are intended to do most of the teaching. The stories include a variety of accounts and reports picked up by the author throughout the years, from Bible reading, commentaries, history, biographies, travels and the media. Biblical references are incorporated in the text, and footnotes for other sources are easily accessible at the bottom of the relevant page.

Hopefully the substance of the Beatitudes is also presented here with a devotional slant – in such a way that 'ordinary folk' will find it useful for meditation. I count myself among such 'ordinary folk', and since this approach helps me, I have assumed it will, at least, help a few others too.

The selecting and arranging of such material has been a fascinating and delightful exercise. My prayer is that the reader will find equal pleasure and edification in reflecting upon what is written here. The fact that I have tried to make the understanding of the Beatitudes a little easier does not imply that the practical application will be easier also – sometimes it may be difficult, and sometimes it will take a lifetime of struggle. Clearly the Beatitudes are very challenging.

THE UPSIDE-DOWN KINGDOM

I was brought up on the old King James Version of the Bible, and was always struck by the words there of the leading Jews in Thessalonica opposed to the missionary work of Paul. They arrested some of the early Christians and brought them before the city officials, complaining, *'These . . . have turned the world upside down' (Acts 17:6b KJV)*. The teaching of Christ on the Beatitudes has been ingeniously termed a 'divine conspiracy'.[1] Many of the Jewish leaders quickly discerned this and it made them feel threatened personally, culturally, politically and religiously. Modern versions translate the Greek here in a slightly different way, interpreting it as '. . . *caused trouble all over the world'* (NIV).

The apostles took this revolutionary message of the kingdom of heaven and kingdom character out into the wider world, and continued to challenge basic human assumptions about personal life, society and religion. If 'upside down' is not literally in the original biblical text, it was effectively present in the practical intention. That is what makes it all so startling – when it is seriously confronted. I cannot forget the words of Mahatma Gandhi, who remarked to a group of missionaries, 'You Christians look after a document containing enough dynamite to blow all civilisation to pieces, turn the world upside down and bring peace to a battle-torn planet. But you treat it as though it is nothing more than a piece of literature.'

ATTITUDES

Jesus gives us these eight Beatitudes as an introduction to his famous Sermon on the Mount in Matthew's Gospel. A glance at Luke's Gospel *(Luke 6:20–49)* shows that he also preached much the same sermon on 'the Plain'. However, with subject matter as fundamental as this, it would be no surprise to find Jesus preaching about it – or parts of it – over and over again wherever he travelled around the country. It

---

[1] Dallas Willard's title for his book on the Sermon on the Mount (HarperCollins, 1998).

was vital that the apostles understood all that he was saying, and could begin reforming their attitudes and reshaping their lives in line with the Beatitudes, before they were sent off to preach the good news across the land and beyond.

An attitude is 'a settled mode of thinking'. To change our attitudes usually requires 'a paradigm shift' (to use Wimber jargon). The Greek for this is *metanoia*, which simply means 'repent' – a word Jesus used frequently. It meant 'to change one's mind'. One prominent politician was asked how he could account for taking a senior position in an institution whose establishment he had campaigned against in an earlier generation. He replied, 'When I realise I am in the wrong, I admit it and change my mind. What do you do?'

Attitudes have a powerful influence on our spiritual, mental and emotional life. Right attitudes affect personal health beneficially. Many cancer sufferers have testified to this even resulting in their healing. Attitudes affect the physical body in other ways also. This is exemplified by the story of a missionary to the Philippines, who related how (in the Second World War) he and his wife were rounded up by the Japanese to be sent to a prisoner-of-war camp. They were told they could take with them only as much food and clothing as they could carry from their home. The missionary's wife weighed just 100 pounds, yet she managed to carry a 200-pound load, consisting mostly of tinned food – 'a load that neither of them could lift again after they had arrived at their destination'.[2]

Normally the body uses about an eighth of its physical reserves, but extra strength may be brought into play by our

---

[2] Selwyn Hughes, *Every Day With Jesus* (CWR, 3rd July 2006).

attitudes – they tap the hidden physical resources of the body. Attitudes are our motivators. They create our identity, our new mindset – our approach to our work and our relationships, to every situation and difficulty.

Clearly Jesus was not teaching a creed here, but rather touching on attitudes that could change the world – something which in later years has been too often overlooked by the church. It is timely today to look again at these attitudes for fresh inspiration as they draw us back to the real basics of Jesus' teaching.

Henri Nouwen comments on the Sermon on the Mount by saying,

> This most famous, thought-provoking sermon ever recorded offers us both a self-portrait of Jesus and an example of the Christian lifestyle that He expected of His disciples. As we keep that before our eyes, we will soon learn what it means to follow Jesus and become like Him.[3]

Another writer thinks 'it is significant that the history of the first century church is called the book of Acts, not the book of truths'.[4] Philip Yancey says almost the same thing as Nouwen:

> The more I study Jesus, the more I realize that the statements contained here (in the Sermon on the Mount) lie at the heart of His message. If I fail to understand this teaching, I fail to understand Him.[5]

---

[3] Henri Nouwen, *Bread for the Journey* (HarperSanFrancisco, 1997).

[4] Erwin Raphael McManus, *An Unstoppable Force* (Group Publishing, 2001), p. 72.

[5] Philip Yancey, *The Jesus I Never Knew* (Zondervan, 1995).

ETHICAL TEACHING

The question is, 'Has the church ever taken this ethical side of the faith seriously enough?' Did the faith become too formal and doctrinaire? Certainly history records Antony escaping into the Egyptian desert (AD 269), the first Christian monk, seeking a more self-denying lifestyle as a witness against the increasing worldliness of the church. Sadly his challenge made little immediate difference.

E. Stanley Jones says,

> With emphasis on doctrines, which left unaffected our way of life, the Christian Church could accept the Emperor Constantine as its prize convert, even though Constantine [after his alleged conversion] murdered his conquered colleague and brother-in-law Lucinius; sentenced to death his eleven-year-old nephew, killed his eldest son Crispus; brought about the death of his second wife; took the nails that were supposed to come from the cross of Christ, and used one in his war-helmet and another on the bridle of his warhorse.[6]

Was such knowledge about him in the public arena? If so, it was extraordinary that the Roman emperor, who confessed to having had a celestial vision in AD 312, was canonised and his memory celebrated 'as equal to the apostles'. He both addressed and presided at the opening of the Council of Nicea (AD 325). This had been called to deal with the heresy of Arianism (a teaching that denied the co-eternity of Christ with God the Father), a heresy tending to split the church. The council framed what was known as the Creed of Nicea, still regarded as the orthodox teaching of the

---

[6] E. Stanley Jones, *Christ of the Mount* (Hodder & Stoughton, 1931), p. 12.

church today. Constantine was also hailed as 'a bishop of the bishops'. Could this title have been given him if the church leaders who had gathered for the council still regarded the Beatitudes as lifestyle markers of Christ and his disciples?

If Constantine could yet feel at ease among such men, could these Christian ideals have still possessed the soul of the church?

THE TRUE FOUNDATION FOR LIFE IN GOD'S KINGDOM

The Sermon on the Mount provides the ethical foundation of God's kingdom of righteousness *(Matthew 6:33)*. Those who follow this way bring light to overcome darkness, salt to inhibit corruption and yeast to change a 'crooked and perverse' society for good. Dean Inge once wrote,

> If Christianity cannot hold us at the place of ethical conduct – if it loses the battle at that place, then what is left is not worth fighting over. For, mind you, if the ethical side of our Gospel is unworkable, then by that very fact, the redemptive side is rendered worthless. The centre and substance of the Christian's ethical conduct are plainly revealed in the Sermon on the Mount.[7]

And William Law,

> Is it not therefore exceeding strange that people should place so much piety in the attendance of public worship, concerning which there is not one precept of our Lord to be found, and yet

___

[7] I cannot discover my original source for this, but am confident that it was a quote from Dean Inge.

neglect these common duties of our ordinary life, which are commanded in every page of the Gospel?[8]

BENEFICIAL IMPACT

An example of the beneficial effects upon English society, where and when the teaching of Christ was taken seriously, can be classically observed in the nineteenth century – the fruits of the Wesleyan revival of the previous century. The historian William E. H. Lecky, although himself a free-thinker, credited the Evangelical Revival with bringing about

> a great moral revolution in England: it planted fervid and enduring religious sentiment in the midst of the most brutal, and most neglected portions of the population, and whatever may have been its defects it undoubtedly . . . imparted . . . a greater energy to the philanthropy of every denomination, both in England and the colonies.

David Thomson writes of the moral conscience of Britain during the same period, and says that

> the most practised form of Christianity at the time was that which was broadly described as evangelicalism, with its emphasis on moral conduct as the test of the good Christian. In this sense it transcended all barriers of a religious sect, and marked the religious outlook of a Quaker like Bright and a High Churchman like Gladstone, a Low Church Tory like Shaftesbury and a Presbyterian like Livingstone. It even coloured the outlook of an agnostic like T. H. Huxley, and a

---

[8] William Law, *A Serious Call to a Devout and Holy Life* (Dent & Sons Ltd, 1728), p.6.

man like Disraeli who, although of the Jewish race, was a practising Christian. Its basis was biblical: its business was ethical. It
was a proud period when the so-called 'non-conformist conscience' was beneficially permeating English life and manners.
But gradually all this was weakened by the growth of free
thinking and rational movements. . .[9]

The enemy, however, always has his ways of counteracting
the things of God *(Ephesians 6:12)*.

One commentator on the Beatitudes has suggested that
we could understand them better by restating them in the
negative, and spelling out the opposite conditions. Some,
Jesus implied, will not be blessed. Their condition could be
described as follows:

Wretched are the spiritually self-sufficient, for theirs is the kingdom of hell.

Wretched are those who deny the tragedy of their sinfulness,
for they will be troubled.

Wretched are the self-centred, for they will be empty.

Wretched are those who ceaselessly justify themselves, for
their efforts will be in vain.

Wretched are the merciless, for no mercy will be shown to
them.

Wretched are those with impure hearts, for they will not see
God.

Wretched are those who reject peace, for they will earn the
title 'sons of Satan'.

Wretched are the uncommitted for convenience's sake, for
their destination is hell.[10]

---

[9] David Thomson, *England in the Nineteenth Century* (Penguin
Books, 1950).

[10] *Life Application Bible Commentary, Matthew* (Tyndale House,
1996), p. 76.

A BOOK FOR REFLECTION

This book is written to help people reflect on their own spiritual health. Some prefer to examine their lives thoroughly and systematically during set times such as Lent; others in their own time. In either case a book of this kind may help us to do some wholesome heart-searching, as we seek to follow the Spirit of God leading us forward in our daily pilgrimage. Profitable reflection on these 'attitudes' could also be shared or discussed in a church cell or a home group of some kind.

These Beatitudes are the highway code for the Christian life. There is a 'beyondness' here that startles and appals the mind. They are by no means multiple choice (select one and forget the rest) – they must be taken as a whole. They are not eight articles of law to get us from earth to heaven, but eight attitudes which will bring heaven down to earth.

A WORD ABOUT 'BLESSED'

I am not qualified to argue the case for linguistic nuances over the interpretation of certain words. But I do admit to having some gut feelings about whether Jesus intended the word 'blessed' or 'happy' to apply to those who have taken the Beatitudes seriously. Different translators have recently opted for an updated interpretation of the rich Greek word *makarios*. The word 'blessed' (that prefixes each beatitude) carries the meaning of being 'singularly favoured' and 'graciously approved of'. Many of the newer versions of the Bible, in seeking to be relevant, prefer the word 'happy' in place of 'blessed', and there is obviously some legitimacy in this, but a serious limitation too.

Such modern Bible translators and paraphrasers may well be right in seeking to find words which are apparently less old fashioned, but by replacing 'blessed' with a more familiar word such as 'happy' we may be exchanging a greater for a lesser. Happiness is undeniably a blessing, but suggests a temporal state of delight and contentment; blessing, on the other hand, suggests an eternal state that is conferred upon us, whether or not the feelings are enduring. 'Blessings' do not exclude happy surprises of delight and ephemeral sensations of bliss, but they clearly do express the impartation of both a present and an eternal asset. Besides, blessing comes from the greater to the lesser, from God to man – a dimension I would be sorry to see overlooked.

But is the word 'blessed' too antiquated for today? I find it fascinating that Matt and Beth Redman have recently published a book directed at today's young people called *Blessed Be Your Name*,[11] a title taken from their own very popular song of the same title. I do not think that Matt Redman would have become one of the most favourite songwriters among the Christian youth in our world today if he was using irrelevant language that was considered out of date!

God's 'blessing' is 'a divine favour' truly desirable and positively obtainable. *'I will not let you go unless you bless me'* *(Genesis 32:26b)*, cried Jacob, to whom being 'blessed' was so vital and enduring that he earlier even deceived his father and brother in order to get it. It may not be instantly

---

[11] Matt and Beth Redman, *Blessed Be Your Name* (Regal Books, 2005), p. 14.

quantifiable, but in review it is measurable by tracing the good hand of God back through one's life. It is important not to lose sight of the Lord's sovereignty in all this. God is pleased when he sees his subjects trying to please him. And the more God is pleased, like any father, the more he grants us his sovereign favour – his blessing.

The Greek word for 'blessed' is *makarios*. This was an early name for the Mediterranean island of Cyprus, which seemed to have had everything the heart could desire. The Cypriots were highly favoured with their island, enjoying secure shelter from high winds, rocky and commanding protection from enemy marauders, proximity to the mainland for emergencies, fish-filled sea, mountain scenery, favourable climate, colourful flowers and luscious fruit, meat and milk – what more could anyone ask for? The islanders were blessed indeed: *'The blessing of the Lord brings wealth, and he adds no trouble to it' (Proverbs 10:22)*. There was evidently a considerable feel-good factor about being in Cyprus in those early times.

As we seek to work out these attitudes in a myriad of practical ways, we shall share that kind of blessing too, knowing periods of happiness, bliss and contentment, and sensing ourselves to be highly favoured and fortunate – yes, continuously and assuredly 'blessed' indeed, as Jesus knew we would be. So 'blessed' is the word we choose to use throughout this book as we reflect on each of these highly challenging Beatitudes.

> *Blessed are all who fear the Lord,*
> *who walk in his ways.*
> *You will eat the fruit of your labour;*
> *blessings and prosperity will be yours.*

Your wife will be like a fruitful vine
  within your house;
your sons will be like olive shoots
  round your table.
Thus is the man blessed
  who fears the Lord.
May the Lord bless you from Zion
  all the days of your life;
may you see the prosperity of Jerusalem,
  and may you live to see your children's children.
(Psalm 128)

CONCLUSION

As a young man I was inspired by the martyrdom of Captain Allen Gardiner. He was the founder of the South American Missionary Society (SAMS), under whose banner Mary and I served for 17 years in Chile – although when it was first founded in 1844 SAMS was called the Patagonian Missionary Society. This intrepid sailor made many false starts at mission work, and on his final venture in Tierra del Fuego, he and his six-man party met yet further and final disaster in their attempt in 1851 to reach the hitherto unreached Fueginos (made up of about four different Indian tribes). All the men died tragically of starvation and exposure. Their emaciated remains were eventually discovered. The body of their leader, Gardiner, was found in the shelter of his battered boat. He had been the last of the party to die. Many pages of his journal were picked up from where they had been wind-strewn across those desolate shores. His final entry for the 5th September 1851 read,

'Great and marvellous are the loving kindnesses of my gracious God unto me. He has preserved me hitherto for four days without any bodily food, without any feelings of hunger or thirst.' Such was the heroism that inspired my generation and no doubt would still inspire today's! From such people I have taken many of my stories for this book.

The place where their remains were found was map-marked as Spaniard Harbour. It was bathed in biting icy waters and bounded by cruel gale-blasted rocks. As a well-trained naval officer, Allen Gardiner had left a message painted in white on the rocks at an even more exposed site where he would have been expected to be rescued. The sign, directing any later search party looking for him, said, 'Dig Below.' And below, in a bottle buried in the sand, was a brief note directing the 'digger'. It read, 'Gone to Spaniard Harbour.'

In this book, I like to think that I have been trying to 'dig below' a bit, to find out how to 'rise above'. My hope is that readers will be able to pick up some encouragement and get fired up by the Holy Spirit from these 'diggings' to help them in pressing on *towards the goal to win the prize for which God has called [us] heavenwards in Christ Jesus' (Philippians 3:13c).*

1

Dark Nights of the Soul

Blessed are the poor in spirit, for theirs is the kingdom of heaven.
(Matthew 5:3)

Why, O Lord, do you stand far off?
   Why do you hide yourself in times of trouble?
(Psalm 10:1)

* * *

My God, my God, why have you forsaken me?
   Why are you so far from saving me,
   so far from the words of my groaning?
O my God, I cry out by day, but you do not answer,
   by night, and am not silent.
(Psalm 22:1)

* * *

My tears have been my food day and night,
while men say to me all day long,
   'Where is your God?'
(Psalm 42:3)

* * *

Each heart knows its own bitterness. (Proverbs 14:10)

* * *

Heartache crushes the spirit. (Proverbs 15:13b)

* * *

It is the heart that is afraid of breaking that never learns to dance. (Old song)

* * *

One can see further through a tear than a telescope. (Anon.)

INTRODUCTION

We cannot give any precise definition of what 'poor in spirit' might mean, since the phrase does not occur elsewhere in the New Testament. Cross-referencing therefore does not really help. Spiritual poverty, or destitution of the soul, is a sign that all self-dependence has been cast aside. The poor in spirit are compelled to acknowledge their spiritual bankruptcy. They recognise that they have no merit to plead, no strings to pull, no power to save themselves. Of such people is the church of Jesus Christ made up. Evidence of self-wretchedness is common in the Bible. We offer two examples – one from the Old and one from the New Testament.

First there is Isaiah in the Temple – a wretched prophet. Isaiah cried,

> *I saw the Lord seated on a throne, high and exalted, and the train of his robe filled the temple. Above him were seraphs, each with six wings: With two wings they covered their faces, with two they covered their feet, and with two they were flying. And they were calling to one another:*

'Holy, holy, holy is the Lord Almighty;
the whole earth is full of his glory.'
At the sound of their voices the doorposts and thresholds shook and the
temple was filled with smoke.
    'Woe to me!' I cried. 'I am ruined! For I am a man of unclean lips
. . . and my eyes have seen the King, the Lord Almighty.' (Isaiah 6:1–5)

Later Isaiah reflected on his visions of God.

> *For this is what the high and lofty One says –*
>   *he who lives for ever, whose name is holy:*
> *'I live in a high and holy place,*
>   *but also with him who is contrite and lowly in spirit,*
> *to revive the spirit of the lowly*
>   *and to revive the heart of the contrite . . .'*
> *(Isaiah 57:15)*

The other Old Testament prophets would have shared similar experiences.

Our second example is from Paul on a mission tour – a wretched apostle.

> *I have the desire to do what is good, but I cannot carry it out . . . For in*
> *my inner being I delight in God's law, but I see another law at work*
> *in the members of my body, waging war against the law of my mind*
> *and making me a prisoner of the law of sin at work within my mem-*
> *bers. What a wretched man I am! Who will rescue me from this body*
> *of death? (Romans 7:18, 22–24)*

The naturally optimistic and cheerful among us may well be tempted to recoil from, or gloss over, this woeful beatitude, but Jesus said it and we cannot ignore it. Indeed, if we have never experienced such brokenheartedness, we have missed out on something very significant.

But how can we ever think of being blessed in such a state? And what benefit could there possibly be for those who are travelling along this way? We shall look at these three questions in the following pages, finishing with a meditation.

Jesus preached the substance of the same sermon in several places. And why not, when it was so foundational to his teaching? In Matthew's Gospel, in the Sermon on the Mount, Jesus talks of 'the poor in spirit'. In Luke's Gospel, however, in the 'sermon on the plain', he is reportedly saying simply, 'Blessed are the poor.' Was Jesus speaking of the same category of people there as in the Sermon on the Mount? If so, could Jesus actually be saying that material poverty is such a blessing? Could the utterly poor really be happy? It is hard to believe that Jesus could truly have meant that – it seems so out of character – but that is what he apparently did say.

WHAT DOES POVERTY MEAN?

In considering poverty of spirit, we must first deal with the nature of material poverty – its aspects, both involuntary and voluntary. And then we must deal with the nature of spiritual poverty – its symptoms and what they may signify.

(1) MATERIAL POVERTY

Material poverty is a deprived state in which people are trapped by circumstances or institutional structures, and apart from the dire problems of eking out a daily existence, they are usually prevented from starting a better lifestyle for themselves. They may also suffer from physical or mental handicaps, or some form of enslavement. Seen as such, pauperism appears to be a curse and hardly a blessing for anyone.

Clearly Christians must maintain a merciful 'bias to the poor', and make every effort to help the needy *(Galatians 2:10)*. Jesus himself had such a 'bias' to the 'oppressed and the marginalised'.[1] Soon after his baptism in the Jordan, when the Holy Spirit came upon him, Jesus prophesied that part of the manifesto of his anointed ministry would include preaching *'good news to the poor'*. His public reading from Isaiah predicted it *(Luke 4:18)*. And his entire ministry illustrated it.

The Dangers of Material Prosperity

At the same time other scriptures warn of the risks of material prosperity: *'Though your riches increase, do not set your heart on them' (Psalm 62:10)*. And the Lord exposes the 'deceitfulness of riches' for being like the thorns that 'choke the word' causing seedlings of new life to die off *(Matthew 13:22)*. Paul draws attention to this danger in his first letter to Timothy:

> But if we have food and clothing, we will be content with that. People who want to get rich fall into temptation and a trap and into many foolish and harmful desires that plunge men into ruin and destruction. For the love of money is a root of all kinds of evil. (1 Timothy 6:8–10)

James adds a serious comment on riches: *'For the sun rises with scorching heat and withers the plant; its blossom falls and its beauty is destroyed. In the same way, the rich man will fade away even while he goes about his business' (James 1:11)*.

---

[1] Mark Stibbe, *Revival* (Monarch, 1998), p. 101.

Bishop Ambrose of Milan (fourth century AD), like many other church fathers, regarded the possessions of the rich as goods stolen from the poor. Basil, a contemporary of Ambrose, also said,

> The bread in your cupboard belongs to the hungry man; the coat hanging unused in your closet belongs to the man who needs it; the shoes rotting in your closet belong to the man who has no shoes; the money which you put in the bank belongs to the poor. You do wrong to everyone you could help but fail to help.

Yet another early church father, John Chrysostom, preached, 'The rich are in possession of the goods of the poor, even if they have acquired them honestly or inherited them legally.' He went on to say that those who do not share are 'a species of bandit'.[2] We do, of course, know how wonderfully rich philanthropists have blessed the world with their wealth and we thank God for them. But they are relatively few.

A Sad Story

Bible history includes a sad story of the great and wise King Solomon. After he finished his public buildings (including the first Temple) he filled them with an abundance of gold. His wisdom and material glory became renowned across the known world – so much so that the Queen of Sheba travelled a long way from Africa to see it for herself. She marvelled at what she saw, and confessed that 'the half was not told me'. But following her departure, Scripture reveals how his prosperity led to his moral and spiritual decline. He had married, and continued to marry, numerous foreign

---

[2] See Jim Wallis, *The Call to Conversion* (Monarch, 2006), p. 200.

women against the commandments of the Lord. One disobedience led to another. The record says matter-of-factly:
'his wives turned his heart after other gods' (1 Kings 11:3–4). His
wealth led to a sense of self-sufficiency and independence
from God. He provoked the Lord and he put himself and his
kingdom under the judgement of God.

The Virtue of Material Poverty

If Jesus was indeed commending material poverty in any
way, it was poverty that was embraced voluntarily for the
sake of the kingdom of heaven – just as he accepted it for
himself when he became poor for our sakes *(2 Corinthians
8:9)*, and the apostles did when they also took up their
crosses of sacrifice and poverty to follow him.

Sadly, within a short time, some of the recently founded
churches had become prosperous and compromised, like
the church of Laodicea: *'You say, "I am rich; I have acquired
wealth and do not need a thing"' (Revelation 3:17)*.

St Antony of Egypt (AD 251?–356) was clearly sickened
by the empty worldliness creeping up on the church. To
escape it he retired to the desert (c. AD 285). Such radical
action drew many other believers to his example. Before
long he was organising his fellow 'eremites' into desert
communities. Such a lifestyle has always attracted the
reflective Christian. From this spontaneous beginning fresh
communities have sprung up ever since, with greater or
lesser degrees of common life – brotherhoods dedicated to
worship and mission under differing religious orders. Such
communities voluntarily made vows of poverty to show
that a person's value is not to be measured by what he or
she possesses, but by what he or she becomes.

'A man's wealth consists not in the abundance of his possessions, but in the fewness of his wants' (anon.). Voluntary poverty demands respect for and solidarity with the poor and the underprivileged of this world. It counters the instinct for power. Love is the motive for voluntary poverty – not just love for God, to become like him who made himself poor for our sakes, but love for our fellow beings, especially the needy.[3]

(2) POVERTY OF SPIRIT

In Matthew's account of the Sermon on the Mount, however, Jesus appears to be talking of the *'poor in spirit'*. And how well the Lord understood the significance of what he was saying. Had he not himself been born in the humblest of human circumstances? *'You know,'* said Peter, *'the grace of our Lord Jesus Christ, that though he was rich, yet for your sakes he became poor, so that you through his poverty might become rich' (2 Corinthians 8:9).* Did he not undergo incalculable depths in personally experiencing 'poverty of spirit'? 'The emotional suffering, self-imposed limitations, low status, exile from His real home, and the fact of living among sinful humans must all point to a profound degree of spiritual poverty.'[4] And finally, what about his utterly appalling cry of desolation from the cross: *'My God, my God, why have you forsaken me?' (Matthew 27:45).* Utter abandonment is the ultimate depth of spiritual poverty.

---

[3] We shall deal much more fully with our Christian obligations to the materially poor in the 'merciful' beatitude.

[4] My thanks to Peggy Knight for these and many other insights included in this book.

Many Are Blind to their Spiritual Poverty

Matthew's Gospel tells us that Jesus *'saw a man named Matthew sitting at the tax collector's booth. "Follow me," he told him.'* Matthew got up and followed him. Now it happened that while Jesus was at table in Matthew's house, many tax collectors and those known as sinners came to join Jesus and his disciples at dinner. The Pharisees saw this and complained to his disciples, *'Why does your teacher eat with tax collectors and "sinners"?'* Overhearing them, Jesus said, *'It is not the healthy who need a doctor, but the sick . . . I have not come to call the righteous, but sinners'* (Matthew 9:9–11).

Jesus comes to those who know they have a need for him – like a doctor who knows his calling is to the sick, not to the fit and able-bodied. We have a theology for the place of prosperity (abundant life – John 10:10) but we also have a theology for the place of poverty in the spirit.

John Flavel puts it in a nutshell: 'When God prepares to fill a soul He first makes it empty. When He intends to enrich a soul He first makes it poor. When He intends to exalt a soul He first makes it sensible to its own miseries, wants and nothingness.'

Examples of Spiritual Poverty

(i) Disappointment

We are not talking about life's natural disappointments, though again these may well be used by God for positive spiritual ends. To cite a familiar cliché, 'Man's disappointments are often God's appointments.' *'We know that in all things God works for the good of those who love him'* (*Romans 8:28*). There are disappointments of a more enduring kind.

John Wesley apparently never received the abiding
assurance of faith experienced by so many of those he loved
and admired. He seemingly had doubts until the very end;
but nevertheless he persevered. John Wesley never
achieved the entire sanctification in this life that he
preached so trustingly to others. He eventually wrote, 'I
have told the world I am not perfect . . . I have never
attained the character that I draw.' Finally, he realised he
could not muster the attitude towards death about which
he had boasted. He wanted to die positively rejoicing, not
just in peace.[5] Everyone will have some degree of regret
over life in retrospect: truth will compel us to admit that we
have been 'unprofitable servants' in too many ways. But
wisdom will keep us focused, as much as possible, on Jesus
– on his mercy and grace.

Pollyanna was written from a Christian perspective, and
there is a very tender chapter in the middle of the book in
which the town minister is discouraged to the point of resignation. Things had not gone well at church, and people
were critical and divided. He rode into the forest to ponder
things, and his spirits were lower than they had ever been.
Pollyanna, playing in the woods, saw him and noticed his
depressed expression.

> 'I know how you feel,' she said as they talked. 'Father used to
> feel like that too, lots of times. I reckon ministers do – most
> generally. He grew mighty discouraged until he found his
> rejoicing texts.'
> 'His what?'

---

[5] Robert G. Tuttle, Jr, *John Wesley: His Life and Theology* (Zondervan,
1978), p. 353.

'Well, that's what father used to call 'em. Of course, the Bible didn't name 'em that, but it's all those that begin, "Be glad in the Lord," or "Rejoice greatly," or "Shout for joy," and all that – you know – such a lot of 'em. Once, when father felt specially bad, he counted 'em. There were eight hundred of 'em.'[6]

(ii) Empty Hopelessness and Misery

Experience of the Christian life usually begins with the troublesome realisation, sudden or gradual, of our own exceeding emptiness. Sooner or later, one way or another, we discover we have nothing in our 'spiritual bank'. Like Mother Hubbard's cupboard, it is bare! We are like the starving prodigal in the 'far country': *'When he [the prodigal son] came to his senses, he said, "How many of my father's hired men have food to spare, and here I am starving to death! I will . . . go back to my father. . ."' (Luke 15:17).* How often has it been just such dire destitution that has driven us back to God?

This is a condition, much like that of the saintly David Brainerd, one of the first missionaries to the North American Indians, whose example had such a profound impact on the first wave of nineteenth-century Protestant missionaries. Even at the early age of seven, Brainerd had an increasing sense of spiritual poverty that eventually drove him to the Lord at the age of 20. This kind of general emptiness, often submerged beneath exciting youthful projects and prospects, can be a kind of gestation period, such poverty of spirit being the spiritual prelude to conversion. Many, though not all, unbelievers have travelled the way of

---

[6] Eleanor Porter, *Pollyanna* (1913).

Brainerd before his conversion to Christ. They have dallied so long over turning to Christ until they have been ground down by their poverty of spirit. The natural man's desperate flight from God is most movingly depicted in Francis Thompson's poem 'The Hound of Heaven', in which he tells his own story:

> I fled Him, down the nights and down the days:
> I fled Him, down the arches of the years;
> I fled Him, down the labyrinthine way
> Of my own mind; and in the midst of tears
> I hid from Him. . .[7]

* * *

Christian's Despair – in the Mire of Despond:

This poverty of spirit is most graphically portrayed in John Bunyan's *Pilgrim's Progress*.[8]

Now I saw in my dreams that, just as they [Christian and Pliable] had ended their conversation, they approached a miry Slough [a muddy swamp] in the plain. Neither of them paid any attention to it, and both suddenly fell into the bog. The Slough's name was 'Despond'. Covered with mud, they wallowed in it for some time. And Christian, because of the burden on his back, began to sink in the mire.

'Oh, Christian, my neighbour!' Pliable cried out. 'Where are you now?'

'To tell you the truth, I don't know,' Christian answered.

Hearing this, Pliable became offended and angrily scolded

---

[7] Francis Thompson, 'The Hound of Heaven' (A. R. Mowbray & Co., 1955).

[8] See Cheryl Ford's retelling of John Bunyan, *The Pilgrim's Progress* (Tyndale House, 1991).

his companion. 'Is this the happiness you have told me about all this time? If we have such terrible misfortune here at the beginning, what must we expect between here and the end of our journey? If I can possibly get out of here with my life, you can possess that wonderful Country for you and me both!'

With that, Pliable gave a desperate struggle or two and was able to get out of the mire on the side of the Slough that faced his home. So away he went, and Christian never saw him again.

Thus Christian was left to roll around in the Slough of Despond by himself. Even then, however, he tried to struggle to the side of the Slough that was farthest from his own home and closer to the Wicket-gate [the direction he had been told to make for by Evangelist where he might find relief from his heavy burden]. He continued to struggle, but could not get out because of the burden that was on his back.

Then I saw in my dream that a man called Help came to him, and he asked Christian what he was doing there.

'Sir,' explained Christian, 'I was instructed to go this way by a man named Evangelist who gave me directions to that Gate up ahead where I might escape the coming wrath. As I was going toward the Gate, I fell in here.'

Christian then reached out his hand and Help pulled him out. Then in his imaginary dream, the writer, John Bunyan, asks Help:

'Since this is the way from the city of Destruction to the Gate, why isn't it fenced off so that poor travellers may go by more safely?'

And he answered, 'This miry Slough is the type that cannot be fenced. It is the lower ground where the scum and filth that accompany conviction of sin continually accumulate. Therefore it was named the "Slough of Despond" because, as the sinner is awakened to his lost condition, many fears, doubts, and discouraging anxieties arise in his soul. All of them come together and settle here in this place, and that is the reason this ground is no good.'[9]

Paul Baker's Despair:

Paul Baker, a senior assistant governor of Pentonville prison, who recently became a Christian, writes in 'UK Focus' about his pre-conversion days as an alcoholic, followed by his later separation from his wife and daughter. Until his conversion, he says, 'Everyone saw me as able and successful, but underneath there was this constant gnawing sense of misery, unhappiness and loneliness.'[10]

Chuck Colson's Despair:

Chuck Colson, a right-hand man to the disgraced US president Richard Nixon, and criminally implicated in the infamous 'Watergate Scandal', had been thought to be enjoying one of the most high-profile careers in the world. He had ready access to the leader of the major world power. He had huge influence. He was considered a leading lawyer of his day. And he ended that phase of his life by going to prison. His former career was over. But before his trial began he discovered Christ, and during his time in prison he found himself helping other prisoners with his legal knowledge. This was the beginning of an inspiring Christian mission for prison inmates. Reviewing his life later, he wrote, 'The real legacy of my life was my biggest failure.'

---

[9] John Bunyan, *The Pilgrim's Progress*, pp. 8–10.

[10] *Church of England Newspaper*, 14th April 2006.

Henri Nouwen's Despair:

In the prologue to a biography of Henri J. M. Nouwen, a Catholic priest and a prolific and popular spiritual writer and counsellor, Michael Ford writes,

> Much of his genius was shaped by an ongoing loneliness and anguish which also afflicted Van Gogh whose painting he greatly admired. Constantly fearing solitude and rejection, especially from those they loved, both men sank at times into deep depression yet, at their lowest ebb, managed to create some of their most inspiring and memorable work.[11]

Nouwen wrote of the impact of van Gogh's personal struggles and a connection with his own:

> Vincent van Gogh painted what I had not dared to look at: he questioned what I had not dared before to speak about, he entered into the spaces of my heart that I had not dared to come close to. By doing so he brought me in touch with many of my fears and gave me the courage to go further and deeper in my search for a God who loves.

(iii) Disillusionment

'If anyone is in Christ, he is a new creation; the old has gone, the new has come!' (2 Corinthians 5:17). We had thought this meant that the old nature had been completely done away with – eradicated. But that was a misunderstanding. We really do have a new life in Christ. And we know we have been changed. At the beginning of the previous verse Paul had just written, 'So from now on we regard no one from a

---

[11] Michael Ford, *Wounded Prophet – A Portrait of Henri J. M. Nouwen* (Darton, Longman & Todd, 1999), p. 1.

worldly point of view.' We have a new perspective, a new heart, a new mind *(Romans 12:2)*, plus a sure and certain hope – a new confidence. All this has come about since our *metanoia* (repentance). We no longer view life from a worldly standpoint. 'In Christ' now we see things very differently. However, we still have the old sinful nature to cope with, as Paul explains when he admits to the inner frustrations with himself:

> *I know that nothing good lives in me, that is, in my sinful nature. For I have the desire to do what is good, but I cannot carry it out. For what I do is not the good I want to do [but] the evil I do not want to do – this I keep on doing. (Romans 7:18–19)*

This is what gets the better of us more often than it should as we seek to follow Christ.

But it does not have to stay that way. We do not have to sin. Paul reminds us quite clearly, *'Sin shall not be your master' (Romans 6:14)*. We are able to overcome temptation if we want to, and the Lord is always there to give us *'grace to help us in our time of need' (Hebrews 4:16)* if we ask for it.

When I was a boy it was explained to me that our two natures (the old and the new) were like two strong horses, tied to the same rope, pulling against each other. If I wanted one of them especially to win, that was the one to feed. I simply had to starve the other. This would ensure that the one I wanted to win would do so. So we endeavour to feed our new nature with Christian fellowship, Bible reading, prayer, worship, the Lord's Supper and service to others, and to weaken the old nature by depriving it of sinful attitudes and actions which help it to thrive.

Many new Christians, in the process of discovering these

realities, have already experienced some inner spiritual poverty before conversion. Others (often the offspring of Christians) seem to bypass this pre-conversion experience in some way, but then it catches up with them later. They find themselves entering a post-conversion disillusionment with 'self' which is often deeply worrying for them. It does not seem attributable to any obvious cause, just 'being out of sorts', downcast, defeated – 'poverty of spirit' again. Like the depressed poet and hymn-writer William Cowper, we cry:

> Where is the blessedness I knew when first I saw the Lord?
> Where is that soul-refreshing view of Jesus and His Word?[12]

What we suddenly realise is that we are struggling with an old nature which we mistakenly believed had been done away with at the cross. Indeed, there is Scripture to support such a straightforward belief: *'the old has gone, the new has come!' (2 Corinthians 5:17)*. But this is one of those paradoxes we meet in the Bible. It is all true, but not all the truth. There is another side to it. Paul is very frank about it: *'I see another law at work in the members of my body, waging war. . .' (Romans 7:22)*. Some Christians have never been sufficiently taught that the battle, which was bad enough before conversion, can actually become even more intense after conversion, and continues so until the day of the general resurrection when all will be changed – 'morphed', to use a modern expression: *'the perishable must clothe itself with the imperishable, and the mortal with immortality' (1 Corinthians 15:53)*.

---

[12] William Cowper, Hymn No. 461, v. 2, *The Methodist Hymnbook* (Methodist Pub. Rev., 1954).

Many a missionary has gone abroad to another culture or nation, having left behind father and mother, houses and lands – everything – and been appalled to find that the old nature has come too. Touch the missionary, and he is still touchy! Overlook her, and she is still resentful! The old nature keeps rearing its ugly head, watchful of its own place and power. When I first went out to the mission field, I think I thought the missionary society was rather lucky to have me. But after six months I began to wonder how on earth they had ever selected such a scumbag sinner! When Christians first discover the depths of their spiritual poverty, the disillusioned soul could easily let the heart become a morbid centre of spiritual confusion: *'Why are you downcast, O my soul? Why so disturbed within me?' (Psalm 42:11)*. In the case of the Christian who has never really experienced the 'slough of despond', the temptation might easily be to give up in despair in those first wild flailings.

The fact is, the Christian life takes us through a continuous war zone of spiritual battles measuring various degrees of intensity. Although there is always grace to help us, if we ask for it in such times of need, this is actually the normal Christian life. We soldier on through life, struggling against this old nature until our dying day. It is all too easy to lose our focus, and start waging war against our brothers and sisters instead of that enemy within. As we mature, we begin to realise how mistaken we have been – how hypocritical, how self-righteous! We all have victories to keep us joyful, but we also suffer shameful defeats that leave us wounded and bleeding once again, and truly 'poor in spirit'.

Catherine Marshall's Despair:

This was the sorry state reflected in Catherine Marshall's experience. We may quickly recognise it in ourselves:

> I fell on my face. There followed months of rebellion against God, sharper questioning than ever . . . I experienced the most intense misery I had ever known. Life went gray . . . Life in the exterior world began going against me . . . Trials have a way of piling up. The question is – why? Once again . . . I was brought back to see that if we don't accept the circumstances [that] God's permissive will has allowed [us to suffer], and ask, 'Lord what is Your will for me in the midst of these circumstances?', then He permits the difficulties to heap up. For most of us that's the only way He can get our attention. In my misery He had my attention all right . . . Finally the words of truth began to break through . . . We must see all of life as coming directly from His Hands. . .[13]

David Brainerd's Testimony:

Thus I was made sensible of my great ignorance and unfitness for public service. I had the most abasing thoughts of myself I think that I have ever had. I thought of myself as the worst wretch that ever lived; it hurt me and pained my very heart that anybody should show me any respect. 'Alas!' methought, 'how sadly they are deceived in me! How miserably would they be disappointed if they knew me inside? Oh my heart!' And in this depressed condition I was forced to go and preach to a considerable assembly [in New York] before some grave and learned ministers; but felt such a pressure from my sense

---

[13] Catherine Marshall, *Something More* (McGraw-Hill Book Company, 1974), pp. 10, 11.

of vileness, ignorance, and unfitness to appear in public that I
was almost overcome with it. My soul grieved for the congregation, that they should be there to hear such a dead dog as I
preach.[14]

(iv) Pruning

There is also a 'spiritual poverty' that results from God's
'pruning'.[15] Perhaps the classic case is that of Job, who had
everything taken from him – his children, his flocks and
herds, his health. Job's reply to Bildad, one of his so-called
'comforters', reveals his 'poverty of spirit': *'As surely as God
lives, who has denied me justice, the Almighty . . . has made me
taste bitterness of soul. . .' (Job 27:2).* Pruning by the gardener
is intended to increase fruitfulness. Job, who had been
exceedingly fruitful, does end up being even more fruitful.
After all his pain, grief and discomfort, the Lord prospered
Job once more, *'and gave him twice as much as he had before . . .
the Lord blessed the latter part of Job's life more than the first. . .'
(Job 42:10b–12a).* But pruning is always and inevitably
painful and brings us very low.

(v) Sowing in Tears

> *Those who sow in tears*
> *will reap with songs of joy.*
> (Psalm 126:5)

It has been said that whenever you find tears in your eyes
it is well to pay close attention to them, especially the

---

[14] Philip E. Howard, *The Life of David Brainerd* (Baker Book House,
1994), p. 105.

[15] The branches of the vine need this pruning, see John 15.

unexpected ones. 'They not only tell you something about the secret of who you are, but more often than not God is speaking to you through them of the mystery of where you have been coming from and summoning you to where, if your soul is being saved, you should go next.'[16]

Selwyn Hughes, world famous for his 40 years of 'Every Day With Jesus' Bible reading notes, describes an experience he had in the early 1960s while viewing the film *Ben Hur*. It was deeply moving for him. He had never dreamed a movie could be a window through which God could come to him. He could not stop weeping as he watched the portrayal of Christ's miracles, and particularly the crucifixion scene. It triggered something in his soul that never left him. 'It was as if my soul was being drawn out in hot, adoring tears of love,' he wrote.

> I had always been grateful for my Saviour's sacrifice for me on Calvary, but in the cinema that day I came to realise more vividly than ever before how Christ's suffering had brought me salvation. It was an epiphany of understanding. I left the cinema with a more vivid realization than ever of what it meant for Christ to be my Saviour.[17]

Other Christian believers suffer from a mysterious and mounting sense of desperation – an emotional turbulence that appears to be genuine 'poverty of spirit' for which there is no other apparent cause. It has been known to lead people to imagine they must be on the verge of some kind of nervous breakdown. Testimonies of many who have

---

[16] Frederick Bruechner, *Whistling in the Dark* (HarperSanFrancisco, 1993).

[17] Selwyn Hughes, *My Story* (CWR, 2005), p.168.

been through this kind of experience indicate that God has indeed been taking them not to a breakdown but to a further spiritual breakthrough. Such times have culminated in visitations of the Holy Spirit that are initiations into something new – a different dimension or a different direction of service or ministry. This may also be accompanied by the release of some unexpected power or gifting – or something along those lines – a paradigm shift in one's mindset; dreams and visions of new forms of outreach in evangelism or new ways of 'doing church'; a new mission in the area of mercy ministries or a new revelation of God for his purposes in history or the community. Such can be illustrated by the fascinating examples we relate below.

Graham Pulkingham's Despair:

Graham was taking over a very run-down Episcopal church, the Church of the Redeemer in Houston, Texas, in the 1960s, where God later did a remarkable redemptive work in the community. He describes the prelude to the breakthrough he personally experienced:

> There were frequent nightly intrusions from the neighbourhood youths – some . . . vandalous, most . . . only mischievous – but now [the vestry]. . . officially closed the building, which became empty and tomb-like except for a few hours each week when public services were held. The church property was in the same dormant condition it had been in when I arrived the September before, with one notable exception – it was defaced and in some places destroyed beyond repair. With increasing frequency I sat alone in the chapel weeping, consumed with grief – a grief encompassing neighbourhood, family and church.

It seemed that everything was lost. Despite that, however, my soul would not tolerate the idea that the gospel had failed to bring healing in these desperate lives. And in the chill of a cellar retreat I responded in fury to my feelings of desolation and abandonment, accusing God of trickery in His dealings with human suffering. Day by day my ears accustomed themselves to emptiness, listening to the incessant hum of the chapel's fluorescent lights as I strained for answers to my questions. Only sobs punctuated the hollow sound of despair. Shaking an angry fist at the God of this dilemma, I demanded to know the cause of my failure. If He heard, I was not aware. Silence was His only answer.

As the weeks passed, loneliness and dread began to settle upon me like a fog. Soon there were timorous pleas for help displacing the inquisition, and a disconsolate soul cried out for comfort. I had begun by requiring of God that He explain His indifference to my failure; I had come round to the place of longing to hear just a word. Opening it at random, (as I read it) I heard the voice of Job utter my complaint, 'I cry out to you, O God, but you do not answer' (Job 30:20–21).[18]

This 'fasting, weeping and mourning' all happened over a protracted period of time. But Graham was beginning to discern a voice that he knew to be God's. Finally, in obedience, he went to seek out Dave Wilkerson at the Brooklyn Teen Challenge Center (his book *The Cross and the Switchblade* tells the story of a remarkable breakthrough among a violent youth gang in New York), and there Graham received an empowering touch of God on his own life and ministry. He carried this back with him to his dwindling

---

[18] Graham Pulkingham, *Gathered for Power* (Hodder & Stoughton, 1972), pp.53, 55, 66–77.

church in Houston. Graham's book *Gathering for Power* tells the story of a wonderful outpouring of God's blessing that ensued in that broken-down community.

Jim Cymbala's Despair:

Jim Cymbala was taking over a run-down New York City slum congregation with no experience at all of leading a church. He wrote of a significant early incident:

> One Sunday night early on I was so depressed by what I saw – even more by what I felt in my spirit – that I literally could not preach. I did not know whether this was a normal experience in the ministry or not; I had no preconceived ideas from Bible college or seminary by which to judge, because I had not been there. We were just blundering along all by ourselves. Even my father-in-law (himself a pastor) did not offer a lot of advice. He often told me, 'Jim, you're just going to have to find your own way, under God, of ministering to people.'
>
> That evening I had been at my lowest, confounded by obstacles, bewildered by the darkness that surrounded us, unable even to continue preaching, I discovered an astonishing truth: God is *attracted to weakness*. He can't resist those who humbly and honestly admit how desperately they need him. Our weakness, in fact, makes room for God's power.
>
> Five minutes into my sermon, I began choking on the words. Tears filled my eyes. Gloom engulfed me. All I could say to the people was, 'I'm sorry . . . I . . . can't preach in this atmosphere . . . Something is terribly wrong . . . I don't know what to say . . . I can't go on. Carol [his wife], would you play something on the piano, and would the rest of you come to this altar? If we don't see God help us, I don't know. . .' With that, I just quit. It was embarrassing, but I couldn't do anything else. . .

With my face planted in my hands, I sobbed. Things were quiet at first, but soon the Spirit of God came down upon us. People began to call upon the Lord, their words motivated by a stirring within. 'God, help us,' we prayed. Carol played the old hymn 'I need Thee, Oh I need Thee', and we sang along. A tide of intercession arose.

Suddenly a young usher came running down the centre aisle and threw himself on the altar. He began to cry as he prayed. When I placed my hand on his shoulder, he looked up, the tears streaming down his face as he said, 'I'm sorry! I'm sorry – I won't do it again! Please forgive me.' Instantly I realized he was apologizing for taking money from the offering plate. I stood speechless for a moment, bewildered by his unexpected confession. It was our first spiritual breakthrough. . .

Read his book – it is really good![19]

Heidi Baker's Despair:

Heidi Baker was (and still is) a missionary in Mozambique with her husband Rolland. They were hungry for revival after many visions had been given to the 300-plus at their children's centre in the country district of Machava. She wrote:

We were *desperate*[20] for more of God. The children's visions were really encouraging but we wanted to see an entire nation come to God. Rolland and I longed to be wherever He [God] was pouring out His Spirit, and managed a trip to Toronto, Canada.

---

[19] Jim Cymbala, *Fresh Wind, Fresh Fire* (Zondervan, 1997), pp. 18–19.

[20] I have marked in italics the words which reveal the poverty of spirit which she seemed to be experiencing.

The first night they were back in Toronto, the preacher suddenly pointed right at Heidi and said, 'God is asking, "Do you want Mozambique?"' Instantly the fire of God fell.

> I was so hot I literally thought I was going to burn up . . . I cried out, *'Lord, I'm dying!'* Then the Lord spoke clearly to my heart: *'Good!' He said, ' I want you dead'*! He wanted me *completely emptied* of self so He could pour even more of His Spirit into my life.
>
> For seven days I was *unable to move.* Rolland had to pick me up and carry me. I had to be carried to the washroom, to the hotel and back in the morning. The weight of His glory was upon me. I felt so heavy I could not lift my head. Some passing by thought it was funny to see me stuck to the floor for so long. If I was put in a chair I would slide off onto the floor again. I was *utterly and completely helpless.* I was *unable to speak* for most of the seven days. This holy, fearful, awesome presence of God completely changed my life. I have never been *so humbled, never felt so poor, so helpless, so vulnerable.* I even needed help to drink water. There was nothing funny about it. It was a most holy time. I learned more in those seven days than in ten years of academic theological study. [She and her husband both have English university doctorates.][21]

David Bracewell's Despair:

A respected rector in Guildford, Surrey, for the past 15 years, leading a full church in the city, David Bracewell shared his testimony in *Anglicans for Renewal* magazine.[22] He wrote of

---

[21] Rolland and Heidi Baker, *Always Enough* (Chosen Books, 2003). If readers are wondering about the value of such an anointing from God, I would recommend their testimony – seeing God's miraculous provision among the poorest people on earth.

[22] *Anglicans for Renewal*, Vol. 79, reprinted here by permission.

the unexpected and prolonged experience through which he was going – a sense of 'poverty of the spirit'. He explained the circumstances:

My life seemed as dry as a stick. . . [He gives various contributory reasons.] Sitting at my kitchen table I seemed trapped. Sue [his wife] came and sat beside me, and I began to pray with gritty desperation that God would close the great gap between what I professed in my ministry and how I felt in my heart and mind. We sat in silence, a silence in which nothing happened, and everything changed. . .

The New Year began with a gathering of the church family to review the year ahead . . . pray . . . dedicate ourselves afresh . . . a grim two hours . . . A respected member spoke of his sense of disquiet. 'We seem to have lost our way. . .' he said. Others stood to add their bit of personal doom and gloom. . .

I chose to abandon my carefully planned preaching series and focus on the Holy Spirit. So it was that on the evening of the 24th January 1993 . . . I began to expound Ezekiel 47 – the water flowing from the Temple that swirls round Ezekiel's ankles, then his knees – then his waist . . . until it is a river . . . becoming a torrent . . . causing everything in its path to spring to life . . . and eventually pouring its freshness into the Dead Sea. I got to verse 9 and read the words, 'Where the river flows everything will live.' And at that point God answered my kitchen table prayer.

My notes became a blur and I began to cry. Since there is nothing in the prayer book that says 'Here the priest may shed tears' the congregation were taken aback. There was an 'Oh no, the vicar's having a turn in the pulpit' sort of silence, during which I gathered myself and stumbled to the end of the sermon. By now, well and truly gone, I invited people to come forward if they would like some Ezekiel-type refreshment from

God. I knelt at my prayer desk expecting nothing, and then rose to announce a hymn. As I turned I saw scores of people standing across the front of the church and others moving down the aisles and more struggling to get out of the pews – in all about 100 people. Never having made a 'successful' appeal before I had no follow-up strategy, so I blew my nose and pronounced the blessing!

During the following weeks news got round that there had been strange goings-on at the evening service . . . next Sunday morning the mood of anticipation was quite extraordinary. Those who gathered to observe the vicar's new style of pulpit performance were not disappointed. A short way into the service my eyes began to prick, my voice wobbled and (as final evidence of supernatural power) I was lost for words. It was most embarrassing, but there was nothing I could do. Once again I stumbled on and at the end invited people to come forward to the chapel for prayer. Again there were queues and for over an hour I heard confessions, dried tears, shed more of my own, laid hands on people and prayed for the joyful, solemn presence of the Holy Spirit – this time of refreshing went on for three months – week after week I would walk . . . and weep bewildering cleansing tears. Sunday by Sunday I would climb the steps and begin to preach what I had prepared, only to reach a point where notes were swept away as God took over my frail words and spoke his Word with awesome clarity and gentle power. . .

But why recount it seven years later? The answer is that the deepest meaning of renewal lies not in the initiatory events, however dramatic, by which God gets our attention, but in his lasting shift of perspective that reveals that we have paid attention, changed our ways and moved on.

It is over seven years since that divine visitation, and now I find myself praying, with some trepidation, that God will do it again. Mercifully that is up to him. But there is no going back. We have received a severe mercy whereby God, in answer to the cry of our hearts, has determined to deny us contentment but grant us glimpses of his glory.

(vi) Thorns

There is a spiritual poverty that derives from what Paul calls a 'thorn in the flesh'. God uses 'thorns' to remind us of the source of any strength we may have. Paul talks about his struggle with a 'thorn', but he does not tell us what it was, although he does say God had shown him that it was *'to keep me from becoming conceited because of . . . surpassing great revelations' (2 Corinthians 12:7)*. If Paul ever wanted to brag about being shown such revelations, about being so successful in mission, so effective and wise in church governance, the Lord would just rein him in with this 'thorn'. Any time he was tempted to begin attributing some fruitfulness, some blessing, some victory in the demolition of an enemy stronghold to his own credit, God could gently apply this 'thorn'. This constantly reminded him, he said, that his strength was *'made perfect in weakness' (2 Corinthians 12:9)*. And so is ours. We need always to remain aware of just how weak we are.

'Thorns' are usually difficult to accept or understand, often humiliating and sometimes shameful to confess. God could deliver us from any 'thorn' at any time, but sometimes he leaves it with us for a long time – sometimes for life, like Jacob's limp *(Genesis 32:31)*. God has plenty of 'thorns' available and suitable for each of us, should they ever become necessary.

A helpful book entitled *The Thorn in the Flesh*[23] suggests a number of these prickly afflictions, including loneliness, unhappy employment, an enemy, a handicap or disability, unsuitable living conditions, a sexual misgiving, a difficult marriage, a chronic illness, a personality problem, money matters, an unwanted calling. Other 'thorns' that the book does not mention come readily to mind: a rebellious child, a stalker, a neighbour from hell, unfulfilled dreams, unanswered prayers, anonymous letters. And readers will doubtless think of many others. In the following paragraphs we add a few examples from the lives of well-known, highly gifted and greatly used Christian leaders.

Charles Spurgeon's Despair:

Charles Spurgeon suffered from depressions increasingly as the years passed by. He once spoke of his bouts of darkness that accompanied his physical suffering with excruciating gout: 'There are dungeons beneath the Castle of Despair.' With all his tremendous responsibility, and in spite of the rich blessing which followed his most fruitful ministry, he suffered terribly from this gout, which frequently attacked him and laid him 'prostrate with depression'. He wrote:

> I am a potter's vessel when it is utterly broken, useless and laid aside. Nights of watching and days of weeping have been mine, but I hope the cloud is passing. Alas! I can only say this for my own personal and light affliction; there is one who lies nearest to my heart [his wife] whose sorrows are not relieved by such a hope.

---

[23] R. T. Kendall, *The Thorn in the Flesh* (Hodder and Stoughton, 1999).

John Wesley's Despair:

In John Wesley's *Journal* he describes the 'thorn' of an unhappy marriage that must have been a constantly painful and humbling experience for him. After many years he confides to his journal the case of his own disastrous relationship with his wife. He writes:

> At this point, though it pains me, I must relate the account regarding the consequences of my marriage. I have put it off long enough. If we ever properly loved each other (and I doubt that we did), it lasted but a few months. My wife was insanely jealous, refusing to accept the tone and advice of my correspondence (especially with young women) in the spirit in which it was written. I could not perform any of my duties in my usual manner.
>
> We lived together only occasionally for twenty years. In 1771 she decided to live with her married daughter in Newcastle, proposing never to return. I could only comment: *'Non eam reliqui: Non dimisi: Non revocabo.'*[24] From that point on (though her daughter persuaded her to return to me) we lived and travelled together only sparingly.
>
> Though she shared our homes both in London and Bristol, for the most part, even while we were together, we were apart. Then, years after our separation, she died. I was not informed until four days later. There have been times when I wished we had never met. I am certain that she must have felt the same way; but surely God will somehow even glorify Himself by this unfortunate match.[25]

---

[24] 'I did not desert her: I did not send her away; I will never recall her.'

[25] Tuttle, Jr, *John Wesley: His Life and Theology.*

Mother Teresa's Despair:

Mother Teresa of Calcutta suffered notably from depression. She was reputed to have had a year of elation when she heard God's call, and 50 years of depression after that. But this took her into a ministry of mercy which blessed every dying Indian she ever nursed, and inspired every heart that ever knew about it. Added to that, she could say at the end of her life that it had been happy! She had felt more than content with her calling from God.

We soon come to recognise that our sense of spiritual poverty has not ceased when we are born again; nor even after significant touches of God's Spirit; nor when we have learned to take 'pruning' or 'thorns' in our stride.

W. E. Sangster recalls that Jesus knew what to do with thorns: he wore them as a crown.

> O Sacred head, now wounded,
> With grief and shame bowed down,
> Now scornfully surrounded
> With thorns, Thine only crown.

(vii) Defeat – Poverty of Spirit follows Falls from Grace

We think of King David finding his way back into a relationship with God. His testimony is in the Psalms:

> *This poor man called, and the Lord heard him,*
> *he saved him out of all his troubles.*
> *(Psalm 34:6)*

> *The Lord is close to the broken-hearted*
> *and saves those who are crushed in spirit.*
> *(Psalm 34:18)*

Then after his affair with Bathsheba, he could cry:

> *Wash away all my iniquity*
> *and cleanse me from my sin. . .*
> *my sin is always before me. . .*
> *Let me hear joy and gladness. . .*
> *The sacrifices of God are a broken spirit;*
> *a broken and contrite heart,*
> *O God, you will not despise.*
> *(Psalm 51:2, 3, 8, 17)*

David recognised that his consequent poverty of spirit was perfectly acceptable in the process of becoming realistic and honest with God, who desires *'truth in the inner parts' (Psalm 51:6)*.

On the 19th January 1999, Jonathan Aitken, newly converted to Christ, entered a plea of guilty to charges of perjury at London's Central Criminal Court, about an illegal act committed before his recent conversion. Immediately, the press began to savage him with extreme ferocity and this, coupled with the prospect of imminent imprisonment, threw him into a state of clinical depression accompanied by physical illness. He was bedridden for a week with flu, pneumonia and, worst of all, an occlusion – a mini-stroke which burst most of the blood vessels in his left eye, severely impairing his sight. Above all, he suffered from deep feelings of guilt. He identified his reactions closely with those of the writer of Psalm 31. In his utter helplessness and guilt, he later wrote, 'All I could do was to pray in faith for God's mercy and forgiveness' – and, like the psalmist, he was granted it. That answer to prayer changed nothing in the unpleasant circumstances he had yet to face, he said, but it changed everything about the way he faced them. 'Fear and trembling were gradually replaced by peaceful acceptance of God's will and a prayerful trust that He would be with me on my prison journey. He was.'[26]

(viii) Life Assessment

The 'poor in spirit' are broken-hearted spiritually, bankrupt inwardly, utterly unworthy mentally and unready to face God. It has been said that 'from infancy to old age the record of every man's life is written in letters of tears'.[27] There is nothing wrong with these seasons of spiritual poverty – so long as we do not shrug them off with resignation, or indulge in self-pity. They should be used, as God always intended them to be used, as spurs to drive us back on the mercy of God, as thorns to keep us humble, or as pruning hooks to keep us fruitful. And none should be surprised or ashamed of these seasons of brokenness. Poverty of spirit is a wholesome blessing to have.

(ix) Sympathy and Sorrow

Meeting others who are weighed down by sorrow can be a heartbreaking experience. Paul's Christian friends were overwhelmed at the thought that if Paul went to Jerusalem he would be arrested and *'they would never see his face again'* *(Acts 20:38b)*. After these fears were confirmed in Jerusalem by the prophecy of Agabus, his friends there entreated him not to stay around. Paul answered them, *'Why are you weeping and breaking my heart? I am ready. . .' (Acts 21:13)*. He knew

---

[26] Jonathan Aitken, *Psalms for People Under Pressure* (Continuum, 2004), p. 67.

[27] M. R. De Haan.

from a succession of prophecies along his way there that it was all in the will of God.

(x) A Desert Experience

Selwyn Hughes reflects on a 'wilderness experience' in his own Christian pilgrimage. He describes this extremely testing time in his biography. It lasted for almost a year in his early ministry. He wrote in *My Story*:

> What troubled me most was that I had begun to lose my desire for prayer and my appetite for the Scriptures. I still read my Bible, but it did not seem to speak to me any more . . . I wondered whether I should give up all thoughts of pursuing the ministry . . . At times it felt like being in a spiritual wrestling match without knowing who was wrestling with me – God or the devil.[28]

Later he defined the 'wilderness experience' as a prolonged or deeply intense period of trial and testing in which a particular providential purpose is being worked out. It is something we are led into by the Lord. God either arranges it or allows us to enter into it, not because he wants to punish us but because he wants to prune us. He does this because it is the only way he can bring his purposes to pass in our lives.

Hughes realised that during this experience he had to prove to himself that he could believe in a God 'who sometimes leads us in ways that are baffling, but can always be trusted to do what is good'. He wrote that he could almost pin-point the day when he came out of the wilderness (the late summer of 1962). 'I had begun to wonder whether there would ever be an end to this spiritual impasse I found

---

[28] Selwyn Hughes, *My Story* (CWR, 2005), pp.178–9.

myself in, or whether I would find myself in this mood for the rest of my life.'

On the day it happened he opened his Bible at the Song of Solomon 2:12–13 and read, *'Flowers appear on the earth; the season of singing has come, the cooing of the doves is heard in our land. The fig tree forms its early fruit; the blossoming vines spread their fragrance. Arise . . .'* That was all, but that was enough.

SEEING THE GOODNESS OF GOD IN OUR BROKENNESS

> It is in our pain and in our brokenness that we all come closest to Christ.[29]

> No one can know the Lord intimately who has not realized the sickness of his own soul.[30]

> It is only when we recognize our great poverty, humble ourselves and cry out for mercy, that we can receive the free gift of life through Jesus. The one thing we can do – must do – is to run from our self-reliance and reach for the Good News.[31]

The human heart is often so stubborn and blind that the Lord in his love for us helps us by a discipline of trials and tribulations. He may even allow us to go through sharper suffering to spur us on to deeper heart-searching. He sometimes puts us on our backs to make us look up! He may lead us through a desert, or along a mysterious, lonely and difficult path, to get us to our destiny – or rather, to his destiny for us.

---

[29] Martin Luther, *Table Talk*, p. 389.

[30] William Temple, *Palm Sunday to Easter* (SPCK), p. 88.

[31] Gary Best, *Naturally Supernatural* (Vineyard International Publishing, 2005), p. 36.

In his famous play *The Death of a Salesman* Arthur Miller traces the life of Willy Loman, a man who spent his life chasing fantasies of success as an irresistible salesman. Loman lived in total denial, and swung between his illusion that the next day would bring the success he had dreamed of, and bouts of despair about his uselessness at the job. He tortured himself that if only he had enough confidence, he would 'make it'. The tragedy was that, if only he had had enough courage to face up to the unrealities of his dreams, and had chosen to pursue something more attainable and practical, he could have made something of his life. As it was, he ended it tragically by suicide. He could never allow himself to go through the vale of tears in recognising the unreality of his dreams – or, indeed, the truth about himself. Had he allowed himself to face that, he could have begun to find true meaning to life and started the building of a realistic future for himself.

God sometimes locks us up to make us search for a way out. Jonathan Aitken was reflecting on Psalm 46 while in prison following his conviction for 'lying on oath about a hotel bill'. Awaiting trial he had surprisingly found God. He writes that 'God's mysterious purposes can be communicated to us in mysterious ways. Tragedies, disasters and catastrophes may seem the most unbearable and unbelievable signals of a new and God-guided purpose in our lives.' He continues by asking, 'Are we willing to listen to those signals, to decode them, and to act upon them?'[32]

John Newton, author of the hymn 'Amazing Grace', was also very perceptive in his understanding of God's dealings

---

[32] Aitken, *Psalms for People Under Pressure*, p. 129.

with man. He published a book of counselling letters and once in addressing a friend he wrote, 'You say you are more disposed to cry, "Misere!" than "Hallelujah". Why not both together? When the treble is praise and heart humiliation is for bass, the melody is pleasant and the harmony is good.'

The purpose of God in showing believers the evil of their own hearts is to impel them to prize more highly the grace and all-sufficiency of Jesus. In this way they go through life *sorrowful yet always rejoicing* *(1 Corinthians 6:10)*. 'Soul exercise' (Newton's name for poverty of spirit) is evidence of a healthy spiritual condition.[33]

> Christians down the ages have discovered the 'treasures of darkness' and have gained a richness of maturity and spirituality that would have been impossible when the sun was shining.[34]

Joseph was sold into slavery by his own jealous brothers, and taken to Egypt where he went through some extraordinary sufferings, until God promoted him to be Pharaoh's right-hand man – 'Number Two' in the nation. When his older brothers went to Egypt later, in a desperate search for corn, they came face to face with their younger brother, now in a position of great power. As they grovelled before him in repentance, Joseph dismissed their weeping:

> *Do not be distressed and do not be angry with yourselves for selling me here, because it was to save lives that God sent me ahead of you. For two years now there has been famine in the land, and for the next five years there will not be ploughing and reaping. But God sent me ahead*

---

[33] See John Newton in *Letters* (Banner of Truth, 1960), pp.10–11.

[34] David Watson, *Fear No Evil* (Hodder & Stougton, 1984), p.120.

of you to preserve for you a remnant on earth and to save your lives by a great deliverance. So then, it was not you who sent me here, but God. (Genesis 45:5–8)

An amazing insight, and a lesson for us all. Joseph could see the hand of God in his life. So many, sadly, fail to see it. *'And we know that in all things God works for the good of those who love him, who have been called according to his purpose' (Romans 8:28).*

The wife of a missionary martyr, Elisabeth Elliot once talked about a time she had spent with Corrie ten Boom. After Elisabeth had recounted something of her experiences and that of her martyred husband Jim (whose story is told in *Through Gates of Splendour*), Corrie held up a piece of embroidery with its back facing Elisabeth – just a jumble of threads that made no sense at all (no pattern or pleasing picture). As she did this she repeated a poem:

> My life is but a weaving betwixt my God and me,
> I do not choose the colours, He worketh steadily.
> Oftimes He weaveth sorrow, and I, in foolish pride,
> Forget He sees the upper and I the underside.

Then she turned the piece over, and there on a purple background was revealed a shining golden crown.

PROMISED REWARD[35]

What could be the benefit of being 'poor in spirit'? Jesus says that *'theirs is the kingdom of heaven'*.

---

[35] I cannot write on this without recommending a wonderful book called *Heaven* by Randy Alcorn and published by Tyndale House, Illinois.

Those who sow in tears
  will reap with songs of joy.
He who goes out weeping,
  carrying seed to sow,
will return with songs of joy,
  carrying sheaves with him.
(Psalm 126:5–6)

Has not God chosen those who are poor in the eyes of the world to be rich in faith and to inherit the kingdom he promised those who love him? (James 2:5)

It is difficult to begin to appreciate what good news this is – an eternal kingdom that is built on *'righteousness, peace and joy in the Holy Spirit' (Romans 14:17)*. *'Then the King will say to those on his right, "Come, you who are blessed by my Father; take your inheritance, the kingdom prepared for you since the creation of the world"' (Matthew 25:34)*. While everything else, the heavens and the earth – the whole of creation – will be thoroughly shaken, the kingdom of God remains 'unshakeable'. *'Therefore, since we are receiving a kingdom that cannot be shaken, let us be thankful, and so worship God acceptably with reverence and awe, for our God is a consuming fire' (Hebrews 12:28)*. And whether we have seen little or much fruit in seeking to advance the kingdom of God, we who count ourselves to be no more than 'worms' have a place in the kingdom of heaven, granted to us solely by his grace.

This kingdom is the kingdom of God.[36] We acknowledge this every time we conclude the Lord's Prayer – *'Yours is the*

---

[36] Referred to by Matthew as the 'kingdom of heaven', out of deference to his Jewish readers who would have considered it blasphemy to pronounce the actual name of God aloud.

kingdom, the power and the glory.' It is a kingdom utterly beyond our earthly comprehension. *'Now we see but a poor reflection as in a mirror; then we shall see face to face. Now I know in part; then I shall know fully, even as I am fully known (1 Corinthians 13:12).*

In his last crusade, after which he collapsed and never preached again, Dwight L. Moody, the great American evangelist, was weak and in pain on the platform, but he threw up his arms before the massed thousands and cried, 'Look at the other world!' He pointed heavenwards in the old familiar gesture: 'No death, no pain, no sorrow, no old age, no sickness, no bending forms, no dimmed eyes, no tears. But joy, peace, love, happiness. No grey hairs. People all young! Think of it! Life! Life! Life without end!'[37] That is just a glimpse of it. That is what is coming – what is waiting for us. Thanks be to God!

MEDITATION

The way to deeper knowledge of God is through the lonely valley of soul poverty and abnegation of all things . . . [such] blessed poor are no longer slaves to the tyranny of things. They have broken the yoke of the oppressor; and this they have done, not by fighting but by surrendering. Though free from all sense of possessing, they yet possess all things. 'Theirs is the kingdom of heaven.' (Anon.)

* * *

Miles Coverdale gives us a profound translation of Psalm 84 in the old 1662 *Book of Common Prayer*: 'Who going through

---

[37] J. C. Pollock, *Moody without Sankey* (Hodder & Stoughton, 1963), p. 268.

the vale of misery use it for a well' (verse 6). The idea behind this is that a person is certainly blessed who 'can use his or her tears of misery as a well or spring from which to drink the waters of spiritual refreshment . . . Adversity is often the gateway to deeper faith'. (Jonathan Aitken)

* * *

Dr Sheila Cassidy has written of how she entered a convent to test her vocation. Was God really calling her to be a nun? She soon found that in fact she was unsuited to such a lifestyle. Reflecting later, she reckoned that the only thing that kept her sane during the time there was a poster showing an extremely unhappy rag doll being put through a mangle, with the caption, 'The truth will set you free – but first it will make you miserable'![38]

* * *

Call me Mara [Bitterness], because the Almighty has made my life very bitter. I went away full, but the Lord has brought me back empty. (Ruth 1:20–21)

* * *

> *Bring my soul out of prison;*
> *that I may give thanks unto thy Name.*
> *(Psalm 142:9, Book of Common Prayer, 1662)*

* * *

> *Blessed are those whose strength is in you,*
> *   who have set their hearts on pilgrimage.*
> *As they pass through the Valley of Baca [weeping],*

---

[38] Sheila Cassidy, *Your Kingdom Come* (Cafod/Darton, Longman and Todd, 1997), p. 72.

they make it a place of springs [refreshing]. . .
They go from strength to strength,
    till each appears before God in Zion.
(Psalm 84:5–6, 7)

* * *

It is God's will that I should cast my cares on Him each day.
He always asks me not to cast my confidence away.
But Oh! How stupidly I act, when taken unawares.
I cast away my confidence – and carry all my cares.
(Anon.)

* * *

Just as I am, without one plea,
But that Thy blood was shed for me,
And that Thou bidst me come to Thee,
O Lamb of God, I come. . .

Just as I am, though tossed about
With many a conflict, many a doubt,
Fightings and fears within, without,
O Lamb of God, I come. . .
(Charlotte Elliott, 1789–1871)

* * *

Following his public reading of Isaiah's prophecy in the Nazareth synagogue, Jesus explained that a part of his ministry would be *'to bind up the broken-hearted'*, so we can be assured that he is ever watchful over our spiritual well-being. He is an 'ever present help in time of need', though the help may not come in ways or by means we imagine.

* * *

I am no longer my own, but Thine.
Put me to what Thou wilt,
Rank me with whom Thou wilt,
Put me to doing, put me to suffering:
Let me be employed for Thee,
Or laid aside for Thee,
Or brought low for Thee:
Let me be full,
Let me be empty:
Let me be all things,
Let me be nothing:
I freely and heartily yield all things
To Thy pleasure and disposal.
And now, O Glorious and Blessed God,
Father, Son and Holy Spirit,
Thou art mine and I am Thine.
So be it.
And the Covenant which I have made on earth,
Let it be ratified in Heaven. Amen.[39]

* * *

Lord, teach me not to be afraid of experiencing the whole gamut of emotions. (Selwyn Hughes)

* * *

John Newton, the converted and repentant slave-trader, famous for the popular hymn 'Amazing Grace', wrote another that beautifully expresses the struggles we have over our broken-heartedness.

I asked the Lord that I might grow
In faith, and love, and every grace,

---

[39] The Methodist Covenant Prayer.

Might more of His salvation know,
And seek more earnestly His face.

'Twas He who taught me thus to pray,
And He, I trust, has answered prayer;
But it has been in such a way
As almost drove me to despair.

I hoped that in some favoured hour,
At once He'd answer my request;
And, by His love's constraining power,
Subdue my sins, and give me rest.

Instead of this, He made me feel
The hidden evils of my heart;
And let the angry powers of hell
Assault my soul in every part.

Yea more with His own hand He seemed
Intent to aggravate my woe;
Crossed all the fair designs I schemed,
Blasted my gourds, and laid me low.

'Lord why is this?' I trembling cried,
'Wilt Thou pursue Thy worm to death?'
''Tis in this way,' the Lord replied,
'I answer prayer for grace and faith.'

'These inward trials I employ,
From self and pride to set thee free;
And break the schemes of earthly joy,
That thou mayest seek thy all in Me.'

* * *

It is in our pain and in our brokenness that we come closest to
Christ. (Martin Luther)

* * *

Marie Balter ends her amazing story *Nobody's Child* with beautiful words whose source I cannot identify – a modern paraphrase of a psalm perhaps: 'I will build an altar unto you, O God, with the broken pieces of my heart.'

* * *

> I turn to you in times of sorrow
> And times of hurt and pain.
> I blame you when all goes wrong
> When there's no sun shining through the rain.
> I tell you my thoughts
> Whether I'm right or wrong.
> You helped me get through
> To stay faithful and stay strong.
> I thank you for always being there
> When I really needed a friend.
> When I needed someone to talk to
> You listened from beginning to end.
> You helped me to get through
> With all the love you give.
> If you weren't there I don't know what I'd do.
> I don't know how I would talk or live.
> It's nice to know you are always there
> Watching over me.
> It's nice to know there's someone else to talk to;
> Someone to set me free
> From all the suffering and evil
> That is here today.
> But I trust you God my Father
> In every single way.
> (Grace Shaw, aged 13)

* * *

O Lord, give me strength in the knowledge of my weakness, light in the hours of my darkness, joy in the seasons of my sadness, solace in the times of my sickness. And with the mercy and grace by which you give your comfort, enable me to comfort others. For Jesus' sake, Amen.

* * *

And he carried me away in the Spirit to a mountain great and high, and showed me the Holy City, Jerusalem, coming down out of heaven from God. It shone with the glory of God. (Revelation 21:10–11)

2

The Slough of Despond

Blessed are those who mourn, for they will be comforted.
(Matthew 5:4)

Then Jacob tore his clothes . . . and mourned for his son [Joseph] many days . . . he refused to be comforted. 'No,' he said, 'in mourning will I go down to the grave to my son.' So his father wept for him. (Genesis 37:34–35)

* * *

I have . . . seen the oppression of my people in Egypt. I have heard their groaning and have come down to set them free. (Acts 7:34)

TEARS

Not now, but in the coming years,
It may be in a better land,
We'll know the meaning of our tears,
And there, sometime, we'll understand.
(Maxine N. Cornelius)

THE DEFINING OF TEARS

What do tears mean? Here are some ideas.

- Mother Teresa talked about the 'gift of tears'.
- Tears are the 'distillation of the soul'. (M. R. De Haan)
- Tears are the 'diamonds of heaven'. (Charles Haddon Spurgeon)
- Tears are 'liquid pain'. (Herbert Lockyer)
- 'Tears win victories – a cold, unfeeling, dry-eyed religion has no influence over the souls of men.' (Anon.)
- 'Those who don't know how to weep with their whole heart don't know how to laugh either.' (Golda Meir)

THE ABSENCE OF TEARS IN OUR CULTURE

> *We played the flute for you,*
> *and you did not dance;*
> *we sang a dirge,*
> *and you did not mourn.*
> *(Matthew 11:17)*

Our own mourning and grief make uncongenial talk in our culture today. We are meant to pretend that we are having a whale of a time – eating better food, driving smarter cars and having exotic holidays, just all enjoying an immensely wonderful existence.

This may explain why, in the case of the death of a young national figure like Princess Diana, there was an unexpected excuse for a mega-expression of long-suppressed and surprisingly widespread grief – much of it personal, but vicariously channelled through the 'occasion'.

A celebrity in mourning, Sheila Hancock, wrote of the

prevalent attitude she found: 'In this country we don't talk about grief. You're not allowed to say, "I feel absolutely devastated and I'd rather die."'[1] But in his Sermon on the Mount Jesus clearly valued the positive relevance of this darkest of life's experiences.

THE ABSENCE OF TEARS IN OUR CHURCHES

Ian Stackhouse has a serious criticism to make about some of our charismatic churches today: 'Charismatic worship is by definition upbeat and strident, with little or no reflection on the place of lament in spiritual development.'[2] John Stott makes a similar observation about evangelicals for another reason: 'I fear', he writes, 'that we evangelical Christians, by making much of grace, sometimes thereby make light of sin.' He continues:

> There is not enough sorrow for sin among us. We should experience more 'godly grief' of Christian penitence, like the eighteenth-century pioneer missionary to the American Indians, David Brainerd. He had written in his journal on 18 October 1740: 'In my morning devotions my soul was exceedingly melted, and bitterly mourned over my exceeding sinfulness and vileness.'[3]

This latter is a genuine concern to which we must return. But the Bible also reveals other examples of mourning for other areas in life too.

---

[1] Sheila Hancock, *The Two of Us: My Life with John Thaw* (Bloomsbury, 2004).

[2] Ian Stackhouse, *The Gospel Driven Church* (Paternoster, 2004), p. 206.

[3] John Stott, *The Message of the Sermon on the Mount* (IVP, 1978), p. 42.

GRIEF

Jesus said, *'Blessed are those who mourn. . .'* There are four occasions recorded in the Gospels when Jesus himself mourned:

(1) At the grave of Lazarus – in grief over the personal loss of his friend.

> *Jesus . . . was deeply moved in spirit and troubled . . . Jesus wept. (John 11:33, 35)*

(2) Over the state of Jerusalem – in grief over the spiritual blindness of some of his hearers.

> *O Jerusalem, Jerusalem, you who kill the prophets and stone those sent to you, how often I have longed to gather your children together, as a hen gathers her chicks under her wings, but you were not willing. Look, your house is left to you desolate. For I tell you, you will not see me again until you say, 'Blessed is he who comes in the name of the Lord.' (Matthew 23:37–39)*

(3) In the Garden of Gethsemane – in grief at facing the unique and imminent suffering and sacrifice of himself on the cross for the sins of the whole world.

> *Then Jesus went with his disciples to a place called Gethsemane, and he said to them, 'Sit here while I go over there and pray.' He took Peter and the two sons of Zebedee along with him, and he began to be sorrowful and troubled. Then he said to them, 'My soul is overwhelmed with sorrow to the point of death. Stay here and keep watch with me.'*
>
> *Going a little farther, he fell with his face to the ground and prayed, 'My Father, if it is possible, may this cup be taken from me. . .' (Matthew 26:36–39)*

(4) On the cross of Calvary. Of course we would not expect to find expressions of grief for personal sin in the sinless Son of God, who *'knew no sin' (2 Corinthians 5:21)*, *'had no sin' (1 John 3:5)* and *'did no sin' (1 Peter 2:22)*. Nearing the end of Jesus' life on earth, when he was on trial, Pilate, the Roman governor, desperate to please the Jewish hierarchy and eager to find some excuse to do as they wanted, had finally to admit, after a full examination of the evidence, that *'I find no fault in Him' (John 19:4 KJV)*. But on the cross, as he bore the sins of the world, he uttered his final agonising cry of grief, *'My God, my God, why have you forsaken me?' (Matthew 27:46)*.

CATEGORIES OF GRIEF

These examples teach us to discern differing categories for grief, and not to limit it just to one. Indeed, it seems there may be some eight distinct categories – each regarding some aspect of loss. We note the following causes.

(1) Grief over the loss of loved ones
(2) Grief over the loss of God's protection and provision
(3) Grief as the sorrow of repentance
(4) Grief at a sense of inadequacy and loss of self-worth
(5) Grief as the cost of love
(6) Grief as a means of becoming attuned to God's heart
(7) Grief as soul travail
(8) Grief over the loss of time and opportunity

Let us look at each category in turn.

(1) Grief over the Loss of Loved Ones

When Martin Luther's daughter Magdalena was only 14 years old and on her deathbed, Luther prayed, 'O God, I love her so, but Thy will be done.' And turning to her, he said, 'Magdalena, my little girl, you would like to stay with your father here and you would be glad to go to your Father in Heaven.' And she said, 'Yes, dear father, as God wills.' And Luther reproached himself, because God had blessed him as no bishop had been blessed in a thousand years. Katie (the girl's mother) stood further away from the bed, overcome by grief. Luther was actually holding his child in his arms as she died. When she was laid to rest, he said, '*Du liebes Lenchen*, you will rise and shine like the stars and the sun. How strange it is to know that she is at peace and all is well and yet to be so sorrowful!'[4]

Mourning the passing of relatives and friends, knowing we shall never meet them again this side of glory, is the mourning with which we are most familiar. To lose a loved one is a devastating crisis – the whole world seems to come crashing down around us. There are heart-searchings, so many regrets. There are resentments and often anger. The broken heart is in turmoil. And we are left with so many questions – why, why and why?

Consider Job. He had just heard that he had lost his seven sons and three daughters, all his sheep, camels, oxen and asses.

At this, Job got up and tore his robe and shaved his head. Then he fell to the ground in worship and said:

---

[4] Roland H. Bainton, *Here I Stand: A Life of Martin Luther* (Mentor Books, 1950), p. 236.

'Naked I came from my mother's womb,
 and naked I shall depart.
The Lord gave and the Lord has taken away;
 may the name of the Lord be praised.'
In all this, Job did not sin by charging God with wrongdoing. (Job 1:21–22)

Following this Job was further afflicted *'with painful sores from the soles of his feet to the top of his head' (Job 2:7).* A yet further degree of distress came from his wife urging him to *'Curse God and die!' (Job 2:9).*

When Job's three friends . . . heard about all the troubles that had come upon him, they set out from their homes and met together by agreement to go and sympathise with him and comfort him. When they saw him from a distance . . . they began to weep aloud, and they tore their robes and sprinkled dust on their heads. Then they sat on the ground with him for seven days and seven nights. No one said a word to him, because they saw how great his suffering was. (Job 2:11–13)

The story (which opens with a peep behind the scenes revealing God's permissive will) continues with strong arguments by Job's friends as to why Job was caused to suffer in this way, with Job protesting all along that he was sure it was not for anything he had done to deserve it.

C. S. Lewis disclosed his own struggle with grief following the death of his wife Joy through cancer. In his book called *A Grief Observed* he reflected on his personal experiences. Few could articulate their grief with his clarity or such daring self-disclosure. He wrote:

My heart and body are crying out; 'Come back, come back!' But I know that this is impossible. I know that the thing I want

I can never get; the old life, the jokes, the drinks, the arguments, the love-making, the tiny, heartbreaking commonplace. . .

Talk to me about the truth of religion and I'll gladly listen. Talk to me about the duty of religion and I'll listen submissively. But don't talk to me of the consolation of religion or I shall suspect that you don't understand. . .

This is one of the most disquieting symptoms. When you are happy, so happy that you have no sense of needing him [God], if you turn to him with praise, you will be welcomed with open arms. But go to him when all other help is vain, and what do you find? A door slammed in your face, and a sound of bolting and double bolting on the inside. After that . . . silence! You may as well turn away!

To whom could this world-famous theologian, this broken-hearted soul, now turn for help? Others had often turned to him, but there seemed to be no one to whom he could turn; neither his disciples, nor his colleagues, nor his friends; neither to his brother, nor to the boys.

I can't talk to the children about her. The moment I try there appears on their faces neither grief, nor love, nor fear, nor pity, but the most fatal of all non-conductors, embarrassment. They look as if I am committing an indecency. They are longing for me to stop.

Then again, his attempts to pray to God about Joy were 'like speaking into a vacuum of nonentity'. He began to think the most terrible thoughts about God for allowing her to be taken, and then not being there for him. But day by day, as he was working and weeping through his grief, dragging it painfully along his *via dolorosa*, he found his conception of

God gradually beginning to change. A note of peace entered his writings which now filled three exercise books. (He filled yet another before he had finished.) But at last he could write:

> I have gradually come to feel that the door is no longer slammed shut and bolted. Was it my own frantic need that slammed it in my face? The time when there is nothing at all in your soul except a cry for help may be just the time when God can't give it. You are like a drowning man who can't be helped because he clutches and grabs. Perhaps your own reiterated cries deafen you to the voice you hoped to hear.

If God did not answer his unanswerable human questions about suffering and grief, it was, at least, 'a rather special sort of "No answer" – more like a silent, certainly not uncompassionate gaze, as though he shook his head, not in refusal, but waiving the question. Like, "Peace child, don't you understand?"'

He ultimately came to realise that his kind of grief could be a selfish thing. He saw that the tears were no longer because his loved one had been taken by God, as he truly believed, but because he did not have her with him any more. This realisation became a turning point for him.[5]

(2) Grief over the Loss of God's Protection and Provision

The priest Ezra, with permission from the king of Persia, started the restoration of the Temple in Jerusalem, and then he heard that those of the people of Israel who had already returned had become involved in the detestable practices of

---

[5] C. S. Lewis, *A Grief Observed* (1961).

their neighbours – and their leaders had led the way in such unfaithfulness. He pours out his grief:

> *When I heard this, I . . . sat there appalled . . . at the evening sacrifice,*
> *I rose from my self-abasement, with my tunic and cloak torn, and fell*
> *on my knees with my hands spread out to the Lord my God and prayed:*
> *'O my God, I am too ashamed and disgraced to lift up my face to you,*
> *my God, because our sins are higher than our heads and our guilt has*
> *reached to the heavens. From the days of our forefathers until now, our*
> *guilt has been great. Because of our sins, we and our kings and our*
> *priests have been subjected to the sword and captivity, to pillage and*
> *humiliation at the hand of foreign kings, as it is today. . .' (Ezra 9:3–7)*

Some years later the Temple building in Jerusalem was still incomplete, and Nehemiah, a Jew and a personal servant of King Artaxerxes, gets a report back on his people there.

> *'Those who survived the exile and are back in the province are in great*
> *trouble and disgrace. The wall of Jerusalem is broken down, and its*
> *gates have been burned with fire.'*
> *When I heard these things, I sat down and wept. For some days I*
> *mourned and fasted and prayed before the God of heaven. Then I said:*
> *'O Lord, God of heaven, the great and awesome God. . .'*
> *(Nehemiah 1:3–5)*

The relevance of mourning to everyday life

In my early attempts at reading the prophets – especially Jeremiah (from the sixth century BC) – I found it hard to get excited about them. I just could not get onto their wavelength. Jeremiah always seemed to be moaning on about something – far too pessimistic for me! And worse still, his depressing prophecies just went on and on. Added to all that there was Lamentations, another (albeit shorter) book of dirges, also believed to have been written by Jeremiah. It had the same tragic tone.

Finally, however, I began to get the message. If Jeremiah was moaning, it was because he was really in mourning about something precious that Israel was losing. If he seemed to be for ever groaning, it was because he was truly grieving over something which was causing everyone to suffer.

Then I saw that the theme of many of the other prophets was equally mournful, although their lamentations were briefer. I looked again at Amos, writing two centuries before Jeremiah, and Haggai, writing two centuries later. They may have been addressing Israel's backsliding leaders, priests and prophets at different periods in history, but they were lamenting very similar conditions and confronting Israel about them, while the contemporary leaders just did not want to know. The prophets predicted that just as night follows day, so the long days of false religion and social evil would be followed by an even longer night of God's judgement. The whole nation had simply forgotten the Lord. They had become faithless to God in all their relationships and responsibilities.

> They sell . . . the needy for a pair of sandals.
> They trample on the heads of the poor
>   as upon the dust of the ground.
> (Amos 2:6–7)

Everything was going wrong, but they completely failed to see, or were determined to overlook, the connection between God's present disfavour towards them and their long-term disobedience towards him. They were experiencing many of the same crises that our 'global village' is experiencing today.

They could not understand that since they as a nation had forsaken God, they were experiencing all the appalling horrors of being God-forsaken. They could not make the connection between the two. But they needed to make that connection and mourn over it. Mourning, with all its vulnerabilities, is an imperative step in the process of repentance leading to change of mind or attitude, whatever the apparent loss or sacrifice involved.

(3) Grief as the Sorrow of Repentance

We have already noted this in John Stott's comment about 'sorrow for sin', quoted above. The shameful awareness that our old nature (the flesh) is still alive and is still seeking to ruin our relationship with the Lord is a deep reality over which we wrestle in hidden inner struggles. As individuals we have no control over the fact of sin in the universe, but as creatures given choices we are responsible for the way we react to it in our own lives.

Because *all have sinned and come short of the glory of God' (Romans 3:23)*, all need to grieve and repent of sin in their own lives. God has said, *'Return to me with all your heart, with fasting and weeping and mourning' (Joel 2:12)*. And again, through Peter, he says, *'Repent, then, and turn to God, so that your sins may be wiped out, that times of refreshing may come from the Lord' (Acts 3:19)*. We are reminded of Paul, who wrote: *'Meanwhile we groan, longing to be clothed with our heavenly dwelling, because when we are clothed, we will not be found naked. For while we are in this tent, we groan and are burdened. . .' (2 Corinthians 5:2–4a)*. Of course, we know that the day is finally coming when we shall be clothed with new, imperishable and glorified bodies *(1 Corinthians 15:53)*.

Bishop James Ryle drives the point home:

> The Lord Jesus calls 'blessed' those that mourn. He means those who sorrow for sin, and grieve daily over their own short-comings. These are they who trouble themselves more about their sin than about anything else on earth. The remembrance of them is grievous to them; the burden of them is intolerable. Blessed are all such! *'The sacrifices of God are a broken spirit and a contrite heart' (Psalm 51:17)*. One day they shall weep no more: *'they shall be comforted'*.[6]

(4) Grief at a Sense of Inadequacy and Loss of Self-Worth

Jeremiah, the weeping prophet, laments the wayward state of the human heart:

> *I know, O LORD, that a man's life is not his own;*
> *it is not for man to direct his steps.*
> (Jeremiah 10:23)

> *The heart is deceitful above all things*
> *and beyond cure.*
> (Jeremiah 17:9)

Before I can become wise, I must first realise my own foolishness. Before I can become strong, I must first recognise my own weakness. Before I can receive power, I must first understand my own powerlessness. Before I can become pure again, I must first recognise my own uncleanness. The

---

[6] J. C. Ryle, *Expository Thoughts on the Gospels – Matthew, Vol. 1* (William Hunt & Co., 1887).

mourning of inadequacy is a weeping that catches the attention of God. The Bible says,

> *The Lord is close to the broken-hearted*
> *and saves those who are crushed in spirit.*
> *(Psalm 34:18)*

(5) Grief as the Cost of Love

Queen Elizabeth II once spoke of 'grief being the cost of love'. She was referring to her loss at the passing of Elizabeth the Queen Mother – her own mother, whom she had loved. We love God, and we grieve when at last we begin to understand how much we have wounded him with our wilfulness.

(6) Grief as a Means of Becoming Attuned to God's Heart

'It is the deepest concern to God to find those who share his feelings. . .'[7] He wants to involve us by allowing us to enter into his grief for the world that he created and loves. 'Becoming attuned to God's heart' may sound a bit cryptic or mystic, but loving God will increasingly move the heart, in a sometimes painful process of discovering his 'wavelength', by having entered that place of grief. We may find ourselves weeping with him. The psalmist appears to have touched base at that point precisely when he wrote,

> *Streams of tears flow from my eyes,*
> *for your law is not obeyed.*
> *(Psalm 119:136)*

---

[7] Arthur Wallis, *God's Chosen Fast* (Victory Press, 1968), p. 37.

This compassionate heartbreak for God's will in the world is what turns our prayer into fruitfulness. Along the *Via Dolorosa* in Jerusalem Jesus bids the weeping women gathered round him to redirect their prayers for him and to start wailing for themselves and their offspring: *'A large number of people followed him, including women who mourned and wailed for him. Jesus turned and said to them, "Daughters of Jerusalem, do not weep for me; weep for yourselves and for your children"' (Luke 23:27–28).*

(7) Grief as Soul Travail

'Man's extremity is God's opportunity.' Many might think that a grown man or woman interceding with loud weeping would be going a bit too far – that praying with tears is a bit 'over the top'. Hannah wept in prayer before the Lord about her childlessness and when, at last, she became pregnant, she turned her heart to God in praise with such a beautiful poetic prayer:

> *He raises the poor from the dust*
> *   and lifts the needy from the ash heap;*
> *he seats them with princes*
> *   and has them inherit a throne of honour.*
> *(1 Samuel 2:8)*

Hannah loved God, and she knew well the cost of a broken heart, having been personally misunderstood and rejected. She knew it, not only from the bitterness of her barrenness, but also from the malice of her husband's other jealous wife. This had been compounded by the casual accusation of drunkenness from Eli the priest. He had misunderstood that her tears were symptoms of deep travailing in her soul in prayer.

Again we can imagine how Jacob experienced such 'soul travail' when he wrestled all night by the brook Jabbok, preparing himself to meet up the next day with his estranged brother Esau. Doubtless he recalled all his double-dealings from the past – and now grieved over them sorely. As a closure to that night of weary wrestling, he adamantly refused to give in and let go of God. And for that he was given a new name, *'Israel, because you have struggled with God and with men and have overcome' (Genesis 32:28).*

Moses was so distressed at the Israelites' faithlessness, he prayed to God, *'Oh, this people have sinned a great sin, and have made them gods of gold. Yet now, if thou wilt forgive their sin; and if not, blot me, I pray thee, out of thy book which thou hast written' (Exodus 32:32 KJV).*

Paul spoke of his great sorrow and the unceasing anguish in his heart, wishing himself accursed and cut off from Christ for the sake of his people, those of his own race, the people of Israel *(Romans 9:2).*

John writes of his sorrow on seeing the vision of the unopened scroll. He had seen *'a mighty angel proclaiming in a loud voice, "Who is worthy to break the seals and open the scroll?" . . . I wept and wept because no one was found who was worthy to open the scroll or look inside' (Revelation 5:2b, 4).*

We do not use the phrase 'soul travail' much today. It implies a continual flow of compassionate prayer arising from the grief of a broken heart for that which seems unattainable. Today it could be travail in prayer for a turnaround in the fortunes of an individual, a family, a nation, or a world that is spiritually lost, that has forsaken its Maker, yet a world that God still loves and grieves over when a single soul is lost *(John 3:16).*

(8) Grief over the Loss of Time and Opportunity

We grieve and mourn because of opportunities missed – the memory of them causes us deep vexation and frustration. We grieve for the consequences of misguided and irreversible neglect, the effects of which may not yet have caught up with us, but which we can already see will adversely affect others in the work of God.

Esau came in feeling famished from hunting and swapped his inheritance as an older brother, his marvellous birthright as Isaac's firstborn, for a mere bowl of Jacob's stew. Later, when he realised the consequences of his folly, *'he burst out with a loud and bitter cry and said to his father, "Bless me – me too, my father!"'* But Isaac said, *'Your brother came deceitfully and took your blessing' (Genesis 27:34–35)*. Afterwards, when he wanted to inherit this blessing, he was rejected. *'He could bring about no change of mind, though he sought the blessing with tears' (Hebrews 12:17)*. Clearly he was still blaming Jacob for the effects of his own foolishness in trading his birthright for a bowl of broth. His weeping was only sorrow for his loss and not repentance for his sin.

So it is really good news when Jesus says that genuine mourners will find comfort. He actually says, *'Blessed are those who mourn, for they will be comforted.'* This paradoxical one-liner would seem to imply a curious state whereby we can be happy and sad at the same time.[8] However, Jesus would have understood this apparent contradiction from his own experience. We read how, *'for the joy set before him*

---

[8] There is an archaic word, *chantepleure*, which means 'to sing and weep at the same time' – a word once current in conversation. See A. Wallace and D. Wallechinsky, *The Back of Lists* (Canongate, 2005).

[he] endured the cross' (Hebrews 12:2), yet he was also *'a man of sorrows and acquainted with grief' (Isaiah 53:3 KJV)*. At any time, anyone meeting him would have been able to be simultaneously exhilarated by his inner joy or comforted by the empathy emanating from his inner sorrow.

WHAT GOOD DOES MOURNING DO?

HOW DOES MOURNING HELP?

(1) It is inevitably a process, a time of transition, of moving on from loss.

(2) It helps us to sense the heart of God. We begin to tune in to God's wavelength.

(3) It urges us to do something about our 'crooked and perverse' generation, and to get others involved in prayer with us to harmonise with God's deep concerns before it is too late.

(4) It spurs us on to warn everyone possible of the imminence of God's wrath and coming judgement – just as the prophets of old did.

> *Put on sackcloth, O priests, and mourn;*
> *wail, you who minister before the altar.*
> *(Joel 1:13)*

> *Blow the trumpet in Zion;*
> *   sound the alarm on my holy hill.*
> *Let all who live in the land tremble,*
> *   for the day of the Lord [judgement] is coming.*
> *(Joel 2:1)*

> *Declare a holy fast,*
> *   call a sacred assembly.*

Gather the people,
consecrate the assembly. . .
(Joel 2:15–16)

You strum away on your harps like David
and improvise on musical instruments.
You drink wine by the bowlful
  and use the finest lotions,
    but you do not grieve over the ruin of Joseph.
(Amos 6:5–6)

WHAT DOES MOURNING CREATE?

One might say that mourning creates three things, three opportunities.

(1) It creates a suitable climate that softens us to reflect and listen to God: *'I am . . . going to allure her* [my people] *. . . into the desert* [the place of deprivation and hardship, where one is more sensitive to the realities of one's life and more aware of the supernatural through the lack of material support] *and speak tenderly to her' (Hosea 2:14).*

(2) It creates a suitable state for repenting and earnest prayer: *'If my people, who are called by my name, will humble themselves and pray and seek my face and turn from their wicked ways, then I will hear from heaven and will forgive their sin and will heal their land' (2 Chronicles 7:14).*

(3) It creates a prelude to God's favour. God has a heart for those who mourn: *'Then the Lord called to the man clothed in linen who had the writing kit at his side and said to him, "Go throughout the city of Jerusalem and put a mark on the*

foreheads of those who grieve and lament over all the detestable things that are done in it"' (Ezekiel 9:3–4).

WHAT IF PEOPLE WON'T ALLOW THEMSELVES TO MOURN?

(1) Such people may experience a famine of hearing the word of God *(Amos 8:11)*. Even if they would listen to God, they cannot hear him. They have *'stopped up their ears' (Zechariah 7:11)*.

(2) Such people may become increasingly cynical – unable to find spiritual satisfaction and, like the Pharisees of old, blind to moral and spiritual realities *(John 9:35–41)*.

(3) Such people may easily become indifferent and hard-hearted – like Pharaoh *(Exodus 7 – 14)*, or 'unresponsive' – like King Josiah *(2 Kings 22:19)*.

(4) Such people will eventually mourn as they fall under God's final judgement *(Amos 5:16–17)* and destruction *(Amos 9:1–4)*.

COMFORT

. . . for they will be comforted. (Matthew 5:4)

WHAT IS COMFORT?

The word 'comfort' in the original is from a Greek verb deriving from the noun *paraklesis* – 'a coming alongside'. This 'coming alongside' is to help or to strengthen us *(John 16:7–16)*. Jesus assures us of the continued presence in the world of a divine 'Comforter'. The Holy Spirit is the Comforter – not so much 'There, there – better soon', but 'I am here and I will be with you through all your troubles'.

The following extract from a book by Susan Hill will serve as an illustration of this kind of comfort.

> Without any warning, the tears rose up and broke out of her, and Potter sat on his chair, saying nothing, and yet being a comfort to her, taking some of her grief on to himself. She wept as she had never wept before in front of any human being, and it was a good thing to do: it was of more value than all the months of solitary mourning. It brought something to an end.[9]

HOW WILL THEY BE COMFORTED?

> *You have heard of Job's perseverance and have seen what the Lord finally brought about. The Lord is full of compassion and mercy. (James 5:11 TNIV)*

The following illustrations will serve to demonstrate some of the ways in which comfort might be brought to those who mourn. If we persevere, God is indeed full of compassion and mercy.

Christian Escapes Despair

In Bunyan's *Pilgrim's Progress*, following their error in taking a short cut through By-Pass Meadow, Christian and Hopeful were arrested for trespassing by Giant Despair, who threw them into the deepest dungeon of Doubting Castle. There they were mercilessly beaten day after day on the orders of Mistrust, the giant's wife, and forced to mourn for many days for their rash folly in leaving the King's highway. They finally escaped the dark dungeon when they discovered, what they had forgotten, that they still had with them

---

[9] Susan Hill, *In the Springtime of the Year* (Penguin, 1977), p. 135.

the Key of Promise. With this they could unlock the dungeon's door, which they did and escaped to freedom.

A Friend at the Right Time

A little girl went out to play with a friend and was late home. Naturally her mother asked her where she had been. The child explained that her friend had fallen and broken her special doll:

'And I stayed to help her.'

'How did you help her?' her curious mother asked.

'I just sat down and helped her to cry!' she replied. (Anon.)

The Source of all Comfort

Paul reminds us again:

> Praise be to the God and Father of our Lord Jesus Christ, the Father of compassion and the God of all comfort, who comforts us in all our troubles, so that we can comfort those in any trouble with the comfort we ourselves have received from God. For just as the sufferings of Christ flow over into our lives, so also through Christ our comfort overflows. (2 Corinthians 1:3–5)

Words of Comfort

The following assurances of comfort are included for our consolation in times of need.

> Even though I walk
>   through the valley of the shadow of death,
> I will fear no evil,
>   for you are with me;
> your rod and your staff,
>   they comfort me.
> (Psalm 23:4)

> *God is our refuge and strength,*
> *an ever-present help in trouble.*
> *Therefore we will not fear. . .*
> *(Psalm 46:1–2a)*

> *May your unfailing love be my comfort.*
> *(Psalm 119:76)*

The prophet Isaiah encourages when he knows that comfort from above is readily available.

> *Comfort, comfort my people,*
> *says your God.*
> *Speak tenderly to Jerusalem,*
> *and proclaim to her*
> *that her hard service has been completed.*
> *(Isaiah 40:1–2a)*

Isaiah prophesied that when the Messiah came, his mission would be to

> *comfort all who mourn,*
> *and provide for those who grieve. . .*
> *(Isaiah 61:2)*

The comfort of the Lord ministers strength to weakness, but brings vexation to the proud. He tends to comfort the discomforted and discomfort the comfortable.

God does not comfort us to make us comfortable, but to make us comforters. (John Henry Jowett, 1817–93)

Blessed are they that comfort, for they have mourned. (Michael Mayne)

Our ultimate comfort is seen in the book of Revelation, when God's kingdom finally comes in all its fullness and glory, and all his creation is healed – when *the dwelling of God is with men' (Revelation 21:3)*, and

> *God . . . will wipe every tear from their eyes. There will be no more death, or mourning or crying or pain, for the old order of things has passed away . . . 'I am making everything new!' (Revelation 21:3–5)*

At times God strengthens by supplying something needed, and at other times he takes away things too heavy for us to carry, or too dangerous for us to handle. The Lord truly comforts us. But he will ease or erase grief in his own way in his own time.

> The Lord showed great pity on me, and made me understand that I must weep all my life. Such is the way of the Lord. (Saint Silouan, 'On Humility')

This same Russian monk, Silouan, who died in 1938 on Mount Athos (Greece), continued to experience great grief in his prayers:

> Weeping in sorrow for the people who do not know the sweetness of a holy and softened heart. My soul burns with longing for the mercy of the Lord to be with all people, for the whole wide universe and all humanity to know how deeply the Lord loves us, like his beloved children.

WEEPING WITH THOSE WHO WEEP

A ROYAL EXAMPLE

Queen Victoria was staying at Balmoral in Scotland, still mourning the death of her husband, when she heard that an old friend, Principal Tulloch, had just passed away. She hastened round to visit his widow. As the Queen entered, a servant announced her visit. Mrs Tulloch, weighed down with grief, was lying on a couch. She struggled to rise to greet this unexpected royal guest. But the Queen raised her hand. 'My dear,' she said, 'don't get up. I am not coming here as a Queen to her subject, but as one woman to another who has also lost her husband.' She was 'coming to be alongside' – to demonstrate that she was thinking of her friend with compassion, and wanting to convey strength and encouragement by her presence.

CORRIE TEN BOOM

Corrie ten Boom was a prisoner in the German concentration camp Ravensbrück during the Second World War. She spent much of her time sharing her faith and consoling the other prisoners as best she could. She told of the day when 250 of the younger women were to be moved on to Munich. She wrote, 'As they formed ranks in front of the barracks I felt as if something inside me were breaking from grief.' No one dared to imagine what their ultimate destiny would be. The Dutch women were replaced by Polish women. 'The latter had suffered a great deal and looked worn and anxious. We could not understand each other's language. Yet we suffered the same afflictions side by side. The same Saviour had borne their griefs also.'

Corrie began again reciting to God concerning her horrible lot in Ravensbrück, with the added burden of her beloved older sister being so ill-treated and ailing there. She listed all her trials in a painful prayer – ending with the words, 'Wilt thou never save us?' Then, to her amazement, the Lord spoke to her audibly – three words in French: 'Rempli de tendresse.' She stopped and looked around. There was no one. It was the Lord. Deeply ashamed, tears of sorrow filled her eyes, but tears of gratitude also for the wonderful sense of his comfort.

> He had spoken his love for me. For me, his rebellious child! He had opened his arms wide and said: 'Filled with tenderness.' No! I was not alone; and I knew that to those who love God all things work together for good.[10]

MOURNING MISUNDERSTOOD

A great British comedian died of an overdose in 1968. His last television monologue, recorded four years before his suicide, was a comical but cynical evaluation of his past life. It was calculated to strike a humorous chord of empathy in his listeners as he talked to himself. It certainly came across as great comedy, but was actually revealing deep tragedy:

> What have you achieved? What have you achieved? You lost your chance, me old son. You contributed absolutely nothing to this life. A waste of time you being here at all. No place for you in Westminster Abbey. The best you can expect is a few daffodils in a jam jar, a rough hewn stone bearing the legend, 'He came and he went and in between – nothing!' Nobody will even notice you're not here. After about a year somebody might say down the pub, 'Where's old Hancock? Haven't seen him around lately.'
> 'Oh, he's dead you know.'
> 'Oh, is he?'
> A right *raison d'être* that is! Nobody will ever know I existed. Nothing to leave behind me! Nothing to pass on! Nobody to mourn me! That's the bitterest blow of all.

---

[10] Summarised from Corrie ten Boom, *The Hiding Place* (Fleming H. Revell Co., 1971).

This man was by then utterly depressed with the emptiness of his life. Tony Hancock died apparently without any repentance. His first step up from that Slough of Despond should have been a cry to God Almighty, who alone could help him. But there seemed to be no sorrow for his life of spiritual neglect; simply self-pity and grief for such self-inflicted meaninglessness and hopelessness.

The starting point in mourning is personal confession and repentance. We must dare to face our own wounds before we attempt to help others. God commands us to take the beam from our own eye before we try to remove anything from the eyes of others.

> O the bliss of the man whose heart is broken for this world's sufferings and for his own sin, for out of his sorrow he will find God.[11]

MEDITATION

> *There is a time for everything,*
> *and a season for every activity under heaven:*
> *a time to be born and a time to die,*
> *a time to plant and a time to uproot,*
> *a time to kill and a time to heal,*
> *a time to tear down and a time to build,*
> *a time to weep and a time to laugh,*
> *a time to mourn and a time to dance.*
> *(Ecclesiastes 3:1–4)*

* * *

---

[11] William Barclay, *The Gospel of Matthew*, vol. 1.

The End of a Dream

Beth Nimmo and Darrell Scott have written a book as parents called *Rachel's Tears*, which is their story of the life and martyrdom of their beautiful teenage daughter in the massacre at the Columbine High School, Denver, on 20th April 1999 – published a year after the tragedy.

Their friend Wes Yoder writes in the foreword:

> Borne on the wings of pain and suffering come many of life's greatest treasures, and these treasures become for us the non-negotiables of our existence on the worn soil of the old world. Forget the lessons and squander the treasures and they must be learned again and again. Keep them and they will be ours for ever . . . Darrell and Beth, as broken as they have been, as many tears as they still pour over their daughter's grave and onto the shoulders of their children and friends, have found a place of comfort and hope. From their broken hearts, the sounds of a new song are being heard. It's a song about love and forgiveness and kindness they pray will be carried as healing to others experiencing sorrow and loss in whatever form they come.

* * *

Comfort ye, comfort ye my people, saith your God. Speak ye comfortably to Jerusalem, and cry unto her, that her warfare is accomplished, that her iniquity is pardoned: for she hath received of the Lord's hand double for all her sins. The voice of him that crieth in the wilderness, Prepare ye the way of the Lord, make straight in the desert a highway for our God. Every valley shall be exalted, and every mountain and hill shall be made low: and the crooked shall be made straight, and the rough places plain: And the glory of the Lord shall be revealed, and all flesh shall see it together: for the mouth of the Lord hath spoken it. (Isaiah 40:1–5 KJV)

* * *

Lord, give us crosses in this life that we may wear crowns in the next. (Anon.)

* * *

Through all the changing scenes of life,
In trouble and in joy,
The praises of my God shall still
My heart and tongue employ.[12]

* * *

O Divine Master, grant that I may not so much seek
To be consoled as to console,
To be understood as to understand,
To be loved as to love;
For it is in giving that we receive;
It is in pardoning that we are pardoned;
It is in dying that we are born to eternal life.
(St Francis of Assisi)

* * *

Pitifully behold the sorrows of our hearts
Mercifully forgive the sins of thy people.[13]

* * *

Father, hear the prayer we offer;
Not for ease that prayer shall be,
But for strength that we may ever
Live our lives courageously.[14]

* * *

---

[12] Tate and Brady, *New English Hymnal*, 1696.
[13] From the Litany in *The Book of Common Prayer*, 1662.
[14] Maria Willis, *New English Hymnal*.

Almighty God, Father of our Lord Jesus Christ, Maker of all
    things, Judge of all men:
We acknowledge and bewail our manifold sins and wickedness,
Which we from time to time most grievously have committed,
By thought, word, and deed, against thy Divine Majesty,
Provoking most justly thy wrath and indignation against us.
We do earnestly repent, and are heartily sorry for these our
    misdoings;
The remembrance of them is grievous unto us;
The burden of them is intolerable.
Have mercy upon us,
Have mercy upon us, most merciful Father;
For thy Son our Lord Jesus Christ's sake,
Forgive us all that is past;
And grant that we may ever hereafter serve and please thee in
    newness of life,
To the honour and glory of thy Name;
Through Jesus Christ our Lord. Amen.[15]

* * *

Grant, O Lord, to all who are bereaved the spirit of faith and
courage, that they may have the strength to meet the days to
come with steadfastness and patience; not sorrowing as those
without hope, but in thankful remembrance of your great
goodness, and in joyful expectation of eternal life with those
they love. And this we ask in the name of Jesus Christ our
Savior . . .[16]

* * *

---

[15] The General Confession during Holy Communion, in *The Book of
Common Prayer*.

[16] Episcopal Church Prayer Book, USA.

Lord Jesus, Son of Man, you know the struggle of our human minds in search of truth and light, our human emotions in search of comfort and compassion and our human spirits in search of freedom: give courage to all who wrestle with uncertainties through the dark nights of the soul, give love and endurance to all who suffer from difficult and despairing circumstances, and hope to all those who suffer injustice. For the sake of your loving and liberating Name – Jesus Christ our Lord. (Anon.)

3

The Death of Dignity

Blessed are the meek, for they will inherit the earth.
(Matthew 5:5)

Breathes there a man with soul seraphic, who never honks
when stalled by traffic? (Anon.)

INTRODUCTION

The prevailing culture of the ancient world regarded meekness as 'the crouching submission of a slave'. And our modern world believes that riches, reputation, success, nobility
and eloquence give people an advantage over others.[1] These
attributes lead people to take pride in a position of power.

Talk of meekness, says Michael Green, 'is revolutionary
stuff':

> It says that victory goes not to the wise nor to the strong, but
> to someone who is so small before God (which is what being
> 'meek' means), that God can afford to exalt him without the
> danger of his becoming spiritually proud.[2]

[1] C.f. Thomas Hobbes (1588–1679) in *Leviathan* (first published 1651).
[2] Michael Green, *Matthew for Today* (Hodder & Stoughton, 1988).

In our modern culture we find nothing like the visual example that Jesus set, or the virtues he spelt out in the Beatitudes. One can best appreciate the alluring magnetism of meekness against the ugly backdrop of pride.

Pride is the only disease known to man that makes everyone sick except the one who has it. (Bud Robinson)

Pride can grow as well upon our virtues as upon our vices, and steals up on us on all occasions. (Anon.)

None are so empty as those who are full of themselves. (Anon.)

When a proud man thinks he is humble, his case is hopeless. (Guy Chevreau)

I will not say a good man is never proud, but a proud man is never good. (William Secker)

There is not in the universe a more ridiculous, nor a more contemptible animal than a proud clergyman. (Henry Fielding)

An old-fashioned revival preacher from the American Deep South is reputed to have announced proudly to his congregation one day, 'Today I'm going to explain to you the inexplicable. I'm going to define the indefinable. I'm going to ponder the imponderable. I'm going to unscrew the inscrutable!'

Pride goes before destruction, a haughty spirit before a fall. (Proverbs 16:18)

A man's pride brings him low, but a man of lowly spirit gains honour. (Proverbs 29:23)

The famous Congregational preacher R. W. Dale warned a novice, 'My lad, remember our temptation is not as a rule money.' Pointing through the open vestry door into the crowded church, he said, 'That is our temptation.' He was referring to the pride at being able to draw such a crowd. The Pharisees who modelled the accepted style of leadership in Jesus' day loved having titles like 'Father', 'Teacher' or 'Rabbi', but Jesus found it obnoxious and condemned it *(Matthew 23:1–12)*. The danger of having a title is that it tends to make one think of oneself as superior – the very opposite of the way Jesus wants us to see ourselves, which is as servants.

Fortunately there are ways of being kept humble. In 1818, a certain Reverend R. Taylor asked his bishop if he could be considered for a parish. He received the startling reply, 'My dear Taylor, the background is the place for you!' Harsh, but it might have been timely. Meekness is an attitude we should attempt to adopt. It is the willingness to take a back seat, indeed the lowest seat, at any social gathering.

To put it in a modern context, I have just heard of a humble but internationally known Christian song-writer and leader of the musical side of worship in a local church, who enquired of a younger guitarist and singer whether he had been leading any worship lately. The young man answered, 'No, not for a few months – the rota has been a bit messed up, and they seem to have overlooked me!' The experienced worship leader smiled at him and in a kindly way commented so wisely, 'Good for the soul, mate! Good for the soul!'

THREE TESTS FOR PRIDE

Pride is a sin of whose presence the guilty person is often least conscious – mainly because he or she has never stopped to think about it, or because no one has ever challenged him or her concerning it. There are, however, three tests by means of which it is soon detected.

(1) STATUS

How do we react when another is selected for an assignment we expected to be given, or for an office we coveted? When another is promoted and we are overlooked? When another outshines us in gifts and accomplishments? King Saul was bitterly jealous and humiliated when the women chanted, *'Saul has slain his thousands, and David his tens of thousands' (1 Samuel 18:7).*

Jesus told a parable to those who were invited to a dinner, when he noticed how they chose the best seats. He said to them,

> *When someone invites you to a wedding feast, do not take the place of honour, for a person more distinguished than you may have been invited. If so, the host who invited both of you will come and say to you, 'Give this man your seat.' Then, humiliated, you will have to take the least important place . . . For everyone who exalts himself will be humbled, and he who humbles himself will be exalted. (Luke 14:7–11)*

Personal Encounters with Meekness

Feeling called to the ordained ministry of the Church of England, I went straight from school for a weekend interview at a theological college in 1947. I was flabbergasted when the principal, showing me to my lodging room, insisted on carrying my bag and opening the door for me – something I would never have imagined my headmaster at school doing!

I once went to speak at Trinity College in the 1980s when George Carey (later the Archbishop of Canterbury) was still the principal there. As the chapel filled with students, George slipped in quietly and, finding all the seats taken up, he simply sat cross-legged in a space on the floor at the front. I could not help reflecting on how those students were being shown a wonderful example of meekness.

Blessed are those who willingly allow themselves to be walked over – not in weakness, but from self-control and genuine humility.

> Meekness is not thinking *less* of yourself, but thinking of yourself *less*! (Anon.)

> The way to up is down! (Donald Barnhouse)

> Jesus specialized in menial tasks that everyone else tried to avoid: washing feet, helping children, fixing breakfast and serving lepers. Nothing was beneath Him, because He came to serve. It was not *in spite of His greatness* that He did it, but *because of His greatness*.[3]

> *Do nothing out of selfish ambition or vain conceit, but in humility consider others better than yourselves. (Philippians 2:3)*

(2) INTEGRITY

In our moments of honest self-criticism we will say many derogatory things about ourselves, and really mean them. But how do we feel when we hear others, especially our rivals, say exactly the same things about us?

William Law, a devotional writer in the days of George I, wrote a book in which he said,

---

[3] Rick Warren, *The Purpose Driven Life* (Zondervan, 2002), p. 260.

Let him but consider, that if the world knew all that of him, which he knows of himself; if they saw what vanity and passions govern his inside, and what secret tempers sully and corrupt his best actions; he would have no more pretence to be honoured and admired for his goodness and wisdom. . .

This is so true, and so known to the hearts of almost all people, that nothing would appear more dreadful to them than to have their hearts thus fully discovered to the eyes of all beholders.[4]

The psalmist wrote,

Surely you desire truth in the inner parts. (Psalm 51:6)

(3) CRITICISM

Does criticism arouse hostility and resentment in our hearts, and cause us to fly off into immediate self-justification?[5] Obviously no one is recommending that we should go round criticising each other *(Romans 14:10)*, unless we are specifically asked for criticism by someone who wants help in that way. We all have too many beams in our own eyes to cope with before we can think of removing specks from the eyes of others. Where we have been treated unjustly, we forgive, and where it is our fault, we ask forgiveness.

But if we find ourselves being criticised (often it may even be unfair criticism), we should not respond in kind. We do what we can to amend our life wherever necessary, and then we forget it. John Wimber once shared his response to a similar problem that was currently bugging

---

[4] William Law, *A Serious Call to a Devout and Holy Life* (Dent & Sons Ltd, 1728), p.211.

[5] See Oswald Sanders, *Spiritual Leadership* (Moody Press, 1947).

me: 'I just think of Paul when he was in Malta,' he said. *'A viper . . . fastened itself on his hand . . . Paul shook the snake off into the fire and suffered no ill effects' (Acts 28:3b, 5).*

Personal Check-up

John Stott wrote,

> I myself am happy to recite the General Confession in church and call myself a 'miserable sinner'. It causes me no great problem. I can take it in my stride. But let someone else come up to me after church and call me a miserable sinner, and I want to punch him on the nose! In other words, I am not prepared to allow other people to think or speak of me what I have just acknowledged before God that I am. There is a basic hypocrisy here; there always is when meekness is absent.[6]

How would you react in such a situation?

If we claim to be without sin, we deceive ourselves and the truth is not in us. (1 John 1:8)

THE MEANING OF MEEKNESS

I first began to discover what meekness meant in a practical way when I had to learn to ride a horse. This was necessary in the rural outpost where I started as a missionary in Chile, in order to reach some of our ever more outward-bound churches. The word for meekness in Spanish is *manso*. When applied to a horse, it means that the animal has been 'broken in'. Once broken in, it will not resist when being saddled, or suddenly rear up when being ridden. Being so

---

[6] John Stott, *The Message of the Sermon on the Mount* (IVP, 1978).

new to the horsey world, I was very grateful to be given a *manso* steed to ride. It certainly made life much easier, and far safer. I could never have coped with one of those 'bucking broncos' we watched at the rodeos. But I have to confess here that my wife would probably say that I did not cope all that well on horseback in any case! She said the horse must know who is master. I told her the horse had found that out already! It may have been *manso* with some, but it sometimes seemed malevolent with me.

Taking this thought of a tamed and trained animal, William Barclay applied it to the person who has every instinct, every impulse, every passion under control: 'Blessed is the man who is entirely self-controlled.' But there are some even more significant translations of the word 'meek' (*praus*) in the New Testament: for example, *Matthew 11:29, 21:5* and *1 Peter 3:4*. It can mean 'humble', 'gentle', 'considerate', 'courteous' – revealing a sense of moral insignificance, as opposed to being self-centred, haughty or conceited.

OLD TESTAMENT REFERENCES TO MEEKNESS

The man Moses was very meek *(Numbers 12:3)*, but he was no weakling. Indeed, he showed tremendous strength and proved to be one of the world's most significant generals ever. Look at the bold way he confronted Pharaoh, or the fearless way he rebuked his followers. Yet in his prayers to God he could say, *'Blot me out of the book you have written'* (*Exodus 32:32*).

There are many psalms which extol meekness, including the following verses (taken from the KJV):

The meek shall eat and be satisfied. (Psalm 22:26)

The meek will he guide in judgement:
and the meek will he teach his way. (Psalm 25:9)

When God arose . . . to save all the meek. . . (Psalm 76:9)

The Lord lifteth up the meek. (Psalm 147:6)

He will beautify the meek with salvation. (Psalm 149:4)

And the prophet Zephaniah urged his listeners:

Seek righteousness. Seek meekness. (Zephaniah 2:3)

NEW TESTAMENT REFERENCES TO MEEKNESS

Jesus does not appear to have explained exactly what he meant by 'meekness' when he preached the Sermon on the Mount, but further on in Matthew's Gospel he gives us the example of his own life – an example of gentleness and humility. He says,

Come to me, all you who are weary and burdened, and I will give you rest. Take my yoke upon you and learn from me, for I am gentle and humble in heart, and you will find rest for your souls. For my yoke is easy and my burden is light. (Matthew 11:28–30)

The burdens borne by mankind, male or female, rich or poor, can be heavy and crushing. They may often be hidden or unseen, but they adversely affect the heart and the mind by reaching the body from within. Among those stressful burdens that readily come to mind are pride, self-image, artificiality – the latter haunted by the secret fear that some day an enemy or a friend will catch a glimpse into our poor, empty and polluted souls. Then there are the impositions of manipulators and those in authority over us, like *'the Phar-isees who sit in Moses' seat . . . They tie up heavy loads and put them on men's shoulders, but they themselves are not willing to lift a finger to move them' (Matthew 23:2–4).*

There are also the burdens of anxiety which seem very heavy for some. Meekness is the Christ-like way to respond to our own and other people's burdens in life; and he invites us to just keep casting these worries and fears onto him, encouraging others to do the same. *'Cast all your anxiety on him because he cares for you' (1 Peter 5:7).*

Jesus said,

> *But I tell you, Do not resist an evil person. If someone strikes you on the right cheek, turn to him the other also. And if someone wants to sue you and take your tunic, let him have your cloak as well. If someone forces you to go one mile, go with him two miles. Give to the one who asks you, and do not turn away from the one who wants to borrow from you. (Matthew 5:39)*

Paul commended such meek behaviour:

> *The fruit of the Spirit is love, joy, peace, patience, kindness, goodness, faithfulness, gentleness and self-control. (Galatians 5:22–23)*

And again:

> *As God's chosen people, holy and dearly loved, clothe yourselves with compassion, kindness, humility, gentleness and patience. (Colossians 3:12)*

James wrote:

> *Receive with meekness the engrafted word. (James 1:21 KJV)*

And again:

The wisdom that comes from heaven is first of all pure; then peace-loving, considerate, submissive, full of mercy and good fruit, impartial and sincere. (James 3:17)

James surely envisaged a meek person!

ARE WE WILLING TO WAIVE OUR RIGHTS?

Meekness means not being a wimp, but being willing to waive one's personal rights. There were a few things we missionary recruits were warned about before we went abroad to serve the Lord. We may not have understood them well at the time, but the reason for them became very plain once we reached our spheres of work. It took most of us a while to learn the language. It took a little longer to learn about the culture of our new host environments. Probably it took much more time to face up to our attitude over our 'rights'.

I had first been challenged over this through reading a book written by an American missionary, Mabel Williamson. She had been working with the China Inland Mission. The book was called *Have We No Rights?* It was one of the most uncomfortable books I had read in preparing for the mission field – in fact, I never finished it. Surely we had some rights? But no! We are never called to compromise God's principles, or to ignore the rights of others, but we may be called to forgo our own. It is the only way to get on with fellow missionaries, the only way to cope with those who have authority over us, and the only way to integrate with the nationals in the new culture in which we have been called to work.

Our attitude in this area expresses the Christian lifestyle

that we want to share in a far more telling way than if we were to spell it out in words. It means *'to walk humbly with [our] God' (Micah 6:8)*, being willing to subjugate our defensive scruples and submit quietly and obediently to him. It means learning to *'turn the other cheek'*, *'to go the second mile'*. The writer to the Hebrews brushes off all our pained objections with a casual aside: *'Take cheerfully the spoiling of your goods' (Hebrews 10:34)*. Such is the attitude God requires from his servants.

SOME ASPECTS OF MEEKNESS

Billy Graham suggests some aspects of meekness, which may help us to understand a little more about what it means. We include his titles,[7] followed by our own adaptations and amplifications.

(1) Meekness Means Gentleness

> A man can never be a true gentleman in manner until he is a true gentleman at heart. (Charles Dickens)

From the time of Henry VIII, the ruling classes in England became known as 'the gentry'. These country gentlemen lived in their manor houses, governed the counties, and acted as justices of the peace. They are not to be confused with the gentlefolk – a parallel cultural stream with Christian values, not necessarily separate from the gentry. They were included in some of their number and displayed some of their virtues. However, there were a number of upwardly mobile working-class Christians (which included many

---

[7] Taken from Billy Graham, *The Secret of Happiness* (Word Publishing, 1958), pp. 67ff.

clergy). This culture of gentlefolk grew during the rise of seventeenth-century Puritanism and increased following the eighteenth-century Wesleyan Revival.

It is not often realised that William Wilberforce, who led the movement for the abolition of slavery, also worked for a reform of manners. He was concerned about the use of bad language in public and wanted to ensure people showed respect for each other in society. The culture of gentility was taken up by Christian families sickened by the sheer corruption, coarseness, debauchery and injustice of the society around them. They believed that mainly through the processes of being light and salt, society could be wholesomely affected.

Christian parents consciously reared their children to cultivate a gentle lifestyle of self-control over appetites, tongue and temper; modesty in dress, personal distinctions and accomplishments; deference, honour and respect for superiors and their fellow beings; chivalry towards, and protection for, the female sex; good manners in society, fair play, team spirit and graciousness when losing at sport. They were encouraged to engage in noble activities and to pioneer worthy objectives – to climb mountains and sail oceans. They followed 'improving' pursuits – education, appreciation of the arts and skills in handicrafts, hobbies, involvement in athletics and sports, and appreciation of nature. They were genteel and refined in their tastes. It was a genuinely uplifting culture. They were trusted in their business enterprises because of their honest dealings between themselves and with others. They acted as leaven to a society which made its impact abroad. An Englishman's word was his bond in business. There was a story that the Pathans, in what is now Pakistan, actually believed that Englishmen had a strange impediment – they could not lie!

The story is told of William Balfour, a businessman in Chile during the mid-nineteenth century, who told one of his office clerks to return a certain contract to a competing trading house and ask them to rewrite it. 'Explain to them that this draft is far too much in our favour!' he commanded.

> Nothing is so strong as gentleness; nothing so gentle as real strength. (Francis de Sales)

One of my colleagues, Barry Kissell, told me how he used to play squash with John Perry, my predecessor as vicar at St Andrew's, Chorleywood (and later the Bishop of Chelmsford). Apparently, one day, on returning to the changing rooms after a game, they found vomit spewed across the floor. Without having any idea as to who the sick man had been, John expressed real concern for him, and proceeded to find a mop, bucket and water and clear it all up without further ado – a very genteel thing to do.

(2) Meekness Involves Yieldedness

To yield means to relinquish, to abandon, to give up. It is the very antithesis of the four 'selfs' promoted today: self-justification, self-vindication, self-assertiveness and self-centredness.

We can read in Romans:

> *As you have yielded your members servants to uncleanness and to iniquity . . . even so now yield your members servants to righteousness unto holiness. (Romans 6:19 KJV)*

Therefore I urge you . . . in view of God's mercy, to offer your bodies as living sacrifices, holy and pleasing to God – this is your spiritual act of worship. Do not conform any longer to the pattern of this world, but be transformed by the renewing of your mind. Then you will be able to test and approve what God's will is – his good, pleasing and perfect will. (Romans 12:1–2)

Yieldedness involves accepting what God does or does not do, what he gives or withholds – without grumbling or resisting.

In acceptance lieth peace. (Amy Carmichael)

(3) Meekness Denotes Forbearance

Like the chirrup of the house sparrow, this word 'forbearance' has almost slipped from our modern vocabulary. The Bible exhorts us to act and react *'with all lowliness and meekness, with longsuffering, forbearing one another in love' (Ephesians 4:2 KJV)*. The meek person puts up with difficult people. *'Let your gentleness be evident to all' (Philippians 4:5)*. Those who are meek are known for their tolerance with regard to their own rights and position.

(4) Meekness Implies Patience

Impatience has produced a new crop of broken homes, a million or more new ulcers, and has set the stage for many wars. In no area of our lives has lack of patience been more damaging than on the domestic scene. *'Let patience have her perfect work, that you may be perfect and entire, wanting nothing' (James 1:4 KJV)*.

All men commend patience, although few be willing to practise it. (Thomas à Kempis)

Be patient enough to live one day at a time as Jesus taught us, letting yesterday go, and leaving tomorrow until it arrives. (John F. Newton)

(5) Meekness Requires Self-Effacement

When Bishop Frank Houghton was researching the life of Amy Carmichael (of Donavur, South India), he expressed his surprise at finding that among a lifetime's collection of personal effects there were many photographs depicting friends and acquaintances, but there were none of Amy herself.

It was said of Eric Liddell, the missionary and champion athlete, whose story is told in the well-known film *Chariots of Fire*, that 'he was . . . ridiculously humble in victory, utterly generous in defeat'.

> The world is a better place as a result of Michelangelo not having said, 'I don't do ceilings!' (Edward McCabe)

(6) Meekness is God-given

Meekness is given by God in exchange for self-surrender. S. I. McMillen once said, 'Surrendering one's will to the divine will may seem a negative process, but it gives positive dividends.'

Blessed is the person who has his or her life 'under wraps' – that person has self-control. Jesus showed the way by his own example:

> *This took place to fulfil what was spoken through the prophet:*
> *'Say to the Daughter of Zion,*
> *"See, your king comes to you,*

gentle [meek] and riding on a donkey,
on a colt, the foal of a donkey.''
(Matthew 21:4–5)

Jesus (who is the truth) could say of himself, *'I am meek and lowly in heart' (Matthew 11:29 KJV)*.

John Wesley was very attracted by the meekness he saw in the Moravian missionaries from Germany whom he met on his voyage to North America. He made a significant note in his journal for Friday the 17th October 1735:

> I began to learn German, in order to converse (a little) with the Moravians, six-and-twenty of whom we have on board . . . I had long before observed the great seriousness of their behaviour. Of their humility they had given a continual proof by performing those servile offices for the other passengers, which none of the English would undertake; for which they desired, and would receive no pay, saying 'it was good for their proud hearts', and their loving Saviour had done more for them. And every day had given them occasion of showing a meekness which no injury could move. If they were pushed, struck, or thrown down, they rose again and went away; but no complaint was found in their mouth.[8]

An Illustration from the Life of Abraham

Abraham was chosen by God to go to a place that he would later receive as his inheritance. So he set off, taking his nephew Lot with him. They journeyed as far as Bethel – between Bethel and Ai. Both of them now had flocks and herds and tents, and the land could no longer support them both dwelling together. Indeed, there were sparks flying

---

[8] John Wesley, *Journals*.

between their herdsmen over pastures and wells. A serious decision had to be made.

> *So Abram said to Lot, 'Let's not have any quarrelling between you and me, or between your herdsmen and mine, for we are brothers. Is not the whole land before you? Let's part company. If you go to the left, I'll go to the right; if you go to the right, I'll go to the left.' (Genesis 13:8–9)*

Lot surveyed his surroundings and, seeing that the Jordan valley was well watered, he chose that way and Abraham meekly agreed. They said 'goodbye' and Lot went east, where in fact he encountered a great deal of trouble. Abram agreed to go in the other direction even though God had said to him, *'All the land that you see I will give to you and your offspring for ever' (Genesis 13:15).*

Blessed are the meek – those who allow others to walk over them, not in weakness, but from self-control.

(7) Meekness is Humility that has Matured

> O the bliss of the man who is always angry at the right time and never at the wrong time, who has every instinct and impulse and passion under control because he himself is God-controlled, who has the humility to realize his own ignorance and his own weaknesses, for such a man is a prince among men.[9]

Meekness is humility that has matured through self-control.

> Humility does not consist in having a worse opinion of ourselves than we deserve, or in abasing ourselves lower than we really are; but as all virtue is founded in truth, so humility is founded in a true and just sense of our weakness, misery and sin. He that rightly feels and lives in this sense of his condition, lives in humility.[10]

---

[9] Barclay, *The Gospel of Matthew.*
[10] Law, *A Serious Call to a Devout and Holy Life*, p.209.

A Humble Doctor

Dr Stanley Smith was a missionary pioneer in Uganda and Rwanda. His original vision for his life's work came to him when he was a British army medical officer there during the First World War. This continued after the founding of the Rwanda Mission as a branch of the Church Missionary Society. Stanley Smith retired at a great age in 1977. He came to live with his daughter Nora and his son-in-law Bishop Dick Lyth in Chorleywood, Hertfordshire.

He died in their home the following year, and there were eleven bishops present at his funeral in St Andrew's Church – mostly from Uganda, Rwanda and Burundi. They were already in England at the Lambeth Conference for bishops being convened at the time. At the funeral, the tributes and addresses went on for so long that the undertaker at last began signalling frantically to me from the back of the church, pointing to his watch. The time allotted at the crematorium would be past before the mourners had arrived with the coffin. I had to interrupt the service and announce that, while we would continue with our celebration in the church, the family would leave with the coffin for the cremation in Amersham, a few miles away.

I apologised to Dick afterwards, explaining that I really had not known quite what to do. I did not want to be disrespectful to our African friends, but I had to do something about the undertaker. Dick agreed that it had been the only thing to do, and added with a smile that his father-in-law would have approved – it had always been typical of him to slip away quietly in the middle of celebrations in his honour!

I shall never forget my first visit to see this godly man

soon after he had arrived in the parish. He was sitting at his table and – to use his own words – 'writing a letter to the church of Uganda'. I began to feel a little wary and recoiled slightly before this humble servant, thinking, I am ashamed now to confess, that he must have gone a little 'batty' in his old age and was imagining himself to be a kind of apostle. It seemed a little preposterous! I was rejecting any idea of this man possibly likening himself to St Paul. But suddenly it clicked. Yes! I was in fact in the presence of an apostle of the church, though such a self-effacing one that he would never have suggested that of himself. I have since been assured by African bishops and missionaries that Dr Smith's letter would indeed have been read out and prayed over in all the churches of Uganda and Rwanda. His utter meekness had blinded me to the possibility of an apostolic ministry.

A Meek Monk

Another example of mature meekness may be seen in the life of St Francis of Assisi, the thirteenth-century founder of the religious order named after him. He was never an administrator or the typical leader, but nonetheless had a vast following. History records a conversation with one of St Francis's colleagues.

> Brother Masseo looked earnestly at Francis and asked wonderingly, 'Why you? Why you?' This he repeated again and again as if to mock him.
> 'What are you saying?' Francis cried at last.
> 'I am saying that everybody follows you, everyone desires to see you, hear you, obey you, and yet for all that, you are neither beautiful, nor learned, nor of noble family. Whence comes it that it should be you whom the world desires to follow?'

When Francis heard these words he was filled with joy, raised his eyes to heaven and, after remaining a long time absorbed in contemplation, knelt praising and blessing God with extraordinary fervour. Then turning to Brother Masseo, said: 'You wish to know? It is because the eyes of the Most High have willed it so. He continually watches the good and the wicked, and, as His most holy eyes have not found among sinners any smaller man, nor any more insufficient and sinful, therefore He has chosen me to accomplish the marvellous work which God has undertaken; He chose me because He could find none more worthless, and He wished to confound the nobility and the grandeur, the strength, the beauty and the learning of this world.'[11]

Although he did not use the word 'meekness', that was what he was so finely describing. Someone once said, 'God has a history of choosing the insignificant to accomplish the impossible.'

A Dying Missionary

We catch an honest glimpse of meekness in William Carey, the pioneer Baptist missionary (1761–1834), a former shoemaker turned preacher and prodigious Bible translator in Bengal. Besides a lifetime of much impressive translation work in many Indian tongues, one of the great reforms that he pioneered in India was the abolition of *sati* – the prevailing custom of burning alive the widow together with the corpse of her deceased husband on the same funeral pyre.

Dr Alexander Duff, the famous educationalist, was one of the many distinguished callers to see this saint as he lay

---

[11] J. Oswald Sanders, *Leadership*.

dying in 1834. Leaving the room after one of his last visits, he heard a faint voice gently calling him back: 'Mr Duff,' said Carey softly. 'Mr Duff! You have been speaking about Dr Carey, Dr Carey. When I am gone, say nothing about Dr Carey – speak about Dr Carey's Saviour.' Carey's self-chosen epitaph for the headstone over his burial site read:

A Wretched, Poor and Helpless Worm, on Thy Kind Arms I Fall.

A worm! A humble self-assessment indeed. Could it possibly be false humility? No. Just a plain self-assessment of moral insignificance, in line with King David's own self-evaluation, *'I am a worm and not a man' (Psalm 22:6)*, and Isaiah's characterisation of the nation of Israel, *'O worm . . . O little Israel' (Isaiah 41:14)*, or Bildad's generalisation of man when talking to Job: any man born of a woman *'is but a maggot – a son of man, who is only a worm' (Job 25:6)*.

Carey had, like John the Baptist, spent his life paving the way for the gospel. He could say like John, *'He must become greater; I must become less' (John 3:30)*. Paul epitomised this quality too when he described himself as the *'least of the apostles' (1 Corinthians 15:9)* and the *'chief of sinners' (1 Timothy 1:15)*. Yes, 'worm' fitted the bill very well in those days. Probably 'nerd' would be a more fitting self-appraisal today.

A man who truly knows himself realises his own worthlessness and takes no pleasure in the praises of men . . . A true understanding and humble estimate of oneself is the highest and most valuable of all lessons.[12]

---

[12] Thomas à Kempis, *The Imitation of Christ* (Penguin Classics, 1952), p.28.

(8) Occasionally Meekness Could Actually Be a Matter of Life or Death

There is a story attributed to Martin Luther about two mountain goats that met each other on a narrow ledge just wide enough for one of the animals to pass. On one side was a sheer cliff, and on the other a steep wall of rock. These two goats came face to face, and it was impossible for either to turn or to back up. Had they been humans, they would probably have started butting each other until one of them plunged to their death in the depths below. But, according to Luther, the goats had more sense than that. One of them simply lay down on the trail and let the other literally walk over it – and through that simple act of meekness both were able to continue on their way without any problem.

PROMISED REWARD

Such meekness as we have described above makes the disciple of God gentle, humble, sensitive and patient in all his or her relationships.

One of the clearest expositions of meekness and its reward is seen in Psalm 37.

> *For evil men will be cut off,*
> *but those who hope in the Lord will inherit the land.*
> *A little while, and the wicked will be no more. . .*
> *But the meek will inherit the land*
> *and enjoy great peace.*
> *(Psalm 37:9–11)*

Jesus himself was clearly quoting from this psalm when he included it among the Beatitudes *(Matthew 5:5).*

The recurring biblical theme of inheriting the land comes from the Old Testament. With the coming of Christ, the 'land' became the symbol of something far more than the physical territory promised to Israel. Now the people of any colour, place or culture can inherit eternal life in the kingdom of heaven *(Matthew 25:34)*. Those who have nothing in this world, but who humbly trust and obey God, will have everything in the age to come, when there will be a new heaven and a new earth (c.f. *Revelation 21 and 22*).

Meek people understand their true state before God. They do not look down on themselves, for they know they are the sons and daughters of God – his true heirs by God's grace. But neither do they think too highly of themselves – they do not forget what and where they were when the Lord found them and saved them. Nor can they forget the many times they have failed the Lord during their lifetimes, so that they say of themselves, *'We are unprofitable servants'* *(Luke 17:10b KJV)*. We certainly do not merit this amazing reward granted to us by God's grace.

It is not the arrogant, the wealthy, the harsh and domineering people, regarded by the world as the winners, who will get everything. Instead the meek, the apparent losers, are the ones who will inherit the earth. Surprise, surprise! But, as with their King, *'the stone you builders rejected . . . has become the capstone' (Acts 4:11)*.

It seems strange that commentators have not enlarged more fully on this wonderful promise awaiting the meek. Perhaps this is because in effect it is the same promise given in two of the other Beatitudes (regarding the poor in spirit and the persecuted). 'The promised land' has to be the new heaven and earth.

Charles Spurgeon comments on this:

> When the Lord takes it into His own possession and enjoyment, they [the meek] shall succeed Him in the possession and enjoyment of it. It is their right and it shall descend to them by right, by inheritance. It is the Lord's right, and by the Lord shall descend to them as their right. They cannot have it yet, for the Lord hath it not yet; but when the Lord hath it, it shall fairly descend to them. This accursed earth they shall never have, but when it is taken into the hands of the Lord, and blessed by the Lord, then it shall be theirs, then it shall be inherited by the children of blessing.[13]

A quaint remark by John Pennington on this theme taken from Psalm 37 does enhance our thinking about the inheritance of the meek. I have adapted it slightly to make it more immediately comprehensible.

> Not the hot stirring spirits who bustle for the world shall have it, but the meek who are thrust up and down from corner to corner and hardly suffered to remain anywhere quietly in it. This earth, which they seem most deprived of, *they only* shall enjoy. When the Lord hath made it worth the having, then none (i.e. of the proud or self-assertive) shall have it but they ... *'The meek shall inherit the earth.'* The earth is the Lord's; these are the children of the Lord, and they shall inherit his earth.

Jesus considered those who were of a humble, patient and contented spirit as being truly meek. They have been willing to forgo recognition here below. They can bear injuries without resentment. They are not quick to take offence.

---

[13] C. H. Spurgeon, *The Treasury of David*, vol. 2 (Marshall Bros), p. 186.

The meek can never be losers in the long run. One day they shall *'reign on the earth' (Revelation 5:10).*

MEDITATION

He was oppressed, and he was afflicted,
*   yet he opened not his mouth;*
like a lamb that is led to the slaughter,
*   and like a sheep that before its shearers is dumb,*
*   so he opened not his mouth.*
By oppression and judgement he was taken away;
*   and as for his generation, who considered*
that he was cut off out of the land of the living,
*   stricken for the transgression of my people?*
And they made his grave with the wicked
*   and with a rich man in his death,*
although he had done no violence,
*   and there was no deceit in his mouth.*
(Isaiah 53:7–9 RSV)

* * *

But whatever was to my profit I now consider loss . . . compared to the surpassing greatness of knowing Christ Jesus my Lord, for whose sake I have lost all things. I consider them rubbish, that I may gain Christ. . . (Philippians 3:7–8)

* * *

Meekness and majesty,
Manhood and deity,
In perfect harmony,
The Man who is God.
Lord of eternity dwells in humanity,
Kneels in humility and washes our feet.

O what a mystery, meekness and majesty.
Bow down and worship for this is your God.[14]
(Graham Kendrick)

* * *

When I survey the wondrous cross,
On which the Prince of Glory died,
My richest gain I count but loss,
And pour contempt on all my pride.
(Isaac Watts)

* * *

From all blindness of heart; from pride, vainglory, and
hypocrisy; from envy, hatred, and malice and all uncharitable-
ness, Good Lord, deliver us...[15]

* * *

Lord, make me childlike. Deliver me from the urge to compete
with another for place or prestige or position. I would be simple and artless as a little child. Deliver me from pose and pretence. Forgive me for thinking of myself. Help me to forget
myself, and find my true peace in beholding Thee. That Thou
mayest answer this prayer I humble myself before Thee. Lay
upon me the easy yoke of self-forgetfulness, that through it I
may find rest. Amen. (A. W. Tozer)

---

[14] 'Meekness and Majesty' by Graham Kendrick © 1986 Thankyou
Music. Adm. by worshiptogether.com songs excl. UK & Europe, adm.
by Kingswaysongs.com tym@kingsway.co.uk. Used by permission.
[15] From the Litany, in *The Book of Common Prayer.*

4

A Diet to Change the Nation

Blessed are those who hunger and thirst for righteousness,
for they will be filled.
(Matthew 5:6)

INTRODUCTION

Hayward was a man who saw nothing for himself, but only through a literary atmosphere, and he was dangerous because he had deceived himself into sincerity. He honestly mistook his sensuality for romantic emotion, his vacillation for artistic temperament, and his idleness for philosophic charm. His mind, vulgar in its effort at refinement, saw everything a little larger than life-size, with the outlines blurred in a golden mist of sentimentality. He lied, and never knew that he lied, and when it was pointed out to him, said that lies were beautiful. He was an idealist.[1]

Somerset Maugham's character Hayward seems to have been totally devoid of any sense of righteousness. Although perhaps abnormal in many ways, he is not alone.

---

[1] Somerset Maugham, *Of Human Bondage.*

RIGHTEOUSNESS

'Noah was a righteous man, blameless among the people of his time, and he walked with God' (Genesis 6:10). Noah consistently followed the will of God as it had been revealed to him. 'Since the creation of the world God's invisible qualities – his eternal power and divine nature – have been clearly seen, being understood from what has been made, so that men are without excuse' (Romans 1:20). 'The requirements of the law are written on their hearts, their consciences also bearing witness' (Romans 2:15b). Noah believed in God as the transcendent source of authority for the laws of righteousness.

RIGHTEOUSNESS IS FUNDAMENTAL

Jesus said, 'Seek first his kingdom and his righteousness' (Matthew 6:33). Unrighteous lifestyles plainly and specifically exclude mankind from God's kingdom (1 Corinthians 6:9–10; Galatians 5:19). But righteousness is fundamental in God's kingdom. If the world becomes aware of the kingdom of God, and is grudgingly drawn to it, it is because it is attracted to righteousness. Jesus' definition of righteousness was summed up in two commandments – loving God and loving one's neighbour as oneself (Matthew 22:37, 39). Men and women of righteousness are accountable to authority – to God directly and through parents, governments, church leaders, police, teachers, etc. The only exception to this would be if any authority tried to compel a righteous man or woman to do something unrighteous. In that case there is a moral case for protest. Peter and John were warned by the Jerusalem council 'not to speak . . . at all *in the name of Jesus'.* They responded, *'Judge for yourselves whether it is right in God's sight to obey you rather than God. For we cannot help speaking about what we have seen and heard' (Acts 4:19–20).*

When the first young Christian men were brought to the king of Uganda, he questioned them before they were martyred for their faith. 'Does not your faith tell you that you should obey your king in all things?' he said. Their reply was simple: 'We have heard that there is a King of kings and we must follow him.'[2]

In this chapter we shall be discussing what personal righteousness is and where it comes from, considering what Jesus meant by 'hunger and thirst', and finally thinking about the meaning of being 'filled' and how we would know if we were.

PERSONAL RIGHTEOUSNESS

Taking personal righteousness first, there are three aspects to consider: legal, moral and social.

LEGAL RIGHTEOUSNESS

From God's perspective, *legal* righteousness is justification, a right relationship with him. We need to develop a basic understanding of the righteousness of God from three perspectives: as an attribute, as an activity and as an achievement.

Divine Attribute

Our God is a righteous God. The Bible talks about it constantly.

---

[2] Charles Cleverly, *The Passion that Shapes Nations* (Kingsway, 2005), p. 102.

Righteousness and justice are the foundation of your throne.
(Psalm 89:14)

Your throne, O God, will last for ever and ever;
*   a sceptre of justice will be the sceptre of your kingdom.*
You love righteousness and hate wickedness.
(Psalm 45:6–7a)

This is the name by which he will be called:
*   'The Lord Our Righteousness'.*
(Jeremiah 23:6)

Seek first his kingdom and his righteousness. . . (Matthew 6:33)

Righteous Father. . . (John 17:25)

The more we consider this, the more we realise how unrighteous we ourselves are, however much we may try to dress ourselves up as something better. *'All our righteous acts are like filthy rags' (Isaiah 64:6).* God sees straight through the outward appearance of our bodies to the inmost thoughts of our hearts – and says *'the heart is deceitful above all things and beyond cure' (Jeremiah 17:9).* Paul sums up our inner character when he says, *'All have sinned and fall short of the glory of God' (Romans 3:23).*

Divine Activity

Yet God has come to our rescue. He first took our humanity and then our sin to the cross of Calvary, to cancel a debt we could not pay and still live. So the gospel really is good news: *'We have an advocate with the Father, Jesus Christ the righteous: and he is the propitiation for our sins' (1 John 2:1–2 KJV).*

Divine Achievement

In the world in which we live we can understand the function of *secular* righteousness (in the context of person-to-person conduct). A crime is committed. You are arrested and charged. If you have not committed the crime, you are found not guilty. There is no penalty to pay. You are acquitted. This differs from the *legal* righteousness we have discussed above. You did commit sin. You are guilty. There is a penalty to be paid. This has been paid already by Christ. You are acquitted, through his death on the cross. Christ clothes us in his righteousness like a garment which covers our own filthy garments *(Isaiah 64:6)*. We simply receive it by faith with thanksgiving. It is confirmed by the witness of the Holy Spirit in our hearts that we are indeed God's children *(Romans 8:16)*, and by the testimony of our own lips *(Matthew 10:32)*. Just as *'Abraham believed God, and it was credited to him as righteousness' (Romans 4:3)*, so also with us:

> *The words 'it was credited to him' were written not for him [Abraham] alone, but also for us, to whom God will credit righteousness – for us who believe in him who raised Jesus our Lord from the dead. He was delivered over to death for our sins and was raised to life for our justification. (Romans 4:22–25)*

This simple belief has been, and still is, a life-changing experience for all who will commit to it. Paul's masterly treatment of the whole subject of God's righteousness is set out in the epistle to the Romans. Professor F. F. Bruce, in his introduction to a commentary on this epistle, gives brief accounts of men who struggled with the whole question of God's righteousness, then came into a right relationship with God and in turn made their own major contributions to theology or mission in the world. Their stories are told below.

St Augustine

In the summer of AD 386, Augustine, a native of North Africa, and then for two years a professor of rhetoric in Milan (now part of Italy), sat weeping in the garden of his friend Alypius. He was almost persuaded in his mind to begin a new life, yet lacking the resolve to break with the old. It was this Augustine who had famously prayed, 'Lord, give me chastity, but not yet!' As he sat, he heard a child singing in a neighbouring house, *'Tolle, lege! Tolle, lege!'* ('Take up and read! Take up and read!') The child was probably playing some kind of a game, but God used it as his own voice to speak to Augustine. As a result Augustine found himself taking up the scroll which lay at his friend's side, and his eye caught sight of the words, *'Not in rioting and drunkenness, not in chambering and wantonness, not in strife and envying. But put on the Lord Jesus Christ, and make not provision for the flesh, to fulfil the lusts thereof' (Romans 13:13b–14 KJV).* 'No further would I read,' Augustine tells us, 'nor had I any need; instantly, at the end of this sentence, a clear light flooded my heart, and all the darkness of doubt vanished away.'[3]

The impact of this experience on Augustine's life, and the influence for good that followed, has been highly significant for the world. Especially for an Augustinian monk named Martin Luther, many centuries later. . .

---

[3] F. F. Bruce, *The Epistle of Paul to the Romans* (Tyndale Press, 1963), p. 58.

Martin Luther

Martin Luther, an Augustinian monk and a professor of sacred theology at the University of Wittenberg, Germany, began to expound Paul's epistle to the Romans to his students in November 1515. During his lecture preparations he came increasingly to appreciate the centrality of the doctrine of justification by faith. He wrote,

> I greatly longed to understand Paul's Epistle to the Romans, and nothing stood in the way but one expression, 'the righteousness of God', because I took it to mean that righteousness whereby God is righteous and deals righteously in punishing the unrighteous . . . Night and day I pondered until . . . I grasped the truth that the righteousness of God is that righteousness whereby, through grace and sheer mercy, He justifies us by faith. Thereupon I felt myself to be reborn and to have gone through the open doors into paradise. The whole of Scripture took on a new meaning, and whereas before 'the righteousness of God' had filled me with hate, now it became to me inexpressibly sweet in greater love. This passage of Paul became to me a gateway to heaven.[4]

This renewing insight by Martin Luther led to the sixteenth-century Reformation in Europe and had many later repercussions. The following account is but one example.

John Wesley

On the evening of the 24th May 1738 John Wesley 'went very unwillingly' to a society in Aldersgate Street, London, where someone was reading Luther's 'Preface to the Epistle to the Romans'. Wesley later wrote in his journal,

---

[4] Ibid., p.59.

About a quarter before nine, while he was describing the change which God works in the heart through faith in Christ, I felt my heart strangely warmed. I felt I did trust in Christ, Christ alone, for my salvation; and an assurance was given me that he had taken my sins away, even mine; and saved me from the law of sin and death.[5]

That experience in the life of Wesley was the event above all others in England which launched the extraordinary Evangelical Revival of the eighteenth century. Indeed, without such a movement of God, Britain might well have suffered a similar bloody revolution to that which took place in France soon after.

Augustine, Luther and Wesley launched great spiritual movements which have left their mark on world history. But similar experiences have happened, and continue to happen, to very ordinary people as the truth of this gospel has opened the eyes of millions.

THE MORAL ASPECT

Once this righteousness has been credited to us, we begin to discover that there is a *moral* dimension to it. This was the original design of the Creator for the common life of the human family. Moral righteousness is that way of living which pleases God. It is based on the command to love and the claims of justice. It is the righteousness of character and conduct that is fundamental to a holy lifestyle.

David Aikman, a former Beijing bureau chief for *Time* magazine, relates the surprising account of some 18 American

---

[5] Ibid.

tourists visiting China in 2002. In Beijing they attended a lecture delivered by a Chinese scholar from a premier academic research institute, the Chinese Academy of Social Sciences (CASS). The scholar amazed them when he explained that his team had been asked by the Chinese authorities to research and explain the pre-eminence of the West.

> We studied everything we could from the historical, political, economic, and cultural perspective. At first, we thought it was because you had more powerful guns than we had. Then we thought it was because you had the best political system. Next we focused on your economic system. But in the past twenty years we have realised that the heart of your culture is your religion – Christianity. That explains why the West has been so powerful. The Christian moral foundation of social and cultural life was what made possible the emergence of capitalism, and then the successful transition to democratic politics. We don't have any doubt about this.[6]

Ethics professor David Gushee, at Union University, Jackson, Tennessee, is quoted as saying,

> Evangelicals should think more about ethics, because it is fundamental to Scripture, and relatively neglected among us compared to, for example, our interest in church growth, evangelism, missions and doctrine . . . This neglect relates directly to our moral sloppiness both in our attitudes and our behaviour, resulting in a disastrous indistinctness from the world.[7]

Paul pressed the point over and over:

---

[6] David Aikman, *Jesus in Beijing* (Regency Publishing Inc., 2003), p. 5.
[7] *Christianity Today*, February 2006.

Do not offer the parts of your body to sin, as instruments of wickedness, but rather offer yourselves to God, as those who have been brought from death to life; and offer the parts of your body to him as instruments of righteousness. (Romans 6:13)

Righteousness is foundational to ethics. Without God the world has no perfect moral-giver who can enlighten or refine our consciences, and to whom we are accountable. Forsake God and his righteousness, and a God-forsaken life soon becomes too awful to contemplate.

This is true of individuals and society. The unknown author of the book of Judges (maybe Samuel) records a period in Israel's history when *'every man did what was right in his own eyes' (Judges 21:25 RSV)*. Anyone who has lived through such a chaotic time of anarchy in any country will know just how terrifying it can become for daily living. After the cruel oppression of Israel *(Judges 4:3)*, *'the roads were abandoned; travellers took to winding paths. Village life in Israel ceased' (Judges 5:6)*. How frustrating and dangerous for agriculture and business, and how paralysing for a nation. Without righteousness our world is heading for terror and tyranny. King Solomon wisely observed, *'Righteousness exalts a nation' (Proverbs 14:34)*. Conversely, moral pollution affects nations and the whole of creation negatively and destructively. When the nations repent, God heals the land once more *(2 Chronicles 7:14)*. Seen in this light, one soon realises that the whole question of righteousness is a very serious matter.

What Jesus had to say about human good and evil was of sufficient depth, power and justification to dominate European culture and its offshoots for two millennia. Nobody even has an idea of what 'Europe' and the 'Western world' would mean apart from Jesus and his words.[8]

A modern historian wrote in the 1970s,

> The most potent figure, not only in the history of religion, but in world history as a whole, is Jesus Christ: the maker of one of the few revolutions which have lasted. Millions of men and women for century after century have found his life and teaching overwhelmingly significant and moving, and there is ample reason . . . in this later twentieth century why this should still be so.[9]

The philosopher Friedrich Nietzsche has usually been regarded as 'a bitter opponent of Jesus'.

> But he clearly recognized his indispensable role to the civilization into which Nietzsche himself had been born. He also understood that the modern world was moving away from its foundations of the Christian tradition of moral goodness, and that cataclysmic changes were to come because of this. They have come and they are coming.[10]

No Easy Answers

We are touching here on something which is a real challenge for believers today. Doing the right thing is sometimes very difficult to square with modern life. The practical outworking is never simple and straightforward. As a young curate in Wallington, Surrey, I once said at a Bible study

---

[8] Dallas Willard, *The Divine Conspiracy* (HarperCollins, 1998), p. 145.

[9] Michael Grant, *Jesus: An Historian's Review of the Gospel* (Charles Scribner & Sons, 1977), p. 1.

[10] Willard, op cit.

that it was always wrong to lie. An ex-army veteran and one-time prisoner-of-war in a Japanese camp, obviously thought differently. 'What if', he asked, 'one of your fellow countrymen was trying to escape from a Japanese concentration camp and an enemy search party asked you if you had seen the escapee when you knew he was hiding under your bed at that actual moment? Would you betray him to an almost certain death?' I had to admit that in those circumstances I would not have done so. A little girl in Sunday school expressed the human dilemma well with the following formula when asked what a lie is. She replied, 'A lie is an abomination to God but a very present help in time of trouble!'

Many years later I read what Richard Wurmbrand, who spent 14 years in a Romanian communist prison cell, had to say about lying to his torturers. He obviously had no scruples about how to react:

> If we have the right to resist the tyrant and deny him the possibility of continuing to live, even more do we have the right to oppose his inquisitive delving into what he is not entitled to know – the secret activities of the church. We can lie to the communist persecutor. Not that it ever becomes right to lie. But is it wrong to prefer your personal purity to responsibility for your neighbour? If you speak the truth you put your neighbour in prison. If you speak the truth you make the existence of the underground church impossible and deprive whole nations of the Gospel . . . We cannot assume the responsibility of telling the truth to tyrants, because it will help them to torture and kill Christians.
>
> I will not justify lying either, but I will gladly accept its responsibility before God. I discover that I am able to live with

my conscience after having lied. [It was] not a choice between good and evil, but only between two evils. Though we sometimes have a duty to lie, still we have the absolute duty of truthfulness. It is a grave sin to trespass against either duty![11]

There is an intriguing example of a contrary line of action spelt out by Corrie ten Boom, a local opposition leader against the Nazi invaders occupying her home town of Haarlem, Holland, during the Second World War. This Christian family were hiding Jews in their own home. The hiding place was entered by a trapdoor covered by a piece of carpet under the kitchen table. They were sitting chatting at that very table with their friend Cocky at exactly the moment when two German soldiers burst in without warning. They were searching for the two Jewish men who had just been hidden beneath the trapdoor. Corrie was very nervous because she knew that her friend, a sincere Christian, simply would not be able to lie about the presence of the men if questioned. And the Germans looked straight at her and demanded to know where the men were hidden. Corrie became extremely worried as Cocky weakly pointed towards the covered trapdoor and said, 'Under the table!' Quickly the Germans lifted the edge of the tablecloth and glanced beneath it. Nothing suspicious there! They saw it as a diversionary tactic to waste their time and, turning sharply, strode from the house, snarling, 'Don't take us for fools!'[12] The Jewish escapees went undiscovered.

---

[11] Richard Wurmbrand, *Alone with God* (Hodder & Stoughton, 1988), pp. 34–35.

[12] See Corrie ten Boom, *The Hiding Place* (Fleming H. Revell Co., 1971), pp. 90–91.

Complex Issues

There is no place for smugness in this area. There is no way of reducing Christian ethics to a clear system with graduated solutions. There are no simple commands or separate prescriptions for each and every particular case. Plenty of complex issues could be cited, but reflection on the following four real-life examples should be enough to start with.

(1) The manager of a local superstore in England is asked for the keys of his office safe under duress. If he does not comply, he is told that his wife and children, who have been tied up at home, will be hurt, mutilated or killed. He hands over the keys. His family is saved. All the money in the safe is stolen.

(2) A very needy single mother in Africa, with no means of support, is offered money for sex by a man who will then give the money to her to buy treatment for her dying baby. She offers her body, he gives her the money, and the baby survives.

(3) Survivors from an air crash in the snow-capped Andes in 1972 realise they will die unless they get food. They hear on their radio that the air search for them has been abandoned. The only possibility is to eat the flesh of fellow passengers who are already dead. Some did that, reluctantly, and survived.[13]

(4) An old-age pensioner protests about the run-down state of her drug- and criminal-infested street. The only way she can draw the council's attention to the problem is by refusing to pay her rates.[14]

---

[13] See Nando Parrado, 'Alive', *Reader's Digest UK*, July 2006, p. 145.
[14] *Daily Telegraph*, 7th, 28th, 29th June 2006.

Paul teaches that where it is not clear about whether something is right or wrong, we need to act wisely. There was a question in one of Paul's churches about eating meat when it was known that the animal had been offered to an idol during its butchering – a common practice among some pagan societies. Paul said, *'Each one should be fully convinced in his own mind' (Romans 14:5b)*. Discussing this question with the Corinthians, he added a caveat, *'Be careful, however, that the exercising of your freedom does not become a stumbling-block to the weak' (1 Corinthians 8:9)*. In other words, feel free to bless such meat with thanksgiving to God and eat it, but do not flaunt your freedom before fellow believers who may be shocked, scandalised or upset that Christians should eat such meat under any circumstances – a common enough problem in some church circles, even today.

Although it may appear overcautious in certain contexts, when mature Christians are advising those younger in the faith, it is good, scripturally justified counsel to advise them, 'If in doubt . . . don't.'

Finding the Right Perspective

Has it surprised the reader as strange that as soon as the Jerusalem council *(Acts 15)* had resolved the problem as to whether Gentile converts needed to be circumcised or not, and it was declared unnecessary, since we are not saved by keeping the law but by God's grace, Paul (in the very next chapter) sets off on a missionary journey with the young Timothy, whose mother was Jewish but whose father was Greek, and Paul had Timothy circumcised. He, of all men, knew only too well that it was not necessary to be circumcised to be saved, but here, it seems, it was on his initiative that Timothy was circumcised. Paul had a different perspective: namely that it would be counterproductive to upset his Jewish listeners before they had even heard the gospel.

Paul's freedom has created a precedent for others.

There is a Christian medical mission in Kenya today that offers circumcision to young men who need to prove their manhood (as their tradition demands) in that way. They have a social ritual to mark an older boy's 'coming out' into adulthood. The alternative method offered by the Christian mission is a hygienic operation, whereas the traditional method risks the spreading of AIDS, since the operations are all usually performed with the same knife. Obviously the whole subject raises new issues.

Sometimes it is hard to figure out quite how to do the right thing sensitively.

Some of the first missionaries in India had concentrated on winning converts among the highest caste – the Brahmins. The belief was that the gospel would seep down into the lower classes once it had taken root, but the early Brahmin converts kept the gospel to themselves – they apparently closed their ears to the cries of the outcasts. Later missionaries came with what we would consider a more Christian approach. But the reasoning of the first missionaries had seemed sensible to them at the time.

An American soldier won the Croix de Guerre in France, but refused to wear it. 'No!' he said. 'I was no good back at home. I let my sister and my widowed mother support me. I was a dead beat. This medal is for something I did here at the Front, but I am not going to wear it here. I am going back home first to show my mother that I can make good at home and then I will wear it on parade.'

Help to Clarify Thinking

C. S. Lewis offered some very clear advice in his excellent book *Mere Christianity*.

> The first thing to get clear about Christian morality between man and man is that in this department Christ did not come to preach any brand new morality. The Golden Rule of the New Testament (Do as you would be done by) is a summing up of what every one, at bottom, has always known to be right. Really great moral teachers never do introduce new moralities: it is quacks and cranks who do that. As Dr Johnson said, 'People need to be reminded more often than they need to be instructed.' The real job of every moral teacher is to keep on bringing us back, time after time, to the old, simple principles which we are all so anxious not to see; like bringing a horse back and back to the fence it has refused to jump or bringing a child back and back to the bit in its lesson that it wants to shirk.[15]

A recent article in a Sunday newspaper revealed how common it is today to shoplift. The journalist tells how she visited her friend Rob, who excused his stealing Evian water from Sainsbury's on the grounds that 'anyway, your other friends are doing it too'. The writer spent the next few days

> phoning, cross-examining and discovering to my surprise that Rob was right. Though they are employed, tax-paying, respectable citizens, more than half my friends confessed to pilfering. A psychologist pal said she snipped security tags from Top Shop T-shirts; a male friend in PR said he pocketed CDs from HMV; another girl claimed she'd got away with hundreds

---

[15] C. S. Lewis, *Mere Christianity* (Fontana Press, 1962), p. 74.

of free books. 'Come on,' she said, 'everyone does it. I mean, who actually pays for newspapers in WH Smith?'[16]

These new attitudes seem far removed from the old catechism used in preparation for confirmation, which taught us 'to keep our hands from picking and stealing'! What has happened to the command, *'You shall not steal' (Exodus 20:15)*? C. S. Lewis writes further,

> The second thing to get clear is that Christianity has not, and does not profess to have, a detailed political programme for applying 'Do as you would be done by' to a particular society at a particular moment. It could not have. [Righteousness] is meant for all men at all times and the particular programme which suited one place or time would not suit another.[17]

It should be stressed that 'Scripture gives us basic principles, not always (or often) direct ethical instructions. Sometimes this seems confusing, but the outworking of the principles (in this case doing what is right), though risky, can be challenging and exciting.'

Signposts

There are certain obvious God-given helps to point the way.

(1) We have the revelation of nature and our consciences to guide us.
(2) We have experienced the new birth through the work of the Holy Spirit and therefore have enlightened consciences to guide us.

---

[16] Mary Wakefield, 'My friends are thieves – and proud of it', *Sunday Telegraph*, 9th July 2006.

[17] Lewis, *Mere Christianity*, p. 74.

(3) We seek to have our hearts cleansed from all known sins, and constantly rededicate our lives to righteousness.

(4) We seek to have our minds well versed in Holy Scripture.

(5) We seek God's mind in prayer, asking for wisdom from above, for *'the wisdom that comes from heaven is first of all pure; then peace-loving, considerate, submissive, full of mercy and good fruit, impartial and sincere' (James 3:17).*

Making the right decision

The following points may help as we try to make the right choices.

(1) We try to listen to God, *'For God does speak – now one way, now another' (Job 33:14).* Jesus says, *'My sheep listen to my voice' (John 10:27).*

(2) We must hear both sides of a case, and listen to others who express opinions also, so that we may *'comprehend with all saints' (Ephesians 3:18 KJV).* *'A wise man listens to advice' (Proverbs 12:15b).* *'Plans fail for lack of counsel, but with many advisers they succeed' (Proverbs 15:22).*

(3) We maintain our sanctified common sense and Christian love.

(4) We consider pretexts from past experience, history and other cultures.

(5) We prayerfully assess the perceived balance of all these insights.

Making the right decision in some cases may seem difficult, but we can usually tackle the issues with a conscience void of offence before God – for *'motives are weighed by the Lord' (Proverbs 16:2b).* If we reflect on all these aspects, they will lead us to the mind of Christ.

In his book *Gathered for Power*, Graham Pulkingham, who was used by God to build up a remarkable redemptive community in the run-down Church of the Redeemer, Houston, Texas, in the 1960s and 70s, tells of a transforming experience of the Holy Spirit which caused him to become enchanted with the word of God, and how he came to recognise when God was speaking to him.

As it was with David, the King of Israel, it [daily meditation on the Bible] had become a delight to my soul and each morning my mind was renewed by it as I awakened eager to hear what God was going to say that day. There had developed a prophetic ring to Scripture which was exciting. The word of God always had a place of importance to me, especially in preaching, but now it was taking on a whole new significance; God himself was speaking to my innermost being, and listening to his words, how could I doubt the vision imparted through his own lips?

Weeks became months and I grew confident of the voice that was speaking during those nightly trysts. There was not a single doubt that it was the voice of God. However, no sounds were heard; no impressions were received, no feeling stimulated from the environment of creatures around me. No. Properly speaking it was not a voice that sounded any more than there were words I was listening to. It was the Person of God my spirit heard, Spirit to spirit, a still, small voice behind the wind and thunder, and behind the words of the Bible too. I knew the thoughts I was identifying as God's voice were experienced in the same way as were all my thoughts, feelings, desires and imaginings. I knew also that God was using the familiar means to communicate with me. It was in the terms of my humanity. He was revealing his mind to the condition of my life and I was learning a new level of trust in him and in myself. A most important discovery was unfolding before me . . .[18]

SOCIAL ACTION

Finally, as we consider aspects of righteousness, we address the practicalities of their application in social contexts. But first, what does the Bible have to say about social issues?

The areas of major social concern in the old covenant, as set out in the book of Deuteronomy, are as follows.[19]

(1) *Personhood*. Everyone's person is to be secure *(5:17; 24:7; 27:18)*.

(2) *False accusation*. Everyone is to be secure against slander and false accusation *(5:20; 19:15–21)*.

(3) *Women*. No woman is to be taken advantage of within her subordinate status in society *(21:10–14; 22:13–30; 24:1–5)*.

(4) *Punishment*. Punishment for wrongdoing shall not be so excessive that the culprit is dehumanised *(25:15)*.

(5) *Dignity*. Every Israelite is God's freedman and servant and has the right to be honoured and safeguarded *(15:12–18)*.

(6) *Inheritance*. Every Israelite's inheritance in the Promised Land is to be secure *(25:5–10)*.

(7) *Property*. Everyone's property is to be secure *(22:1–4; 25:13–15)*.

---

[18] Graham Pulkingham, *Gathered for Power* (Hodder & Stoughton, 1972), p.65.

[19] Taken from the *Pocket-Sized Edition of the New International Version* (Zondervan, 1989), p. 223. My list omits their many other references in the Old Testament.

(8) *Fruit of labour.* Everyone is to receive the fruit of his labours *(24:14; 25:4).*

(9) *Fruit of the ground.* Everyone is to share the fruit of the ground *(14:28–29; 24:19–21).*

(10) *Rest on the Sabbath.* Everyone, down to the humblest servant and the resident alien, is to share in the weekly rest of God's Sabbath *(5:12–15).*

(11) *Marriage.* The marriage relationship is to be kept inviolate *(5:18; 22:13–30).*

(12) *Fair trial.* Everyone is to have free access to the courts, and is to be afforded a fair trial *(1:17; 10:17–18; 16:18–20; 17:8–13; 19:15–21).*

(13) *Social order.* Every person's God-given place in the social order is to be honoured *(17:8–13).*

(14) *Law.* No one shall be above the law, not even the king *(17:8–20).*

(15) *Animals.* Concern for the welfare of other creatures is to be extended to the animal world *(22:4, 6–7; 25:4).*

These were all areas of social concern under the old covenant. Today we live under the new covenant, which the writer to the Hebrews is at pains to demonstrate is even better than the old covenant: *'Jesus has become the guarantee of a better covenant' (Hebrews 7:22).*

Social righteousness is clearly a call to action: it is concerned with seeking the liberation of people from oppression; respect for personal rights; the promotion of civil rights; justice in the law courts; integrity in business dealings; honour in the home and family affairs; responsible care for the creation and opposition to blatant corruption. This is something we have to watch out for and work at most of the time, on a lesser or larger scale. It may frequently involve difficult decisions concerning questions for which we may not yet have the answers, but for which we should continue to pray. We may often make a stand, and later wish we had made it in a wiser, more gracious, more loving, or more sensitive way. It is always helpful, too, to learn from the insights and approach of others regarding how, or how not, to set about it in the particular context involved.

Practical Applications

Sin-buster in Sodom

Not all reforming programmes are wisely conducted; not all are successful. Some fail from lack of support. We may often be surprised at the response of others when we might have expected something very different. The following account will probably help some readers to recall parallels in their own experience.

The subtitle above is taken from Arthur Blessitt's book *Turned on to Jesus*. Blessitt may be better remembered as the evangelist who walked halfway round the world carrying a cross. Before taking up his cross in this way, he had been a church leader in Nevada.

While Arthur Blessitt was pastor of a church in Nevada, he sensed the time had come to wage a war on the rampant prostitution in his locality. 'I doubted I could successfully fight the men and madams who profited mightily from the world's oldest profession,' he wrote, 'yet the stand had to be made.'

He began by denouncing on his radio programme the

existence of nine local brothels. He openly disclosed the names of all the officials in the city and county who were taking bribes to allow the houses to remain in operation. 'The sheriff alone was enriching himself by thousands of dollars a month. I named names and challenged them to sue me – none did.' Not surprisingly, the story created a sensation. Television and radio reporters and representatives from almost every newspaper rushed into Elko, Nevada, to investigate. The district attorney's response to them was: 'Our position is the less said about the matter the better.'

Blessitt was appalled by the responses of some of his fellow pastors as reported in the press. 'Prostitution presents no particular problem,' said one minister. 'We're not bothered by prostitution. I've been here five years and I'd say it's the lesser of two evils,' said another. Yet another said, 'I can't afford to oppose gambling or prostitution. My church would run me off. I've got too many people involved in those businesses.' The comment which troubled Blessitt the most was, 'It's none of my affair. I just preach the Gospel!'[20]

Blessitt's life was threatened; his reputation was slandered. His campaign failed. But in the process, though we may question his method, he had put down a marker for righteousness. And he lived on to fight another day.

A Battle Won

Not all campaigns are doomed to failure. History records many notable successes. I have on my desk beside me the wonderful story of Martin Luther King, who waged a

---

[20] Arthur Blessitt, *Turned on to Jesus* (Word Books, 1972), pp. 97–98.

non-violent struggle for the equality of rights for both blacks and whites in the USA during the 1960s. 'Probably King's movement was the last chance white America had to accept a revolution within its society on peaceful lines.'[21] That battle was won. But in the process King's life was lost. There is usually a cost involved when we stand up for righteousness – but there is a more serious cost long term when we do not. In the eighteenth century Edmund Burke wrote succinctly, 'The only thing necessary for the triumph of evil is for good people to do nothing.' Martin Luther King said something similar: 'We shall have to repent in this generation, not so much for the evil deeds of the wicked people, but for the appalling silence of the good people.'

In the early twentieth century, Lutheran pastor Martin Niemöller wrote of life under Hitler's Nazi regime:

> In Germany, they came for the communists and I didn't speak up because I was not a communist. Then they came for the Jews, and I didn't speak up because I wasn't a Jew. Then they came for the trade unionists, and I didn't speak up because I was not a trade unionist. Then they came for the Catholics, and I didn't speak up because I was not a Catholic. Then they came for me because I was a Protestant, and by that time there was no one left to speak up.

Backseat Protesters on a Bus

Alan Hargrave, a one-time missionary in South America, tells of his experience in Bolivia when taking a ride on a bus.

> I take the No. 2 bus from the top of Sopocachi into the centre of town. It is strange living in La Paz, Bolivia, after Argentina.

---

[21] Kenneth Slack, *Martin Luther King* (SCM Press, 1970), p. 114.

This is not a Latin culture with a few indigenous people; this is an Aymara Indian culture with some Latin influences. I watch as women with huge, multi-layered skirts, bowler hats, babies slung in the brightly coloured cloth on their backs, and heavy bags of shopping in their hands, get on and off the bus.

I stiffen slightly as, at the next stop, a man in an army uniform, with a gun under his arm, gets on the bus. I have seen the police and army in action in the dark days of the 'desaparecidos' in Argentina. Someone is taken off. The bus moves on. They are never seen again. Everyone else remains silent, too intimidated to talk openly about such things for fear of who may be listening, who may be next . . . they are suddenly removed without warning. Then there is no court of appeal. No access to lawyers. No visits from family. No one to listen as you cry out from the electric bed. Not even a grave to visit and remember.

As the man gets on, to my utter astonishment, a woman from the back of the bus shouts out: 'Driver, don't let that military pig on our bus!' I brace myself, waiting for the shooting to start. Instead another woman chips in: 'Aren't you ashamed of yourself, working for that scum?' 'Yes,' says another woman, standing up, 'I pity your mother, having a son like you. Get yourself off our bus.' By now half the bus is on their feet. They are beginning to jostle the man. He does not lift his gun. He tries to say that the situation isn't his fault. He's just doing his job. Just obeying orders. But his voice is drowned out by the growing chorus. Within minutes he is man-handled off the bus! The women sit down with smiles of satisfaction, smacking their formidable palms. 'That showed him!' We drive on. I look behind. The soldier is dusting himself down as he walks sheepishly back into town.[22]

---

[22] Alan Hargrave, *Almighty Passion* (Triangle SPCK, 2002), pp. 68–69.

The Whistleblower

Time magazine recently highlighted the singular role of US captain Ian Fishback.[23] Unable to square what he knew of systemic interrogation abuses in the global war on terror, he saw it as his duty to question company and battalion commanders, lawyers and other officials up the chain of command all the way to the Secretary of the Army. Undaunted by arguments that explicit anti-torture standards would limit the ability to wage war, and in spite of a warning 'to remember that the honour of the unit was at stake', Fishback persevered until true honour was restored. After 17 months of frustration and failure to get his superiors' attention, he went outside his chain of command to Senator John McCain, who in turn successfully spearheaded 'anti-torture' legislation. Fishback, who is called one of *Time*'s 'Persons of the Year 2006', wrote, 'I would die fighting rather than give up even the smallest part of the idea that is America.'

A Price to Pay

Mary Schiavo was a married mother with a small daughter and expecting her second child. She had been recently appointed Inspector General of the Department of Transportation for the US Government. From reports received in her office she soon became increasingly concerned about the safety of some of the lower cost commercial airline flights made possible, apparently, by the purchase of old planes patched up with counterfeit parts. She even discovered that ValuJet had circulated a memo to their directors that their own statistics showed the company safety records to be four

---

[23] *Time* magazine, 8th May 2006.

times worse than any other airline. Nevertheless ValuJet continued to assure the public that every precaution was being taken to protect travellers. On the 12th May 1996, she sent *Time* magazine an article entitled 'I Just Don't Like to Fly'. This was followed almost immediately by a tragic air crash – ValuJet – 110 presumed dead. She was soon to discover the power of this well-funded industry backed by so many political supporters. Instead of the focus being on ValuJet, the focus turned on Mary Schiavo herself, who with so many extra pressures now on her felt forced to resign her job on the 18th July 1996. Mary returned home with a new baby boy but to face the further cost of her marriage break-up.

Rape Victim Seeks Justice

Examples of standing up for righteousness are not limited to Christians. Mukhtaran Bibi[24] is a Pakistani woman raised in poverty. Her personal tragedy began in 2002, when her brother was accused of walking with a girl from a higher tribal group. In a culture in which female bodies are battle-grounds for male honour, the village court ruled that he should be punished with the public rape of his sister Bibi. She was consequently taken, stripped and assaulted by four men, and further shamed by being paraded naked through the village street.

There are perhaps thousands of such 'honour crimes' in Pakistan each year. Survivors are more likely to kill them-selves, or be killed by their families, than resort to a legal system that requires four male adult eyewitnesses to testify to rape – otherwise the victim can be convicted of fornication

---

[24] Ibid.

and adultery. But Bibi did go to court. Her courage attracted attention and support from the international media and women's groups, and her attackers were convicted by the law. With the compensation money, added to contributions from those who had read about her struggle, she created a girls' school. Now, aged 33, she has become a skilled organiser and trusted leader, and a magnet for other women escaping violence. But she is far from safe. Only global pressure forced Pakistan to give her a passport so she could meet women abroad, and she still receives death threats from those who view her as a danger to the nation's image and social order. She depends on ordinary supporters to keep herself alive and her work going. Praying for her will assure even greater and better protection.

New York Mayor Sees Justice Done

Fiorello LaGuardia, after whom a New York airport has been named, was the mayor of New York throughout the worst years of the Great Depression and the whole of the Second World War. One bitterly cold night in 1935 he turned up at a court that served the poorest part of the city, where he dismissed the judge for the evening and sat on the bench himself. Within a few minutes a tattered old woman was brought before him charged with stealing a loaf of bread. She told LaGuardia that her daughter's husband had deserted her, her daughter was sick and her daughter's children were starving. That was why she had stolen the bread. The shopkeeper refused to drop the charges. 'It's a bad neighbourhood, your honour. She must be punished to teach the other people a lesson.'

LaGuardia sighed and turned to the woman. 'I'll have to

punish you,' he said. 'The law makes no exceptions. Ten dollars, or ten days in jail.' Even as he pronounced sentence, he reached into his wallet for a ten-dollar note and tossed it into his famous sombrero. 'Here is the ten-dollar fine which I now remit, and furthermore I'm going to fine everyone in this court room 50 cents, for living in a town where a grandmother has to steal bread in order to feed her grandchildren. Mr Bailiff, collect the fines, and give them to the defendant!'

The following day the newspapers carried the story of how $47.50 had been passed over to a bewildered old lady who had stolen a loaf of bread to feed her grandchildren – 50 cents of which had been contributed by a red-faced store owner – while some 70 petty criminals, people with traffic violations, and New York policemen, each of whom had just paid 50 cents for the privilege of being in court, gave the mayor a standing ovation![25]

STUMBLING BLOCKS

There are plenty of stumbling blocks to righteousness, and these are outlined briefly below.

Sinful Pleasures

Sinful pleasures undermine our resolve for the things of God. Paul lamented the sad case of one of his former fellow workers: *'Demas, because he loved this world, has deserted me. . .'* *(2 Timothy 4:10).*

Our lack of enthusiasm for godly things may be attributed partly to laziness, partly to lack of self-control, and partly to

---

[25] Story taken from Brennan Manning, *The Ragamuffin Gospel* (Authentic, 2004), p. 69.

failure in a disciplined perseverance. And sometimes we are even so busy in the Lord's work that we have no time to discuss things with him, or to seek his counsel about his business! We are too preoccupied in 'doing our own thing' for the Lord!

Nothing will get done if we just cannot be bothered; when we do not want to put ourselves out. We just 'pass by on the other side', unwilling to get involved.

Self-sufficiency and Complacency

Complacency also impairs our hunger for God. This was the problem with the church at Laodicea: *'You say, "I am rich; I have acquired wealth and do not need a thing." But you do not realise that you are wretched, pitiful, poor, blind and naked' (Revelation 3:17).*

'Nothing is more fundamental to wholesome society than righteousness. Nothing is more repulsive than self-righteousness.'[26] And nothing is more soul-destroying than parading one's own righteousness or preaching one's own good deeds. *'I am not like other men . . . I fast twice a week and give a tenth of all I get' (Luke 18:12)*; *'Nor is it honourable to seek one's own honour' (Proverbs 25:27b)*. Indeed, while we should be tireless in protecting the rights of others, and encouraging others in the good they do, we should turn away from the natural temptation to fight over what we consider to be our own personal rights, or to promote ourselves on the basis of our righteous achievements: *'So you also, when you have done everything . . . should say, "We are unworthy servants. . ."' (Luke 17:10).*

---

[26] Richard Dortch, *Integrity: How I Lost and Found It* (New Leaf Press, 1991), p. 313.

Secret Sin

This easily erodes resolve for costly commitment in social action. Judas, one of the twelve apostles, strongly protested the needs of the poor when expensive ointment was poured over Jesus – but all the while, as we learn later, he was secretly plundering for himself the funds that had been intended for the poor *(John 12:6)*. He started by secretly betraying the poor, and ended up by openly betraying Christ.

Richard Dortch, a highly respected minister in the Assemblies of God (USA), served time in prison for shielding Jimmy Bakker, who had apparently once had an affair with a woman before Dortch joined the team. Dortch was compromised by his evasion of the truth about money used to pay off the woman, in order to protect Jimmy Bakker, and to save what he felt was the greater good of Heritage USA, a magnificent Christian project funded from gifts via Jimmy and Tammy Bakker's very popular television programme. Dortch became so intoxicated with the growth of Heritage USA; so enamoured with what was developing around him, that he refused to see what was happening. He observed later that in the many years he had served as a leader he had noticed that almost everyone who had fallen, both leader and layman, did so because they believed that an exception would be made in their case. They could pick and choose. They could sin, even if only occasionally, even for a good cause, and it might make no difference to their Christian work and witness. They could have a public persona and no one would ever see the other side of their lives.[27]

---

[27] See Richard Dortch, *Integrity: How I Lost and Found It* (New Leaf Press, 1991).

Secret sin is one of the 'dampers' inclining us to *'neglect the more important matters of the law' (Matthew 23:23).*

Natural Fear

Baroness Cox sits in the House of Lords, Westminster, but travels widely into some of the most dangerous areas across the globe, in the cause of Christian Solidarity International. She sees for herself the condition of the oppressed living under tyrannical regimes around the world. In 1995 she was the recipient of the Wilberforce Award, which recognised her as 'an individual who has made a difference in the face of formidable societal problems and injustices'. Eager to dispel any image of heroism, Lady Cox admits to having a 'fit of faithless, fearful dread' before going on her dangerous missions.

> I don't want to go. Home is very comfortable, with clean water, electric light, warmth, clean clothes. To wrench yourself away and go voluntarily into a conflict zone, you recoil against it. I don't particularly want to go out and get my guts blown out. I don't really want to go and get malaria.[28]

Prejudice

Prejudice literally means prejudging – consciously or unconsciously. We must recognise, and renounce, any particular prejudice or grievance or other vested interest, apart from what we sincerely believe to be the will of God.

---

[28] Benedict Rogers, Christian Solidarity International website, www.csi-int.org.

HUNGER AND THIRST

A QUESTION OF APPETITE

Here we are talking about appetites. We all know what appetites are. We respond regularly to their demands. We know how easy it is to misuse them. One can fail to eat, and starve. One can overeat, and suffer. One can become addicted, and let life get out of control. One can eat the wrong things, and harm oneself. We need to learn to be discerning and disciplined about diet – eating food in moderation, eating food that is good for us.

Jesus urges us to hunger and thirst after *righteousness*, the healthiest of all soul diets. In the process of 'going for it', we will seek to avoid all self-righteousness, hypocrisy, fanaticism, or seeking fulfilment in unrighteous ways.

In the garden of Eden all the trees growing there were good to eat from, except one – and in spite of all that was on offer, the forbidden fruit was the very fruit which Eve, then Adam, felt they simply had to sample. That wrongful act was the first example in the Bible of unrighteousness. God had offered them freely the 'tree of life'; they chose the forbidden food of death.

We have many spiritual appetites parallel to the natural ones common to us all. Jesus said, '*I am the bread of life. He who comes to me will never go hungry, and he who believes in me will never be thirsty*' *(John 6:35).*

We truly receive the spiritual refreshment that Jesus promises here, and indeed we are satisfied – but our hunger and thirst, like any appetite, will reoccur. Clearly the promise of Jesus that we '*will never be thirsty*' again can only be properly understood if we accept the implication that it means 'so long as the thirsty person *keeps* drinking of that same fountain of life'. We will never hunger again, so long as we keep feeding on Christ – just as the repeated sacrament of the Lord's Supper teaches us to feed on Christ in our hearts 'as *often* as we eat this bread and drink this cup. . .'.

Hunger for bread and thirst for water are as natural as the panting for air of a gasping man, the passionate desire of a lover, the groaning for relief of a sick patient, the endless dreams of a prisoner, the burning zeal of an athlete, or the longing for rest of a tired and weary soul.

Those who truly hunger and thirst after righteousness experience that yearning in at least three forms:

(1) *A longing to be righteous* – to be forgiven and accepted by God; to be right with God; to have a good relationship with him.

(2) *A longing to do what is right* – to do what God commands, imitating and reflecting God's righteousness in our lifestyles.

(3) *A longing to see that right is being done* – to help to bring about God's will of justice and peace into our broken and wounded world.

Maybe we feel we have lost our appetite. Then we should simply repent and seek the company of those who have it. They are the salt of the earth, and salt makes those that taste it thirsty. We can pray with them when they pray, eat with them what they eat, stay with them where they stay, play with them when they play. If *'Bad company corrupts good character' (1 Corinthians 15:33)*, then conversely good company corrects bad character. Such are the disciplines needed to retrieve a healthy appetite.

I was recently drawn to a headline in the daily paper concerning a former champion sportsman. There was a question about whether he would be training for the next Olympics. The caption read: 'I'M TAKING 12 MONTHS OFF TO FIND THAT HUNGER!' These words were supposed to have come from the lips of an Olympic sportsman who already had four gold medals. He was withdrawing from training for the Beijing Olympics, because a repeat of his success would demand even more personal commitment than he had needed for the previous trophies of former Olympic contests. He felt he could no longer give that commitment to his coach, his teammates and his country. He was reported to have said, 'For the first time in my career the hunger I need is not there.'

How about the Christian's hunger and thirst after righteousness (*Matthew 5:6*)? How much is one willing to sweat and sacrifice for that?

WHAT KIND OF HUNGER AND THIRST SHOULD WE BE LOOKING FOR?

Perhaps the question should be, 'What are we hungering and thirsting after?' We have everything a machine age can provide, yet boredom and unhappiness have reached an all-time high in our nation, while morals have plunged to an all-time low. We have dulled our hunger and quenched our thirst by striving after money, security, success, fame and sex. We have exchanged long-term satisfaction for short-term gratification – two very different prizes!

As believers we should be hungering and thirsting to know our righteous God better, to understand him more comprehensively, to praise him more wholeheartedly, to have an ever-improving spiritual relationship with him, and to bless him for saving us. There must be a longing to be *legally righteous* – to be forgiven and to be right with God, and to keep unsoiled the garments of righteousness with which he graciously covers us by faith.

Furthermore, we need that spiritual hunger and thirst for *moral righteousness* – to do what God is demanding, *'to fulfil all righteousness' (Matthew 3:15)*, to be holy.

This will be followed closely by a yearning after *social righteousness*. We are to be *'filled with the fruit of righteousness...' (Philippians 1:11)*, which is sown *'in peace' (James 3:18)*, by seeing that justice is being done in the law courts; that mercy is ministered in our communities; that people are being liberated from oppression; that there is integrity in our business dealings, and honour and fairness in the family; that there is order and respect in our schools; and that righteousness is flourishing in our nation. Such is the commitment to the righteousness that Jesus' disciples have been commissioned to bring in – even before the second coming of Christ in his fullness and glory, and the final judgement, after which the kingdom of righteousness will be established in the heavens and on the earth for ever.

RECOVERING OUR TASTE

Fyodor Dostoevsky, the famous Russian novelist, was once blindfolded and led out to face the Tzar's firing squad, totally unaware, like all the others, that only blanks were being used. So the blindfolded prisoners heard the shots being fired, but survived death. Having undergone the process of dying without being killed, Dostoevsky found the after-effects to be life transforming. His senses were sharpened to such an extent that he was able to savour food with far more relish, he could listen to birds singing with greater sensitivity and appreciation, and he found the colouring and shading of leaves trembling in the gentle breezes ever more fascinating. The whole experience thoroughly refined his tastes and enabled him to capture things more intensely, to convey things more richly in his writing. Powerful experiences of the Holy Spirit have often been found to produce similar effects.

PROMISED REWARD – 'THEY WILL BE FILLED'

FILLED WITH SATISFACTION

One might describe 'being filled' as 'being satisfied', and a good way to appreciate the meaning of 'satisfaction' is to observe the contrast with dissatisfaction. Haggai describes such a case when he depicts the remnant in Jerusalem. He points out to them what is happening because they have unrighteously neglected the rebuilding of the Temple, and have selfishly concentrated on building their own nice houses. He urges them to consider seriously what is happening among them, saying:

> Give careful thought to your ways. You have planted much, but have harvested little. You eat, but never have enough. You drink, but never have your fill. You put on clothes, but are not warm. You earn wages, only to put them in a purse with holes in it. (Haggai 1:5b–6)

Selwyn Hughes writes:

It is a fact that I believe to be incontrovertible that there is a moment in our lives when we begin to realise that the things of earth and time cannot satisfy us. Christian psychologists refer to this as an 'existential moment', a time when we begin to realise that deep down within our souls crave for something that this world cannot give us. For me that 'existential moment' came when I was bordering on 13 years old.[29]

C. S. Lewis once wrote, 'I find in myself desires which nothing in this world can satisfy. The only logical explanation is that I was made for another world.'[30]

Another definition of satisfaction could be 'holy contentment'.

> He satisfies the thirsty
>   and fills the hungry with good things.
> (Psalm 107:9)

Godliness with contentment is great gain. (1 Timothy 6:6)

I know what it is to be in need, and I know what it is to have plenty. I have learned the secret of being content in any and every situation, whether well fed or hungry, whether living in plenty or in want. (Philippians 4:12)

Billy Bray, the poor but very effective Cornish tin-miner-cum-evangelist, used to receive any second-hand clothes he was given so gratefully – whatever the shape, state or size. He would thank the donor with a happy smile and explain that he was sure it would fit him exactly, because 'Me and fashion quarrelled years ago and have never made it up!' He rejoiced infectiously (often dancing) in the blessings of Christ, whatever the circumstances.

I once shared a room at a conference in Peru with Juan

---

[29] Selwyn Hughes, *My Story* (CWR, 2005), p.21.
[30] C. S. Lewis, *The Problem of Pain*.

Carlos Ortiz, an Argentinian pastor, now working in California among Mexican immigrants. He just radiated refreshing contentment. Every morning as he woke up, he would start praising God over and over. He was a contagiously happy Christian breathing contentment – so good to be with!

Like King David, the believer simply *delights himself in the Lord (Psalm 37:4)*, and finds that the Lord is delightful. The same psalm is bursting with the blessings of the righteous.

He [the Lord] will make your righteousness shine like the dawn...
Better the little that the righteous have
    than the wealth of many wicked...
the Lord upholds the righteous...
The mouth of the righteous man utters wisdom,
    and his tongue speaks what is just...
The salvation of the righteous comes from the Lord;
    he is their stronghold in time of trouble.
The Lord helps them and delivers them;
    he delivers them from the wicked and saves them,
    because they take refuge in him.
(vv. 6, 16, 17b, 30, 39–40)

All this helps us to see what is involved in being filled, being content – the ingredients of satisfaction, including the removal of the usual causes for worry.

YOU WILL KNOW 'SATISFACTION' WHEN YOU HAVE IT

But how can we ever describe what it feels like to be spiritually satisfied? Maybe this story will offer a clue. A young housewife was driving away from her home when she spotted what looked like a handbag in a puddle in the road. She retrieved it and discovered that it contained, among other things, money, credit cards and a mobile phone. The owner's home address was there too, so the young lady took it round there. As the door was opened, she enquired if the owner of the handbag was in, but the husband explained that she was out shopping. The young lady replied, 'I doubt whether she has been able to do much shopping, because this is her handbag.' The man looked at it and its contents, and agreed that it was. As the young lady was about to leave, he extracted a generous sum of money and offered it to her, but the young lady declined it, saying, 'No, I just hope that if I ever lose *my* handbag, someone might find it and do the same for me.' That night, as she finished telling her family about the handbag saga, she added, 'And, do you know, I have just felt *so good* all day.' Doing genuine good and being good to others brings its own reward – *the feel-good factor*.

WHAT DOES SATISFACTION MEAN?

We all know when we have been satisfied by a good meal. We have that contented feeling. We express happiness in our demeanour; we express pleasantness in our behaviour; and we express thankfulness in our conversation. So we might assume that being righteous, doing what is right and seeing that right is being done, could well be crowned with feeling blessed, being at peace and being thankful – in other words, with satisfaction. Being satisfied means we are:

No longer hungry, but replete.
No longer thirsty, but refreshed.
No longer restless, but settled.

No longer wrestling, but peaceful.

No longer sad, but happy.

No longer insecure, but safe.

No longer aimless, but focused.

No longer bored, but busy.

No longer vengeful, but forgiving.

No longer vulnerable, but protected.

No longer futile, but hopeful.

No longer empty, but full.

No longer feeling life has passed us by, but sensing fresh opportunities ahead of us.

And there is more:

We remember Israel's thanksgiving for restoration after years in captivity:

> *Our mouths were filled with laughter,*
> *our tongues with songs of joy.*
> *(Psalm 126:2)*

We remember Mary's thanksgiving after the Lord's promise to her of a child:

> *He has filled the hungry with good things*
> *but has sent the rich away empty.*
> *(Luke 1:53)*

We would not be surprised if the righteous sometimes suffered for their faith *(1 Peter 4:12)*, but we would be surprised if they were not *satisfied* by it. But in the final analysis, although there can be no total satisfaction in this life, there is certainly ever the joyful anticipation of the kingdom to come. Even Paul could admit:

Brothers, I do not consider myself yet to have taken hold of it. But one thing I do: Forgetting what is behind and straining towards what is ahead, I press on towards the goal to win the prize for which God has called me heavenwards in Christ Jesus. (Philippians 3:13–14)

If total satisfaction could have been found in this life, it might well have become counterproductive – *'If you find honey, eat just enough. . .' (Proverbs 25:16, 27).* Ultimately the longing for righteousness is a yearning for unbroken fellowship with our righteous God – through knowing God in Christ fully. The psalmist put it so well:

> *In righteousness I shall see your face;*
> > *when I awake, I shall be satisfied with seeing your likeness.*
> *(Psalm 17:15)*

MEDITATION

O the bliss of the man who longs for total righteousness as a starving man longs for food, and a dying man thirsts for living water – for that man will truly be satisfied.[31]

* * *

Justice will dwell in the desert
  and righteousness live in the fertile field.
The fruit of righteousness will be peace;
  the effect of righteousness will be quietness and confidence for ever.
My people will live in peaceful dwelling-places,
  in secure homes,
  in undisturbed places of rest.

---

[31] William Barclay, *Gospel of Matthew Vol. 1* (Saint Andrew Press, 1956), p.97.

Though hail flattens the forest
  and the city is levelled completely,
how blessed you will be,
  sowing your seed by every stream,
  and letting your cattle and donkeys range free.
(Isaiah 32:16–20)

* * *

When He shall come with trumpet sound,
O, may I then in Him be found;
Clothed in His righteousness alone,
Faultless to stand before the throne.

* * *

If my soul has turned perversely to the dark;
If I have left some brother wounded by the way;
If I have preferred my aims to Thine;
If I have been impatient and would not wait;
If I have marred the pattern drawn out for my life;
If I have cost tears to those I loved;
If my heart has mourned against Thy will,
O Lord forgive.
(F. B. Meyer)

* * *

I would be true, for there are those who trust me;
I would be pure, for there are those who care;
I would be strong, for there are those who suffer;
I would be brave, for there is much to dare.
I would be friend of all – the foe and the friendless;
I would be giving, and forget the gift;
I would be humble, for I know my weakness;
I would look up, and laugh, and love, and lift.
(Howard Walter)

* * *

Now may our God and Father himself and our Lord Jesus clear the way for us to come to you. May the Lord make your love increase and overflow for each other and for everyone else, just as ours does for you. May he strengthen your hearts so that you will be blameless and holy in the presence of our God and Father when our Lord Jesus comes with all his holy ones. (1 Thessalonians 3:11–13)

* * *

We pray, our Father, for all those whose freedom has been taken from them:

For those who are suffering imprisonment, whether for their own crime, for conscience's sake or through tyranny;

For all whose vision of your world is seen through bars, and in whose hearts the lamp of hope burns low.

We pray for all those who stand up to defend them in the name of righteousness.

O God of mercy, give help according to their need, and graciously hear our prayers – for Jesus Christ's sake. Amen.

5

Revenge Is Never Sweet

Blessed are the merciful,
for they will be shown mercy.
(Matthew 5:7)

In wrath remember mercy. (Habakkuk 3:2)

INTRODUCTION

An estranged young man left home. His father later set out to find him, searching for months all over Spain without success. Finally, in desperation, the father put an advert in the local newspaper: 'Dear Paco, meet me in front of this newspaper office at noon on Saturday. *All is forgiven.* I love you. Your father.' On the day the paper was put on sale, some 800 young men named Paco showed up, looking for forgiveness and love from their estranged fathers! How many folk are out there desperate for mercy, especially the mercy of forgiveness and reconciliation?

A WORLD WITHOUT MERCY

If we take the various meanings of mercy as differing aspects of the same word, and consider a world without 'kindness', 'loving kindness', 'unfailing love', 'tenderness' and 'faithfulness', that world would be a cold, harsh and inhuman place.

A FATHER WHO REFUSED TO BEAR A GRUDGE

On Remembrance Day 1987, Enniskillen, in Northern Ireland, was torn apart by an IRA bomb. Eleven people were killed and many more injured. Among those who died was a 20-year-old nurse, Marie Wilson, home for the weekend from Belfast's Victoria Hospital. Among the injured was her father Gordon. His words that evening were echoed round the world across the television screens:

> I bear no ill will. I bear no grudge. Dirty sort of talk is not going to bring her back to life. She was a great lassie. She loved her profession. She was a pet, and she is dead. She is in heaven, and we will meet again. Don't ask me please for a purpose. I don't have a purpose. I don't have an answer. But I know that there has to be a plan. If I didn't think that, I would commit suicide. It is part of a greater plan and God is good. And we shall meet again.

This father was wanting no kind of revenge. That is not to say that the powers-that-be on earth should slacken their efforts to identify the criminals, and see them duly punished.

A LEADER WHO WENT THE 'SECOND MILE'

Nelson Mandela went the 'second mile' in his antipathy towards revenge. All who met him following his 27 years of prison life witnessed to his amazing and magnetic authority. As president of South Africa he visited his former tormentors in their homes, and invited his former guards to his official house. A commentator remarked, 'He never sought to harm those who harmed him, or to punish his abusers. He looked forward to justice, not backward to revenge.'

A MOTHER WHO KNEW THE MEANING OF MERCY

There was a young man in Napoleon's army who committed a deed so terrible that it was worthy of death. The day before he was scheduled for the firing squad, the young man's mother went to the general and pleaded for mercy for her son.

Napoleon replied, 'Woman, your son does not deserve mercy.'

'I know,' replied the woman. 'If he deserved it, it would not be mercy.'

THE GREATEST COMMANDMENT

When Jesus was asked which was the greatest commandment, he replied, '"Love the Lord your God. . ." This is the first and greatest commandment. And the second is like it: "Love your neighbour as yourself"' (Matthew 22:37). Love – 'unfailing loving kindness' – is fundamental to the meaning of mercy. It is sympathy: feeling for others, putting yourself in their place; and action: doing for others what you would wish them to do for you, doing whatever you can to help in a practical way.

Mercy emanates from the heart of God. It is his loving nature to have mercy. This revelation, the scarlet thread of God's merciful nature, runs through both the Old Testament and the New.

Early on in Israel's history Moses was shown by God that

in the Holy of Holies in the tabernacle meeting place there was to be a 'mercy seat'. The mercy of God, his love and his readiness to forgive, is the real story of the Bible. This led on to the New Testament story of the cross of Calvary where the sinless Son of God offered himself, once and for all, for our sins, so that the whole of sinful mankind could experience his love and forgiveness.

WHAT IS MERCY?

In Hebrew, the language of most of the Old Testament, the word 'mercy' is also translated 'kindness', 'loving kindness', 'unfailing love', 'tenderness' and 'faithfulness'. The word occurs about 250 times in the Bible and most frequently it signifies God's mercy. Mercy is having compassion for people – even one's enemies.

Jesus taught an important lesson on forgiveness in his parable of the 'Unmerciful Servant'. A servant who owed much was forgiven much, but then refused to forgive a man who owed him only a little. For that the first man was cast into prison until his debt was paid up, fully and finally. The parable ends with the words, *'This is how my heavenly Father will treat each of you unless you forgive your brother from your heart' (Matthew 18:35).*

This chapter focuses on five major strands of mercy:

(1) Compassion
(2) Forgiveness
(3) Stewardship
(4) Healing
(5) Social action

(1) COMPASSION

> *Because of the Lord's great love we are not consumed,*
>   *for his compassions never fail.*
> *They are new every morning;*
>   *great is your faithfulness.*
> *(Lamentations 3:22–23)*

God has a heart of compassion and desires to find the same in his people.

Teachers of the law came to Jesus and asked him which was the greatest commandment. Jesus answered, *'Love the Lord your God . . . Love your neighbour as yourself' (Mark 12:30).* Several times the Gospels refer to Jesus having compassion on people and acting on it. On one occasion Jesus looked on a mass of people and said, *'I have compassion for these people; they have already been with me three days and have nothing to eat' (Mark 8:2).* And Jesus fed the five thousand – a miracle! Another time, Jesus spotted the grief-stricken widow of Nain, whose twelve-year-old daughter had died. The gospel tells us how he had compassion on the mother and he proceeded to raise the girl back to life: *'When the Lord saw her, his heart went out to her and he said, "Don't cry"' (Luke 7:13).* He was clearly moved to action by his compassion.

Raphael McManus describes how compassion works: 'Love produces servanthood. Servanthood sees sacrifice as a privilege.'[1]

(2) FORGIVENESS

Forgiveness is obviously a strong element in the gospel

---

[1] Erwin Raphael McManus, *An Unstoppable Force* (Group Publishing, 2001), p. 158.

stories, but it is not without problems when we seek it or need to put it into practice.

Difficulties about Forgiveness

Robert McAfee Brown once listened to an impassioned address before the memorial of those Jews who lost their lives defending the Warsaw ghetto. The theme was 'Never forget, never forgive!'. The West had found it very difficult to come to terms with the unspeakable treatment of six million Jews by the Nazis during the Second World War.

At that time the world was seeking for a more precise understanding of the Nazi atrocities. What at first nobody could believe, chiefly because the mind could not comprehend the enormity of it, slowly became authenticated by fresh evidence. It gradually dawned that the Nazis committed crimes which were so monstrous as to be incredible.

But ere long priests, philanthropists and philosophers implored the world to forgive the Nazis. Most of these altruists had probably never even had their ears boxed, but nevertheless found compassion for the murderers of innocent millions. The priests said indeed that the criminals would have to appear before the Divine Judge, and that they could therefore dispense with earthly verdicts against them, which eminently suited the Nazis' book. Since they did not believe in God[2] they had no fear of Divine Judgment. It was only earthly justice that they feared.[3]

---

[2] Actually some Nazis, and some of their supporters, did believe in God, and we have read of at least one man's later struggle with his conscience on his deathbed, but that may well have been too much for some to accept.

[3] Simon Wiesenthal, *The Sunflower: On the Possibilities and Limits of Forgiveness* (Schocken Books Inc., 1997), p. 85.

Differing Attitudes Towards Forgiveness

A Vicar Who Could Not Forgive

In the first months of 2006 a Bristol vicar resigned from her parish as she struggled with forgiveness. She had lost her daughter in the terrorist attacks on the London Underground the previous summer, and still could not find it in her heart to forgive the person responsible. The bishop accepted her resignation and commended her integrity. So do we all. And who could not but feel the greatest sympathy for her?

For some people grief is so overwhelming that it is almost impossible at the time to disentangle the need to own and express the grief and the need to release forgiveness. An added complication in the vicar's case was that she never knew, and would never know, the man who committed the assassination, and even if she could forgive, the recipient could never receive that forgiveness. After all, he and his fellow murderers had deliberately plotted to effect maximum carnage with the bombs that were strapped to their own bodies for simultaneous self-destruction. Unlike the atheist Nazis, those terrorists were supposed to be enjoying paradise with 70 virgins each as a reward for their sacrifice in the cause of Allah.

It would take a while for many of us to work through the emotional traumas and the imponderable moral processes following such a tragedy.

A Christian Who Struggled to Forgive

The Second World War was over and Corrie ten Boom was sharing her testimony of God's amazing grace to her and her ailing sister through all the terrible sufferings during their years of concentration camp imprisonment. She writes:

> It was at a church service in Munich that I saw him, the former S.S. man who had stood guard at the shower room door in the processing centre at Ravensbrück. He was the first of our actual jailers that I had seen since that time. And suddenly it was all there – the roomful of mocking men, the heaps of clothing, Betsie's pain-blanched face.
>
> He came up to me as the church was emptying, beaming and bowing. 'How grateful I am for your message *Fraulein,*' he said. 'To think that, as you say, He has washed my sins away!'
>
> His hand was thrust out to shake mine. And I, who had preached so often to the people in Bloemendaal the need to forgive, kept my hand at my side.
>
> Even as the angry, vengeful thoughts boiled through me, I saw the sin of them. Jesus Christ had died for this man . . . Lord Jesus, I prayed, forgive me and help me to forgive him.
>
> I tried to smile, I struggled to raise my hand. I could not. I felt nothing, not the slightest spark of warmth or charity. And so again I breathed a silent prayer. Jesus, I cannot forgive him. Give me Your forgiveness.
>
> As I took his hand the most incredible thing happened. From my shoulder along my arm and through my hand a current seemed to pass from me to him, while into my heart sprang a love for this stranger that almost overwhelmed me.
>
> And so I discovered that it is not on our forgiveness any more than on our goodness that the world's healing hinges, but on His. When He tells us to love our enemies, He gives us, along with the command, the love itself.[4]

---

[4] Corrie ten Boom, *The Hiding Place* (Fleming H. Revell, 1971), p. 238.

But can it always be as simple as that?

A Missionary Who Wished She Had Learned the Importance of Forgiveness Earlier

C. T. Studd's daughter Edith Buxton once wrote:

> I wish I had learned earlier about forgiveness, both giving and receiving it and the freedom of spirit it can bring. You cannot have a happy old age without it. My daughter once wrote these words: 'When a situation has broken down in hurt and bitterness, and disagreement is so deep there seems no solution on earth – there remains forgiveness.'
>
> Through our absorption with this business of life, we play in the shallows and lose the depth of dimension. Laying aside traditional language, we need to go deep down into things, the things that really concern us, and face up to those unresolved conflicts within, the uncertainties and disturbances of our inner life. We need to look, long and deep, into the smallness and the emptiness of life, and face our fears. These may be fear of annihilation, fear of death, even fear of life itself. Then there are the guilt feelings that perhaps lie deepest of all. And into these black depths Christ comes to lighten our darkness, to take us by the hand and lead us to the love and mercy of God. In that moment of openness and acceptance of our smallness, our fears and guilt, we are released and receive grace to live life to its completion.[5]

Dilemmas about Forgiveness

Peter was uptight and put his question directly: *'Lord, how many times shall I forgive my brother when he sins against me? Up*

---

[5] Edith Buxton, *Reluctant Missionary* (Lutterworth Press, 1968), pp. 173–4.

to seven times?' (The rabbis taught three times.) Jesus answered, *'I tell you, not seven times, but seventy-seven times [or seventy times seven]' (Matthew 18:21).*

What is not specific here is whether the forgiveness was to be *unconditional* – what if there had been no signs of repentance? Nor is it clear whether such *unlimited* mercy was for a repeated serial offence or a series of different offences. The answer to the latter question must be partly resolved by asking ourselves how long and how much we need God to go on forgiving us for *our* offences against *him*. But an answer to the former question is ultimately unimportant for us.

The Difference Forgiveness Can Make to Society

After their father Jacob's death, the brothers started to fear that Joseph, still the second most powerful man in Egypt, might now think about taking revenge for their cruel mistreatment of him as a boy. Joseph, however, graciously confirmed his forgiveness and mercy towards them all *(Genesis 50:15–21).*

Forgiveness counters all fear of revenge and creates the grounds for reconciliation. In the imperfect world in which we live there will always be the need for forgiveness and reconciliation between individuals, families, communities and nations.

But this is still only one side of the coin. We have not yet fully answered the moral question as to whether there is any obligation to forgive others if there are no signs of repentance on their part. Should forgiveness not be conditional upon the offender being in the proper spirit in which to receive it – showing some signs of repentance and even offering some practical recompense where recompense might be expected? But we are talking about forgiveness here – not necessarily reconciliation.

Jesus set us a staggering precedent when he prayed for his own executioners: *'Father, forgive them, for they do not know what they are doing' (Luke 23:34)*, which appears to negate the assumption that the person being forgiven must be in any particular condition for receiving the forgiveness.

When the disciples begged Jesus to teach them how to pray, he told them: *'When you pray, say . . . "Forgive us our sins, for we also forgive everyone who sins against us"' (Luke 11:2–4)*. It could be assumed here that any who have experienced God's forgiveness would naturally be understanding of how mercy works, and would be forgiving of all those who had sinned against them also. So Jesus teaches that his forgiveness of us is indeed conditional, but that the condition is our readiness to forgive all those who have sinned against us: *'If you forgive men when they sin against you, your heavenly Father will also forgive you' (Matthew 6:14)*.

> This is not because we can merit mercy by showing mercy, or forgiveness by being forgiving, but because we cannot receive the mercy and forgiveness of God unless we repent, and we cannot claim to have repented of our sins so long as we remain unmerciful (and unforgiving) towards the sins of others.[6]

The 'Unmerciful Servant' in the parable is condemned for his unwillingness to forgive a trifling debt in comparison with the greater debt which his master had cancelled on his account. The master said to him, *'I cancelled [forgave] all that*

---

[6] John Stott, *The Message of the Sermon on the Mount* (IVP, 1978).

debt of yours . . . Shouldn't you have had mercy on your fellow-servant just as I had on you?' (Matthew 18:32–33).

A Father Who Forgave Unconditionally

The Reverend John and Lisa Mosey lost their daughter to a terrorist bomb on board an airliner which blew up over Lockerbie in 1988. When approached by journalists who asked him repeatedly how he could forgive such 'animals' for doing this to their daughter, John Mosey replied, 'I am a Christian, and that means every wrong I have ever done has been forgiven by God. If he can forgive all the wrong that I have ever done, then I must forgive others.'

The Sisters Who Forgave Unconditionally

During the Red Guard era in China (1966–9) many Christians were arrested and executed. Two girls, Chiu-Chiu-Hsiu and Ho-Hsiu-Tzu from Jiangxi in mainland China, were among them. They were taken into the prison yard to hear their sentence announced. A fellow prisoner watched the scene from his cell. He described how their faces shone with an amazing radiance, looking beautiful. He knew they were fearful of the process of death, but they had both bravely resolved to submit to their execution without renouncing their faith.

Flanked by renegade guards, the executioner finally appeared with a revolver in his hand. It was their own pastor, who had given in to torture and denied his faith in the Lord. He had been sentenced to die with the two girls, but his persecutors had told him that he could save his own life and be released, if he would prove his renunciation by shooting the two girls first. Tragically he had agreed.

The girls bowed respectfully before their pastor. An eye-witness heard them saying,

> Before you kill us we want to thank you from the bottom of our hearts for all that you have done for us. You baptised us; you taught the way to eternal life, you gave us Holy Communion from those same hands in which you now hold that gun. You also taught us that Christians are sometimes weak and commit terrible sins, but that they can be forgiven again. When you regret what you are about to do to us, don't do what Judas did and kill yourself, but think about how Peter, who betrayed Jesus, and repented. God bless you, and remember our last thoughts are not indignation against your failure. Everyone has his hours of darkness. May God reward you for all the good you have done to us. We die with thankfulness to God in our hearts for you. But for you we would never have known forgiveness and found God's grace, and had such assurance of life after death.

Then they bowed again as their former pastor obeyed his orders to shoot them in the head. He was himself later executed by his communist captors.[7]

While truly admiring such an example, and fully believing they meant every word of it, and knowing that God has been wonderfully glorified through it, some would still find it extremely difficult to imagine themselves being able to undertake such a merciful act, and almost incredible that anyone else could actually do it.

Release for the Person Doing the Forgiving

There is, however, yet another dimension to the 'unconditional forgiveness' question. When we forgive others out of

---

[7] I have taken this story word for word from some reliable source, but regrettably have since lost the details.

the mercy we have received, we are ourselves released in some way – we are set free, a miraculous personal blessing. There remains no root of bitterness in us over the offence; no desire for payback in kind or worse, no unattended hurt over which to waste more pity, no 'canker of the soul' to eat into the heart of the offended person. 'Revenge' must ever be the Lord's prerogative, however, whenever and if ever he sees fit to exercise it. There is much blessing in forgiving, even though reconciliation may still be practically impossible. Whether offenders receive forgiveness or not is up to them. If they truly repent, no doubt they are fully forgiven, but if not they must remain in an unforgiven state. They have not inwardly repented: they may not have truly accepted the forgiveness. But the person releasing the forgiveness is nevertheless blessed on discovering freedom – no longer bound to the offender in any spiritual or emotionally fraught way.

Relief Comes from Release

Some readers may have watched the final programme of *The Convent* on television.[8] Four women (three of whom had no faith at all) spent 40 days and 40 nights in a convent of the Poor Clares at Arundel in Sussex. Their purpose was to find out whether God had any relevant answers to their lives. The programme followed their stories there. One of the four had been struggling over the whole business of forgiveness, both towards her mother for the way she was treated as a child, and towards others who had hurt her along life's way. After mass each day the priest ended by

---

[8] *The Convent*, BBC2, 9 p.m., Wednesday the 5th July 2006.

offering a blessing to any who would like to come forward to receive it. This particular seeker stayed behind, feeling too unworthy to go forward with the others. It was not until the thirty-eighth day that she at last felt able to release forgiveness, and following mass she finally went forward to be blessed. Viewers could see that her whole appearance was changed, and she looked really happy as she testified afterwards how she had been set free. She had at last begun to feel she was worth something, and she was looking forward to seeing how the experience might work out positively in her life for the future.

Recipe for Retaining Compassion

A revealing comment comes by way of the Dalai Lama, who relates an encounter with a Tibetan monk who had spent 18 years in a Chinese prison and had then escaped to India. The Dalai Lama said, 'I asked him what he felt was the biggest threat or danger while he was in prison. I was amazed by his answer. It was extraordinary and inspiring. I was expecting him to say something else; instead he said that what he most feared was losing his compassion for the Chinese.'[9]

(3) STEWARDSHIP

In God's Economy God Is Central

Stewardship is a solemn trust God has given us. A steward was charged with the management of another man's property. There are many examples of stewards in the Bible. Abraham had a steward named Eliezer *(Genesis 15:2)*, who

---

[9] Wiesenthal, *The Sunflower*, p. 85.

was even entrusted with the task of finding a wife for Abraham's son Isaac.[10] In Luke 16, Jesus told a parable of a bad but cunning steward who was called to give an account of his stewardship.

We are each one of us stewards of what God has entrusted to us. *'Now it is required that those who have been given a trust must prove faithful' (1 Corinthians 4:2).* We too will have to give an account of our stewardship, particularly in using all the gifts God has given to us. I digress a little on the subject of money but the principle is the same with all aspects of stewardship. We are not under law about this, but it is challenging to think that, for a start, the Jews were expected to give a tithe of all that they possessed. After that they gave special thank-offerings when they had received special blessings. At times they got slack about their giving and this signified to God that they were drawing away from him. We can read how the prophet Malachi challenged Israel to return to God. The Israelites said, *'How are we to return?'* Malachi spoke for God when he said,

> *'Will a man rob God? Yet you rob me.*
>
> *'But you ask, "How do we rob you?"*
>
> *'In tithes and offerings. You are under a curse . . . because you are robbing me. Bring the whole tithe into the storehouse, that there may be food in my house. Test me in this,' says the Lord Almighty, 'and see if I will not throw open the floodgates of heaven and pour out so much blessing that you will not have room enough for it. I will prevent pest from devouring your crops, and the vines in your fields will not cast their fruit,' says the Lord Almighty. 'Then all the nations will call you blessed, for yours will be a delightful land.' (Malachi 3:7–12)*

---

[10] For the fascinating story, read Genesis 24.

If the new covenant is better than the old, and the Bible says it is – *'The covenant of which he [Jesus] is mediator is superior to the old one' (Hebrews 8:6b)* – then although we are not under any law to do this, but under this covenant of grace, those who tithe will prove to themselves that God certainly does pour out his blessing when they give generously. The Bible says, *'Freely you have received, freely give' (Matthew 10:8b).* And what is more, *'God loves a cheerful giver' (2 Corinthians 9:7).*

Before I retired I regularly preached on giving each year at St Andrew's, Chorleywood, but I was rather loath to suggest tithing when so many people were already giving so generously. I felt they might think I was putting them under law – the last thing I wanted to imply! However, after some six or seven years there, I was away on a conference in the USA when a man approached me rather apologetically one morning, and told me that he had had a dream in which God told him to go and tell an Anglican leader to teach his people to tithe – and if he did so God would wonderfully bless the church. He said he was sorry to bother me with this 'word from God', but he could not think of any other Anglican at the conference except me. I thanked him and when I got back to Chorleywood I explained what this unknown man had told me and began to teach on tithing. The blessing certainly did increase significantly – so much so that I can only commend the practice highly for any who can bear it. I consider it a vital part of our stewardship as disciples. Jesus talks about it a great deal in the Gospels and one third of the parables Jesus told are dedicated to this theme of stewardship.

Money can be a very 'touchy' subject to many Christians. We can feel guilty if we have it and guilty if we don't. We tend to be shy about telling others how much we earn and particularly reticent about our giving. We often feel that it is right that our Christian leaders tell us about holiness, sexual purity and righteous living, but we get 'very hot under the collar' when money or life-style issues are mentioned. Should these subjects be preached we feel indignant or uncomfortable – or both. It is almost as if our privacy has been invaded. Is this because our whole value system is being questioned?[11]

In the Bible there are 500 verses on faith and a similar number on prayer, but there are more than 2,350 verses on money! Money affects a very large part of our lives and that includes church lives.

'Money is muscle' is a phrase I picked up from my American friend Bishop Chuck Murphey, who went on to explain how the more a church has been given the more there is in hand to get things done for the poor, for increasing ministries in the local church, for resourcing missionaries and church-planting. In fact generous giving is absolutely essential to the health of any church.

There were times, to my surprise, when people came and thanked me for urging them to give to ventures for the Lord. Stewardship might seem sacrificial, but those who practise it find themselves more than blessed for it. And generous giving is fundamental for any works of mercy – for social action. Of course, when we talk of the sacrifices of money, we must obviously also include the sacrifices of time and energy. In fact the principle of faithful stewardship applies to all the gifts God has given to us.

---

[11] Keith Tondeur, *Your Money and Your Life* (SPCK, 1996), p. v.

(4) HEALING

Healing played a major part in the merciful ministry of Jesus. To give but one example, *'As Jesus went on from there, two blind men followed him, calling out, "Have mercy on us, Son of David!"' (Matthew 6:27)*. Jesus touched their eyes and their sight was restored.

When Jesus commissioned the Twelve, and then the Seventy *(Luke 9 – 10)*, he told them among other things to 'heal the sick'. Finally, when he gave the Great Commission he told the disciples to *'go and make disciples . . . teaching them to obey everything I have commanded you' (Matthew 28:19–20)*. That 'everything' would have included the healing of the sick. He had plainly commanded them earlier to heal the sick, and now he was telling them to teach their new disciples, wherever they went, to do the same. In 1 Corinthians 12 Paul refers to the 'gifts of healing' which, among other gifts, were being given to individuals. There is clearly a great commission to heal. Such signs and wonders demonstrate the nature of the coming kingdom in its fullness and glory when we will all be totally healed for ever. There is clearly a great need – especially where some sicknesses defy all medical treatment, and in Third World countries where inhabitants are denied medical treatment altogether because of long distances from medical resources or lack of finances. Of course Christians know they are not able to heal the sick by their own power – *'Why do you stare at us as if by our own power or godliness we had made this man walk?' (Acts 3:12b)* – but only in the name of Jesus and in the power of the Holy Spirit.

(5) SOCIAL ACTION

Most growing churches today are highly involved in social action – which accompanied Jesus' preaching of the good news of the kingdom. James has much to say about this and our obligation to be involved: *'Religion that God our Father accepts as pure and faultless is this: to look after orphans and widows in their distress and to keep oneself from being polluted by the world' (James 1:27),* and again, *'Anyone, then, who knows the good he ought to do and doesn't do it, sins' (James 4:17).*

Being Merciful Rather than Receiving Mercy

We are talking here of 'being merciful' to others rather than receiving mercy from others. Being merciful can apply to a wide range of needy areas. Jesus does not specify them all. He told stories that illustrate how mercy could be shown in various ways. In one he related the case of a traveller who went down from Jerusalem to Jericho, and on the way was mugged by robbers who left him lying by the roadside. While other passers-by (including religious ones) kept their distance, a Samaritan went over to him and cared for him in a practical way. Jesus was clearly commending the Samaritan (an outcast in Jewish eyes) for showing the wounded traveller mercy *(Luke 10:25–37).*

Jesus also modelled being merciful by his lifestyle. He constantly responded to pleas for help and took pity on the hungry, the sick and the outcasts wherever he was.

Opportunities for Being Merciful

There are so many areas which cry out for mercy, some only involving a moment's attention, some involving a lifetime's vocation.

Mother Teresa said,

[I have] come more and more to realize that being *unwanted* is the worst disease that any human being can ever experience. Nowadays we have found medicine for leprosy, and lepers can be cured. There's medicine for TB, and consumption can be cured. But for being *unwanted*, except there are willing hands to serve, and there are loving hearts to love, I don't think this terrible disease can be cured.[12]

Like the woman who anointed Jesus' head, she *'did what she could' (Mark 14:8)*. Mother Teresa spent an inspired lifetime doing *'what she could'* for the dying outcasts in Calcutta.

Jesus told us to love God and to love our neighbours. A 'neighbour' is anyone we may meet on any day in any place. Once, as Jesus was leaving Jericho to go to Jerusalem, a blind man called Bartimaeus cried out desperately for mercy, *'Jesus, Son of David, have mercy on me!'* Jesus said to him, *'What do you want?'* Bartimaeus replied, *'Rabbi, I want to see.'* And Jesus said, *'Your faith has healed you.'* Immediately Bartimaeus received his sight *(Mark 10:46–52)*.

Opportunities for showing mercy and giving help will soon come our way, and we will clearly sense which we are meant to grasp, however sacrificial in time, energy or money: *'If anyone would come after me, he must deny himself' (Matthew 16:24)*. At other times we may feel we just have to let it pass. The disciples once found Jesus on his own, and urged him, *'"Everyone is looking for you!" Jesus replied, "Let us go somewhere else . . . so that I can preach there also"' (Mark 1:37–38)*. He always had a commitment to a higher cause –

---

[12] Mother Teresa, *Peacemaking: Day by Day* (Pax Cristi, USA).

not the need, nor the opportunity, but the bidding of his
Father (John 5:19). This is always the proper attitude to
have and it is important for us to grasp also. Jesus' ministry
of mercy was extraordinary.

The Poor – Always with Us

The challenge is unending and unlimited. Jesus once said,
'The poor you will always have with you' (Mark 14:7). Sadly, it
is only too true, even today, that the poor are still with us –
in spite of all the latest aid programmes around the world.
Jesus was not only referring to the poor unwanted, but
would also have included the unparented, the uncared-for,
the unwashed, the unfed, the unclothed, the unhoused, the
unemployed and the uneducated. His 'mercy-scope' would
also have included drug addicts and victims who have suffered sexual abuse and disasters such as wars, plagues,
droughts, famines, tornadoes, earthquakes and tsunamis.
How often are we 'passing by on the other side', not wanting to know, or ignorantly blaming such people for not
doing more to help themselves?

Being Merciful – a Priority for Us All

Concern for the poor and needy must ever be a priority for
every Christian and every church. It is all too easy to lose
our focus here. Jesus had a passion for the poor. Very early
in his earthly ministry Jesus stood up in the synagogue and
read aloud from Isaiah 61. He then announced that the
prophet was predicting his own anointed mandate. *'The
Spirit of the Lord is on me, because he has anointed me to preach
good news to the poor. . .' (Luke 4:18).* There were other important things to attend to, but he never lost that compassion

for the poor. His ministry revealed 'a bias to the poor', to use the late Bishop David Sheppard's favoured phrase.[13]

We also read how the Christian council at Jerusalem (AD 50) blessed Paul's call to go and work as an apostle to the Gentiles: *'All they asked was that we should continue to remember the poor, the very thing I was eager to do' (Galatians 2:10).*

Evangelicals to the Fore

In his book *England: Before and After Wesley*, J. Wesley Bready comes to the conclusion that the Evangelical Awakening was the true nursing mother of the spirit and character that have created and sustained free institutions throughout the English-speaking world. He calls it 'the moral watershed of Anglo-Saxon history'.[14] John Stott sees social involvement as 'both the child of evangelical religion and the twin sister of evangelism'.[15] Taking their cue from Jesus, who certainly regarded it as one of *'the more important matters of the law' (Matthew 23:23)*, Evangelicals were very much to the fore in recovering for the church a new focus on social action and this continued into the eighteenth and nineteenth centuries. 'Evangelicalism', wrote historian Ian Bradley, 'was the most powerful religious movement in the late eighteenth century.' He tells how the Evangelicals had literally reshaped the social and political structures in the England of the nineteenth century. 'The Saints' (or the 'Clapham

---

[13] David Sheppard, *Bias to the Poor* (Hodder & Stoughton, 1983).

[14] J .Wesley Bready, *England: Before and After Wesley* (Hodder & Stoughton, 1939), pp. 11, 14.

[15] John Stott, *Involvement: Being a Responsible Christian in a Non-Christian Society* (Fleming H. Revell, 1985).

Sect',[16] as they were nicknamed by their contemporaries) were a group of clergy and committed Christian laymen of social, intellectual and financial significance, who felt called to fight injustice wherever they found it. The gradual winning round of public opinion owed much to 'The Saints', whose most popular success – the abolition of the British slave trade in 1807 – was perhaps the most purely altruistic measure ever passed in parliament. This was the result of a 25-year campaign under the direction of William Wilberforce, the slightly built, vivacious Yorkshire MP who became the leader of the Evangelical parliamentarians.

The Saints raised the tone of politics and society out of all recognition. The House of Commons had been manifestly interested only in itself; politics was a corrupt business of borough-mongering and place-seeking; the aristocracy were decadent and debauched. The Evangelical impact on society changed all this. Parliament stopped debating game laws and enclosures in defence of its own personal perceived rights, and began to discuss prison reform and the rights and wrongs of colonial slavery (eventually abolished in 1833). Politics became an exercise in morality; the aristocracy assumed a high seriousness and devoted themselves to good works. Above all, the middle class, which might so easily have lost faith in the prevailing political system, found satisfaction in taking up great moral causes.

'The best in Evangelicalism was what came out in the bitter struggle against vested interest and cynicism. Here it

---

[16] The life of the so-called 'Clapham Sect' roughly coincided with the period during which John Venn held the incumbency of Clapham parish: 1792–1813.

emerged as a radical, dynamic creed compatible only with the keenest intellectual rigour and the most careful conscience-searching.'[17] Not only in politics, but also in urban neighbourhoods, there was increased interest in works of social concern.

A 'Benevolent or Strangers' Friend Society' had been opened by Christians in 1746. The early pioneers in 'good works' were typified by Christian men like John Howard, High Sheriff of Bedfordshire, who in 1773 built model cottages for the poor, promoted educational experiments and developed rural industries. His book *State of the Prisons* (1778) led to major prison reforms and much needed annual inspections. John Wesley had created an organisation to meet the practical concerns of the poor – clothing was distributed, food for the needy was provided, and dispensaries were set up to treat the sick. Legal advice was made available in some cities for the poor. Sunday schools (for secular education) were being popularised by Robert Raikes in the 1770s for the education of poor children who were working on weekdays. William Penn, a Quaker, opened the first asylum for the mentally handicapped in 1796. The eighteenth century, with the Industrial Revolution steaming ahead, had seen a growing awareness of social obligations in the churches, and some significant practical action, not to mention overseas work which included works of mercy as part of the gospel. Meanwhile, Hannah More, the prodigious writer and aristocrat, another evangelical Anglican, wrote books and tracts exposing

---

[17] Ian Bradley, 'The Saints Against Sin', *Christianity Today*, 8th June 1973, pp. 15–16.

many prevailing evil customs and habits, which were widely read during the 1770s and 1780s.

As early as 1818, Elizabeth Fry (a Quaker) was campaigning for the separation of the sexes in prisons, and insisting that female warders supervised the female criminals there. By 1839 she was pioneering rehabilitation schemes for ex-inmates. She had great influence at governmental level for further prison reforms.

Lord Shaftesbury led the way in the factory and coal mining reforms. The Quaker Joseph Lancaster and an Anglican clergyman called Andrew Bell were pioneers independently and founded, respectively, The British and Foreign Schools Society and the National Society of the Church of England for setting up day schools throughout the country. The state did not take responsibility for the education of primary school children until the Forster Act of 1870. In 1830 George Müller, an independent churchman, founded and fed an orphanage with prayer as his only resource, and in 1876 Dr Thomas Barnardo built a village at Ilford to provide homes for waifs and strays. Soon after that he was organising suitable foster homes to accommodate even more of them. In 1865 William Booth began organising the Salvation Army for reaching drunks, prostitutes and those inhabiting the slums 'in darkest England'. William Carlyle, having studied the Franciscan and Wesleyan movements, began a training programme to help laymen in reaching out with the gospel, and founded the Church Army in 1882.

This list is by no means exhaustive. Less notable projects and local ministries of mercy to the poor and needy were many and varied, but there are enough selected examples above to demonstrate that Evangelicals were clearly taking their responsibilities very seriously.

'Between 1850 and 1900 the evangelical movement had become a dominant force in the English-speaking world.'[18] One might even say that Evangelicals in the Church of England actually reached their high point in the 1830s with two evangelical archbishops.[19] But by the turn of the nineteenth century there seems to have begun a decline in vision and commitment to the needs of the poor, at least if we are talking of major pioneer ventures at home. Christian socialism had still not surfaced as the practical agenda for any political party.

Losing Sight of Mercy

So what happened? How did Evangelicals lose sight of such a priority? Seven possible reasons suggest themselves.

(1) Diversionary Factors

There were new bogeys on the horizon by the beginning of the twentieth century. Evangelical energies became partly diverted through their earnest battles with the increasing inroads of Anglo-Catholicism – still regarded as a political intrigue on the part of the Pope in Rome to win back Britain. But this had actually been inspired by the 1830s Oxford Movement under Henry Newman, which had emerged even as the Evangelicals in the Church of England reached the peak of their ecclesiastical power.

---

[18] David W. Bebbington, *The Dominance of Evangelicalism* (IVP, 2006).

[19] Nigel Scotland, *Evangelical Anglicans in the Revolutionary Age, 1789–1901* (Paternoster Press, 2004).

The Oxford Movement was rapidly becoming popular for its resurrection of catholic practices, colourful ritual worship (crudely referred to as 'smells and bells' by hostile critics), and its overt practical commitment to the poor. One of its leaders, Charles Gore, was possibly the most fascinating and most influential English bishop of the early twentieth century, who had formerly held office as the Superior of the Community of the Resurrection and continued his pioneering work for the poor for many years afterwards as the diocesan bishop of Oxford. If, as the diocesan bishop, he needed to stay overnight in a parish, he would not lodge at the vicarage, preferring the simple home of a poor labourer in the parish. By the end of the nineteenth century many other dedicated Anglo-Catholics were taking on slum parishes, determined to help the socially disadvantaged. In the areas of social action, the Anglo-Catholics were seen as 'stealing the Evangelicals' clothes', or at least as having 'stolen a march on them'.

Then there had been the rise of seriously concerned theological liberals, such as the Reverend F. D. Maurice, founder of the London Working Men's College and author of *The Kingdom of Christ*, spelling out the obligations for social reform in his 'incarnational theology' (1843). He was later the Knightsbridge Professor of Moral Philosophy at Cambridge. His friend was the popular Reverend Charles Kingsley of *Tom and the Water Babies* fame. Kingsley's particular concern was with education and sanitation. Together they founded the Christian Socialism movement (1848), raised up to keep the church on course in challenging the government of the day. Individually and through the church they pressed their point, aiming at a combined reform of individuals and society by the application of Christian principles in all relationships. Soon to come was the founding of the Fabian Society in 1884, politically committed to social action. This was the year prior to the death of the great evangelical activist and lay champion Lord Shaftesbury.

From then on, for a while, Evangelicals appeared to have 'lost the plot' regarding concern for the poor and oppressed. This may be partly attributable to a leading layman, Alexander Haldane, who was editor of the increasingly popular evangelical weekly *The Record* (still continued as an inset within the *Church of England Newspaper*). In his opposition to liberalism, Haldane began to give much less attention to humanitarian and social enterprises.[20] Nonetheless, significant individual Evangelicals were still being moved to raise up small hospitals, missions, boys' clubs, youth camps, and so on.

It may also partly be attributed to the fact that many Evangelicals (especially Nonconformists – dubbed the 'Non-Conformist Conscience' by the press) were becoming socially respectable. They had enriched themselves with their industrial enterprises; they had become powerful through their political representation, occupying over 200 seats in the Commons at the turn of the century,[21] and being mainly Liberals politically. Some of these *nouveaux riches* among the industrial barons had been favoured with

---

[20] Prebendary Dr Peter N. L. Pytches, in an unpublished thesis on the 'Development of Anglican Evangelicalism in London 1736–1836' (Open University Library, Milton Keynes).

[21] James Munson, *The Nonconformists – In Search of a Culture* (SPCK, 1991), p. 282.

seats in the House of Lords. Such respectability had all the concomitant social tendencies towards tolerance and accommodation of the status quo. Liberals politically, they had gradually become liberals theologically, losing their fundamental biblical convictions, their conscientious sensitivities and their spiritual cutting edge.

(2) Doctrinal Factors

Evangelicals were also becoming preoccupied by the late nineteenth century with the rise in 'Higher Criticism' emanating from Germany, which was seen to be undermining the authority of the Bible. Then there was Darwinism, which offered an explanation of the world and creation which, if it did not make God unnecessary, at least edged Him off the centre stage. This theory, of vast scope, offering a naturalistic account of creation, would have been dismissed as speculation had it not been for its negative theological implications. Jesus had warned his disciples that his teaching would never be popular in a godless world: *'Woe to you when all men speak well of you' (Luke 6:26)*; especially among the wicked – *'When justice is done, it brings joy to the righteous, but terror to evildoers' (Proverbs 21:15)*. There were plenty of enemies looking for an excuse to undermine their counter-cultural ideology and to thwart their influence.

The 'social gospel' now being trumpeted tended to brush aside concerns for personal salvation. Liberalism was fast becoming the prevailing ideology of the West. Many leaders were worried about splitting their congregations into political camps and swamping the gospel by moral, political and theological compromises.

All this contributed to a change of focus – a sort of

rearguard action – among Evangelicals (less by deliberate intention and more through distraction and dissipation). They had four main fears:

(i) the rising influence of Anglo-Catholicism, now taking the lead in social issues;
(ii) 'Higher Criticism' of the Bible;
(iii) political compromise considered inherent in a social gospel;
(iv) growing preoccupation with 'millenarianism'.

(i) Anglo-Catholicism

Evangelicals wasted a lot of time, energy and resources taking the Anglo-Catholics to court for violations of canon law and failing to take inspiration and encouragement from the good work they were doing.

(ii) Higher Criticism

Evangelicals were caught unawares and, seemingly, lacked academic champions to prepare them to cope with these new challenges. Many younger Evangelicals were even discouraged from reading theology at university for fear they would be led 'off the rails' by their liberal lecturers! It took some time for the next generation to produce adequate intellectual arguments to defend themselves and reveal the fallibilities of their opponents. Meanwhile, Evangelicals had simply become 'defensive' and were talked of, not in terms of what they were 'for', but of what they were 'against'.

(iii) Political Compromise

There were fears that those who got involved in social action projects, and those who supported them, might soon mistakenly assume that a life of such sacrifice and good works merited salvation for the worker. And all 'good' Evangelicals knew that salvation is through the work of Christ alone – something on which they would never compromise. Paul had gone to great pains to ensure that his church plants understood clearly that the gospel was a gift of God – salvation was by grace alone through faith alone. He had spelt this out, most clearly perhaps, in his letter to the Ephesians. *'For it is by grace you have been saved, through faith . . . it is the gift of God – not by works, so that no one can boast. . .' (Ephesians 2:8–9).* At the same time he insisted that *'We are God's workmanship, created in Christ Jesus to do good works' (Ephesians 2:10).* We are to work out what God is working in us.

This clear teaching had been ardently endorsed by James, who stressed both the significance of faith and the relevance of good works: *'Show me your faith without deeds, and I will show you my faith by what I do' (James 2:18b).* We validate the reality of our faith by the visibility of our good works. As Jesus said, *'Let your light shine before men, that they may see your good deeds and praise your Father in heaven' (Matthew 5:16).*

(iv) Millenarianism

This understanding of the 1,000-year period of time at the end of the age, when Christ will reign on earth over a perfect world order, as a literal interpretation of Revelation 20:1–10, created an excited debate about when in world history this might be expected to occur. The interpretations were divided up into premillennialist (before the Second Coming), postmillennialist (after the Second Coming) and amillennialist (the period we are now in), and from that the divisions continued between pre-rapture and post-rapture, and so on. With all these discussions, the Enlightenment idea of progress (as seen in the 'gradualist' approach to social change by those who followed the Clapham view, i.e. that the quality of human life could be improved by social and political action), was giving way to the expectation of a cataclysmic intervention through the Second Coming of Christ – the only true preoccupation to make life worth living!

Although Charles Simeon, a leading and highly influential Evangelical, refused to be majorly distracted by such a few mystical references in the book of Revelation, a growing number of Evangelicals were increasingly preoccupied by this debate throughout the following century. The great hope and prayer was for the return of Christ. All this practically resulted in 'a theology of despair' so far as any future social reforms in this present world were concerned.

(3) Social Structures Factor

A further issue for some Evangelicals was that the early church had never appeared to view the changing of structures as their primary objective. Larry Christenson, a Lutheran minister in the USA, makes a thought-provoking observation here:

> The thought of the church changing the structures of society by direct action is alien to the thought-world of the New Testament. Both with Jesus and with the Apostles we find an almost studied avoidance of what we would call political social involvement. They never lift their voices against Rome, nor are they particularly critical of society, as such. Their counsel for Christians is to respect the secular authorities – the same

authorities who had subjugated most of the known world by force of arms, who dispensed justice to non-Romans by fiat or whim, who upheld the institution of slavery as a matter of course, whose chief concern for the poor was the amount of money they could squeeze out of them in taxes.

In this kind of way the church lived, without offering much either by way of advice or complaint. It was not that they were self-serving supporters of the *status quo*. They simply recognized – as too many present-day social theorists do not – that the structures of society will not succumb to a frontal attack by the church. There is a more effective way – the way of example.[22]

The early Christians submitted to the world order in everything (even slavery), except where the powers-that-be tried to force them to deny the faith, or to do something they knew to be personally immoral. Yet who would deny the rightness of William Wilberforce in organising the abolition of slavery in the UK, or of Martin Luther King in pressing for the abolition of black segregation in the USA? Clearly different men and women are called to see and serve the cause of this world's disadvantaged in differing ways. *'Each of us will give an account of himself to God' (Romans 14:12).*

Another problem with the focus on structural reform, particularly in overseas countries, is the easy abuse. Some of us still remember the huge gifts of grain, sent as emergency relief for the starving Ethiopians under Mengistu, their Marxist leader; grain which was then traded off to Russia (at that time under an embargo from the USA) in exchange for MiG fighter planes! We have read of some

---

[22] Larry Christenson, *A Charismatic Approach to Social Action* (Lakeland, 1973), p. 81.

Third World leaders hoarding vast amounts of freely given and freely transported relief aid in the form of food for the poor, to be disposed of only at times of their leadership's choosing – even if it had passed its shelf-life and was rotting in storage. The motive for keeping it was to reserve it for distribution at a suitable future time when it might serve for some political advantage.

Some years ago, by popular request, we had a generous offering taken up at our New Wine renewal conference for the newly elected leader of an African republic who had formerly been imprisoned as a trade union leader under a previous regime. During his imprisonment he had supposedly been converted to Christ. But after eight years in office, I read, he was being divorced by his wife who was suing him for a two-billion-pound settlement! How would a former trade union leader now president, ever have come by such funds? One can only imagine!

Large sums of money sent abroad to augment overseas governments in the management of disasters needs close scrutiny all the way down the line. A BBC overnight newscast of the 16th August 2006, and a report in the *Daily Telegraph* of the same date, stated that money raised in Britain on behalf of the victims of the previous October's earthquake in Pakistani-controlled Kashmir may have been diverted to help pay for the recent alleged plot to blow up airliners over the Atlantic. The claim is being seriously investigated, and a number have since been charged with involvement in the 'plot'.

And who knows which proposed structural changes will be truly beneficial in the long run? The West may promote 'government of the people, by the people, for the people', but democracy can be too easily abused to the advantage of the powers-that-be where there is no inherent Christian culture of 'fair play' to make it work. So where does this get us? We need to ask which kind of social action the church is being called by God to engage in and how it can be responsibly administered.

Another danger with the social activist approach is that it is essentially paternalistic. In a recent book, *The White Man's Burden: Why the West's Efforts to Aid the Rest Have Done So Much Ill and So Little Good*, William Easterly, a former World Bank hand, gives a comprehensive study of how, despite the record amounts of aid being donated to poor countries, poverty levels are still increasing. He argues that the money is spent unwisely since politicians and charities are more concerned with hitting targets than solving an area's systemic shortcomings. He thinks that what is needed are 'searchers' who can tailor aid for a particular town or region. This is, of course, what the old missionary societies, with local missionaries who were accountable, often did so well – though not on so large a scale. But even that may have been seen as paternalistic. It caused one observer of the inner city scene to remark, 'The activist churches have been less successful in reaching the people of the inner city than the Pentecostal store-front operations, because the activists came in as *benefactors* while the Pentecostals came in as *brothers*.' The Pentecostals saw the need for embracing people to bring them into the household of faith. So as long as large sums of money donated to meet desperate needs are being sent abroad to augment overseas governments in the management of disasters, there needs to be a close scrutiny of their administration all the way down the line.

Wake-up Call

On the positive side, perhaps, the modern wake-up call for many Evangelicals was the inspired 1950s work of David Wilkerson among the violent drug addicts in the New York underworld famous for its street gangs and turf wars.[23] Soon after that Calvary Chapel, in Costa Mesa, became a centre for the remarkable Jesus Movement in California. They opened up a house for drop-outs and dope addicts in 1967, and saw some spectacular changes in the lives of young people – many of whom I personally met later in the 1980s. By then several had become pastors of Vineyard churches. This example of a caring Christian community (highlighted on the cover of a *Time* magazine of the day) was soon to spread to many other parts of North America. The charismatic Church of the Redeemer in Houston, Texas, was an example within the Episcopal Church.

We must not overlook the extraordinary work of individual leaders like the late charismatic Catholic priest Father Ric Thomas, with his relief for the rival gangs who eked out a miserable living from scraps from the stinking refuse dump in Juarez, Mexico just over the border from El Paso. A work described more fully on p. 219. Nor should we forget the marvellous redemptive work among drug addicts begun in the inner city of Hong Kong under Jackie Pullinger, a story made famous through her book *Chasing the Dragon* (1980). Nor the exciting Christian ministry among the many orphaned Muslim children under the

---

[23] David Wilkerson, *The Cross and the Switchblade* (Zondervan, 1964).

leadership of two Christians, Drs Rolland and Heidi Baker, in Mozambique today.

There are ample examples today showing that the Evangelicals have been getting back on course in a serious way since the 1950s – not to mention organisations like World Vision, Tearfund, Samaritan Purse, Care, Christian Outreach and Oasis. Stephen Motsma's research of 'welfare-to-work programmes' in the USA reveals that today there are actually more evangelical programmes than mainline programmes in progress.[24] So how can we know what works of mercy we should be involved in? This is vital if we are not going to waste time, energy and resources on abortive programmes: *'Unless the Lord builds the house, its builders labour in vain' (Psalm 127:1)*, and *'Every plant that my heavenly Father has not planted will be pulled up by the roots' (Matthew 15:13)*. When Jesus visited the Pool of Bethesda, a local 'spa' crowded with sick people, he only healed one man. How did he know whom to heal among all those sick? He explained elsewhere how this was. He looked to his Father and asked him what he should do. *'I tell you the truth, the Son . . . can do only what he sees his Father doing, because whatever the Father does, the Son also does' (John 5:19)*.

Each letter to the seven churches in the book of Revelation ends with the same challenge: *'He who has an ear, let him hear.'* Jesus, the Good Shepherd, said that his *'sheep listen to his voice' (John 10:3)*, so it cannot be too difficult to see or hear what God wants us to be doing. If we humbly seek God's face, he will surely give us signs to show us his will.

---

[24] Stephen Motsma, 'Social Justice Surprise', *Christianity Today*, July 2006.

We then check this out with others, especially our leaders. And if the leaders think it is right, we should go for it!

In theory, it is usually agreed in the wider church that we must mix evangelism with social action, but in practice the dichotomy often proves more formidable; invisible lines are drawn, and camps are set up in opposition to each other.

'Part of our training', said a layman who had been a social activist on behalf of his church for many years, 'was a studied avoidance of any mention of Christ. We were told to do our good thing in such a way that *no one would suspect we were Christians.*'[25] Many church activists have tended to stress social issues and dumb down the preaching of the gospel, though, of course, evangelism is a form of social action in itself. But salt must be tasted to recognise its flavour; light must shine to expose darkness; yeast must be well kneaded into the dough to raise it before baking. Love must be demonstrated in praying, caring, loyalty and thoughtful service to one another in such a way that the world can appreciate the great attraction of God's counter-culture. *'By this all men will know that you are my disciples, if you love one another' (John 13:35).* Some call this 'evangelism by magnetism'![26]

Finally, we can never be serving God faithfully nor be truly effective in his kingdom without sharing the gospel – not so much by preaching something *at* people, but by sensitive personal sharing in answer to possible incidental questions. Peter urges his readers, *'Always be prepared to give an answer to everyone who asks you to give the reason for*

---

[25] Christenson, *A Charismatic Approach to Social Action*, p. 80.

[26] Derek Morphew, in Bible study at New Wine 2006.

the hope that you have. But do this with gentleness and respect'
(1 Peter 3:15).

(4) State Factor

Soon after the Second World War, Clement Attlee's recently elected Labour government introduced the National Health Service, while various governmental departments took over responsibility for other social needs such as housing, unemployment and pensions. As a result many church members came to feel somewhat relieved of their commitment to social issues, considering that the State had now taken over. Many no longer gave to church charities, maintaining that they were already paying to help the poor through their government taxes and did not wish to pay twice over! In some ways the church gradually lost its reputation again for caring for the sick, the poor, the orphans, etc. And without realising it, the church was no longer seen as called to social action at home – only overseas through their missionary societies and 'mercy' ministries.

Whatever the reason, the call to serve the poor was slowly being relegated to the back-burner. Thankfully the revival under Billy Graham in the 1950s reawakened evangelical compassion for the needy and the outcast. Their eyes began to focus once again on the communities around them.

(5) 'Rice Christian' Factor

Reports of missionaries from China implied that some nationals had become 'converts' because they wanted all the practical help missionaries might be able to offer them and their families. Bishop Welldon from Calcutta wrote as early as 1899 that many of his callers at the bishop's residence made predictable requests for 'catechism, baptism and a pair of shoes'! It was not a new problem. Jesus said, *'You are looking for me . . . because you ate the loaves. . .' (John 6:26)*. But whatever the motivation of the hearers, Jesus did not change his practice and used such occasions to give them bread, and to teach about the bread which does not perish – until there came a point when his hearers begged him, *'Sir, from now on give us this bread' (John 6:34)*. We should not allow ourselves necessarily to be put off, whatever other priorities we have, just because ministry to the poor at home or overseas might be abused. The givers are always blessed in any case. But probably confusion over our obligations has weighed on some of those who were feeling less dedicated to the cause of social concern.

(6) Money Factor

Then there was the concern of the local pastor or treasurer. Having only a limited number of people in their congregation, there was a real need for all hands on deck to pay the bills and pull their weight in keeping the ship afloat. They did not want to risk their members getting distracted by putting their time and energy into all and every 'mercy ministry'. How could the local church survive if their members began channelling all their giving to projects outside the church? Archbishop Michael Ramsey's challenging reminder was badly needed: 'The church that lives to itself will die to itself.'

(7) Sacrificial Factor

The showing of mercy on the social 'level' may certainly be costly. I take the liberty of repeating an illustration of this already referred to earlier. Eager to dispel any image of heroism, Baroness Cox, recipient of the 1995 Wilberforce Award which recognises 'an individual who has made a difference in the face of formidable societal problems and injustices', admits to having a 'fit of faithless, fearful dread' before going on her dangerous missions (see *Christian Solidarity Worldwide – Voice of the Voiceless*, which gives reports of her ministry and the cries of the oppressed for help, mercy and prayer).[27]

Getting Back on Track

Slowly Evangelicals have been rediscovering the social aspect of their mission – ministries of mercy to the poor and needy, demonstrating to the world that the kingdom of heaven really is good news for everyone in every way. But it has not been easy for all to get back on track.

Ken Gott, a Pentecostal pastor in Sunderland, reveals very honestly how the Lord, in spite of all the other pressures on him (such as paying off a huge debt on a new church building), led the church forward into a significant sacrificial ministry to the poor. Doubtless many another church leader would empathise with Gott's initial discomfort on receiving such a challenge. He wrote:

> One day a woman came up to me who had been saved in the renewal – a Christian of only six months, whom God was about to use to shame me for my apathy and disobedience! She stood right beside me and said, 'Ken, what are we doing about the poor in this city?' (Pastors just love questions like that!) I

---

[27] Benedict Rogers, *The Unconventional Baroness*, www.csw.org.uk, 2006; and chapter 4 of this book.

said, 'Well, you know, we take up an offering once in a while, and we support one or two little things . . . but *actually* we are not doing anything!'[28]

His church had become sidetracked, and this was a gentle shove back in the right direction.

Helping Hands

In *Life Together*, Dietrich Bonhoeffer says,

The second service that one should perform for another in a Christian community is that of active helpfulness. *'If anyone serves, he should do it with the strength that God provides, so that in all things God may be praised' (1 Peter 4:10).* Initially this means simple assistance in trifling, external matters. There is a multitude of these things that can be done wherever people live together. Nobody is too good for the meanest service. One who worries about the loss of time that such petty, outward acts of helpfulness entail, is usually taking the importance of his own career too solemnly.

William Law made a profound impact upon eighteenth-century English society – especially on John Wesley. In his book *A Serious Call to a Devout and Holy Life*[29] he urges that every day should be viewed as a day of humility by learning to serve others. He counsels us to

condescend to all the weaknesses and infirmities of your fellow creatures, cover their frailties, love their excellencies, encourage their virtues, relieve their wants, rejoice in their prosperities,

---

[28] Ken Gott, *Anointing or Annoying – Searching for the Fruit of Revival* (Destiny Image, Revival Press, 1998), p.90.

[29] William Law, *A Serious Call to a Devout and Holy Life* (1728).

be compassionate in their distress, receive their friendship, overlook their unkindness, forgive their malice, be a servant of servants, and condescend to do the lowest offices to the lowest of mankind.[30]

There are many church members who see themselves as having little money to contribute, but there is a significant gift of 'helps' – a gift included along with administration, mentioned by Paul when writing to the Corinthian church, in his list of spiritual gifts *(1 Corinthians 12:28)*. This gift of 'helps' has been overlooked, undervalued and undeveloped. People actually like doing what they like doing and they like doing what they are gifted at doing. If the church can inspire the use of this multifaceted gift, it would greatly enhance the work of the kingdom of God – especially if the church made a point of being interested in how different members are thus engaged. It would be good to allow the 'helpers' sometimes to share feedback about what they are trying to do, to pray for them in it, to take some interest in how things are going, and even support them financially if necessary. The more acts of mercy being done, the greater the blessing all round!

The Helpful Scout

The Boy Scout movement was started as an adjunct to the YMCA by Robert Baden Powell, a war hero for his strategic holding action at Mafeking in the South African war against the Dutch Boers in 1899.

---

[30] Taken from Richard Foster, *A Celebration of Discipline* (Harper-Collins, 1978).

In August 1909 a Chicago millionaire publisher, William Dickson Boyce, was visiting London. The city was shrouded by one of London's 'pea-soup' fogs. Boyce had lost his way in the murky gloom when he was approached by a twelve-year-old boy carrying a lantern. The boy offered to guide him to the address he was looking for. On finding the place, Boyce was about to hand over a generous tip when the boy checked him politely. 'No Sir, I am a scout. Scouts do not accept tips for Good Turns!'

This led to Boyce filing for incorporation papers for the 'Boy Scouts of America' on the 8th February 1910. The helpful twelve-year-old's name has been lost sight of, but the fact that a whole national movement for good was started abroad as the result of one simple act of kindness is worth remembering. 'Kindness is a language which the deaf can hear and the blind can see' (anon.).

Envisioned While Ironing

Marion Johnston (wife of the Reverend Pat Ashe, at St Mary Priors, Leamington Spa) was ironing in the kitchen. As she did so she watched a television report by Julian Pettifer in Vietnam, on the plight of the Vietnamese refugees. On the screen was a picture of one little boy with a baby on his back, wandering around and lost. At that point her husband came in to get some coffee for a group of some eight men he had called together to discuss the matter of Christian responsibility – a ruse he had developed to help men get involved in work for the Lord. He found his wife looking appalled, and asked her what the matter was. She told him what she had just seen, and said something must be done about those children – it was so terrible for them.

Taking the coffee back to his group, Pat put the problem
to the men there. Some thought it was far too big a task for
them. There were millions of such children in the world!
These things have to be solved at government level! Finally
the vicar summed up the discussion. 'Naught means nothing. Let's not be put off by the millions. Let's try and help
one.'[31] That was the seed thought that blossomed into Project Vietnam Orphans in 1967. The men continued to meet
and pray regularly. A practical start was made and the first
nurses were sent out to Vietnam in 1968. Homes for
orphans were found. Refugee camps were set up. As the
work spread to other Far Eastern countries, the title became
an embarrassment and the charity was re-registered as
Christian Outreach in 1978. This was a relatively small
mercy mission among the millions of needy people – but, as
Jesus taught about yeast, salt and light, these things go a
very long way in the kingdom of God. 'A journey of a thousand miles begins with one small step' (anon.).

The above is an example of a couple with compassion for
the poor, who were inspired by a vision. This was the driving force that enabled them to overcome strong opposition
from those who would normally be sympathetic, and to get
something really helpful going. Later one of their own sons,
who undertook several years of permanent oversight in
various relief programmes, was honoured with an MBE for
his services. Relatively few are honoured in this way, but
when they are, it is to encourage us to emulate the kind of
things that they have done for the good of others.

Visiting today from church to church, one is inspired by

---

[31] Patrick Ashe, *Dust and Ashes*, published in Indonesia 2005, p.216.

the variety of programmes, including soup runs for the hungry, clothing for refugees, furniture repaired and given to battered wives and ex-prisoners, refuge and counselling for drug addicts, AIDS organisations, rescue work for enslaved teenage prostitutes from abroad, meeting places for pregnant teenagers, cleaning-up programmes for deprived parts of the community where volunteers gather up broken glass and dangerous needles, helping the elderly with their gardens and hedges, fitting such equipment as smoke detectors on behalf of the local council – the list is endless. But where a church is listening to God there are plenty of doors that will open.

Miracle in El Paso

Towards the end of the 1970s an inspiring video was being circulated among charismatics in Britain. It was called *Miracle in El Paso*,[32] and had been made for the Pope. It told the story of how the Lord had led a North American Catholic priest, Ric Thomas (d. 2006), to start a social work alongside his evangelism at Juarez in Mexico, on the other side of El Rio Grande. Trucks from Juarez disgorged their hourly loads of city trash at a vast refuse dump there – the usual waste paper, cardboard, tins, plastic and rotting food, iron scraps, pots and pans, rags and nondescript articles of every conceivable sort – even occasionally dead newborn babies. In the heat of the day, the air thick with the stench and flies from so much putrid garbage, two hostile gangs of men eked out a meagre living by saving anything that might be resaleable, and even ate some of the discarded food.

---

[32] See Rene Laurentin, *Miracle in El Paso* (Servant Books, c. 1980).

In the autumn of 1972 Father Ric Thomas was reading Luke's Gospel to a charismatic group in his church.

When you give a luncheon or dinner, do not invite your friends, your brothers or relatives, or your rich neighbours; if you do, they may invite you back and so you will be repaid. But when you give a banquet, invite the poor, the crippled, the lame, the blind, and you will be blessed. Although they cannot repay you, you will be repaid at the resurrection of the righteous. (Luke 14:12–14)

They felt this was a call to the group to share a Christmas dinner with the two poverty-stricken gangs of trash-grubbers who made their living off what they could pick out of that huge stinking garbage dump. Physical blows, injuries and even deaths had resulted from their fighting over garbage. The group made the whole project a matter of earnest prayer. Before they could proceed far with their arrangements, they had to get the two gang leaders who controlled the dump to agree to a truce for the hours between 11.00 a.m. and 4.30 p.m. on Christmas Day. The number of people from both groups was reckoned to total about 150. When the day arrived, however, twice as many turned up as the number of hot meals prepared! The miracle was that, without understanding how it happened, there was enough for all, and so much over that they had to take it to a nearby orphanage. Since then many other miracles have happened. The poor there have been encouraged to mobilise themselves. They have taken charge of their own community – they have installed a drainage system and put up small concrete buildings for each other. All this has led on to many other projects that have inspired other churches since to initiate mercy ministries to the poor and needy around them and beyond. Father Ric Thomas heard God speaking to him through the Gospel he had read, and he acted on it. There is nothing like such projects for convincing unbelievers that the gospel is indeed good news!

PROMISED REWARD

. . . for they shall be shown mercy. (Matthew 5:7)

The merciful receive a merciful reward.

INJURED MAN ON AN ICY MOUNTAIN

Sadhu Sundar Singh, a twentieth-century Hindu who converted to Christ, was once battling his way along a pass on the Tibetan border. Icy winds were blowing and the air was so cold he dared not stop to rest, weary though he was. A Tibetan was with him. They came to a place where the mountain pass narrowed, and they spotted a man lying motionless on a ledge a few feet below them. He had obviously slipped and fallen. 'We must try to help him,' said the sadhu. 'Help him?' snapped the Tibetan scornfully. 'We've got ourselves to think of. We'd die trying to save him.' And he left the sadhu and went his own way.

But the sadhu managed to climb down to the ledge. He found the man unconscious but still alive and somehow dragged him back up to the path. With difficulty he lifted the injured man onto his back. He managed to stagger slowly along the slippery track under the load. 'I could not go fast, but at least I was moving, and the exertion warmed me – and the warmth got through to the man on my back. Eventually I reached the village and got shelter for us both. We were both alive!' But as he struggled on, the sadhu had

passed another traveller fallen beside the path. It was his
Tibetan companion lying there – stone cold and dead.[33] The
sadhu had both shown mercy and received it. His merciful
deed to someone else had mercifully saved his own life also.
Had he ignored the plight of the injured man the sadhu
could so easily have died of the terrible cold, like his Tibetan
companion. Happy are those who show mercy, for they will
receive mercy.

MEDITATION

If I can stop one heart from breaking,
I shall not live in vain:
If I can ease one life from aching,
Or cool one pain,
Or help one fainting robin
Unto his nest again,
I shall not live in vain.
(Emily Dickinson)

* * *

He has showed you, O man, what is good.
And what does the Lord require of you?
To act justly and to love mercy
and to walk humbly with your God.
(Micah 6:8)

* * *

Always give yourselves fully to the work of the Lord, because you know
that your labour in the Lord is not in vain. (1 Corinthians 15:58b)

* * *

---

[33] Phyllis Thompson, *Sadhu Sundar Singh* (OM Publishing, 1992),
p. 121.

Enough for All

John Wimber was once given a vision of a huge honey-comb. It was high in the sky and dripping with honey. All sorts of people were gathered round it, some simply catching it and eating it. Some were taking it away to share with their families and friends. Others were watching on fascinated and yet others were standing by scoffing! He felt that God was saying to him, 'John, that's my mercy. For some it's a blessing and for others it is not, but there is plenty for everyone. The problem is not with the supply – the problem is with the people.'

* * *

A Penitent's Prayer

Lord, I feel so ashamed. There are so many unmerciful things I should not have done that I have done, and so many helpful things I should have done and have left undone. And again there are so many unkind things I should not have said that I have said and so many other good things that I could and should have said but did not say. There were angry and impatient letters, emails and phone calls I should neither have made nor sent and so many encouraging or consoling messages I could have sent. Lord, there have been times when I just could not be bothered to go the second mile, times when I have passed by on the other side to avoid putting myself out, and things I did not want to attend to and pretended that I had not seen. You know my heart through and through – I have been selfish, careless and thoughtless. I have let you down. There are no excuses. Lord Jesus, Son of God, have mercy on me, a sinner. Amen.

6

Here Comes the Bride

Blessed are the pure in heart,
for they will see God.
(Matthew 5:8)

Who may ascend the hill of the Lord?
Who may stand in his holy place?
He who has clean hands and a pure heart,
who does not lift up his soul to an idol
or swear by what is false.
(Psalm 24:3–4)

* * *

The fruit of the Spirit is . . . self-control. (Galatians 5:22)

* * *

Purity of soul cannot be lost without consent. (St Augustine of Hippo)

* * *

Purity is the outcome of sustained spiritual sympathy with God. (Oswald Chambers)

INTRODUCTION

The writer of Psalm 24 seems appalled by his own presumption in seeking the presence of God. He is wondering how he could be so brazen as to desire to enter into the presence of God with all that searching light and all that scorching holiness. The subject of purity is certainly a challenging one. How could anyone even think he could address such a subject? *'Who can say, "I have kept my heart pure; I am clean and without sin"?' (Proverbs 20:9).*

Christians today are so compromised as to what is acceptable, what we listen to, what we look at, what we talk about and the things we do. It is only with awe and trepidation that the issue of purity (usually assumed to mean sexual purity) can be confronted head on.

Addressing the church of Thyatira, John reminds them that

God [has] eyes ... like blazing fire and ... feet ... like burnished bronze ... [and says] I have this against you: You tolerate that woman Jezebel, who calls herself a prophetess. By her teaching she misleads my servants into sexual immorality and the eating of food sacrificed to idols. I have given her time to repent of her immorality, but she is unwilling ... I will strike her children dead. Then all the churches will know that I am he who searches hearts and minds, and I will repay each of you according to your deeds. (Revelation 2:18b–23)

Is there a case for addressing the church of Christ today in similar fashion?

PREPARING THE BRIDE

Recently I read a letter addressed to a member of Union Church, Vina del Mar, Chile, where I had once 'stood in' while their pastor was on long leave. The author of the letter was an Australian who had also been their minister some years later. He had written to a mutual friend in the church there, who gave me the copy that I quote here with his permission. It certainly touched a chord in my own heart, and I suspect it will in my readers.

> I wanted to tell you about my journey in God over these past two years. It has been amazing. I have begun writing a book but who knows when I will finish it? . . . It's called 'Here Comes the Bride' and it is the story about how the Lord is preparing the church to become the bride of Christ.

This Australian minister told how he had been fasting and praying – and seeking God in a new way – since January 2004. This was followed by a powerful encounter with the Lord. From that time, he said,

> Everything about the way I serve Him, and the way we do church, has been affected. I find myself . . . swimming against the tide of popular churches. Our church started to pray and since that time our doors have been open 24 hours a day, seven days a week, as people run shifts of prayer day and night. The manifest presence of the Lord has become so tangible at services that there are times when it is difficult just to stand.

Recently this seasoned pastor had to make a train journey, during which he sensed the Lord speaking to him significantly.

> On both the outward and the return journeys the Lord began to show me things about eternity. I was appalled, terrified and in awe. I saw people who profess Christ going into hell. I saw the terrible, careless way the church has been living and

carousing. I saw the bride of Christ as a dishevelled and loose woman whose lipstick was smeared from her adulteries. The fear of the Lord came upon me.

Back in Brisbane, I stood to preach in my church and [again] the fear of God fell upon the congregation. People have streamed to the altar to get right with God. Scriptures, which now seem as though they have been hidden to me, have suddenly leapt off the pages. I realize how pathetic has been our presentation of our Lord in our preaching. How lightly we have treated sin, and [how] generous we have been toward those who have professed Christ but not walked in His ways.

This Australian's concern for the church has stayed with me and I share it here because of the theme of this chapter – purity, holiness.

Christine Darg recounts an interview with a Coptic priest, Father Zechariah. He was part of a twentieth-century revival in Heliopolis, Egypt. This movement of the Holy Spirit of God followed the priest's own conversion at the age of 59. She asked him how the movement had begun. He told her he had been praying and fasting, and asking God to fill him with the Holy Spirit and to use him. One day he was alone when he sensed God questioning him about what he wanted and expected God to do. A question God seemed to be putting to him was, 'If you are self-centred, and you feel you are proud, why don't you ask me to change your attitude and purify your heart?'

'Good,' replied Father Zechariah. 'Do that, please – purify my intentions, my heart, my everything!'

This was followed by an awful vision of the fires of hell and he was crying to God to save those people he saw on their way there. Soon his church was weeping and crying to

God under the influence of the Holy Spirit. 'And many people from that day started to repent and to beg Jesus to clothe them with his righteousness, asking for the blood of Jesus to purify them.'[1] This was the start of a revival that lasted for about 15 years (no precise dates are given).

DEFILING THE BRIDE

The call to inner purity is for everyone. It applies to rich and poor, high and low, man and woman, young and old, whether from the north or the south, the east or the west.

A preacher in the USA once declared that the average American male had a sexual fantasy every twelve minutes. If that statistic is correct, it would probably be the same right across the adult male world. This is a constant challenge even and especially for leaders in the church of Christ. Billy Graham has said that 75 per cent of Christian leaders who come out of the ministry do so on the grounds of sexual misconduct. Who knows how many believers also destroy their own souls in the same way? John gives us an awful warning of end-time finalities: *'Let him who is vile continue to be vile . . . Outside are . . . those who practise magic arts, the sexually immoral. . .' (Revelation 22:11–15).* We need to consider every way we can to keep ourselves pure. Such is the deceitfulness of the human heart!

A sad report, recently published in *Christianity Today*,[2] tells of an archbishop, the leader of a charismatic denomination, who had been removed from office purportedly for

---

[1] Christine Darg, *The Jesus Visions – Signs and Wonders in the Muslim World*.

[2] *Christianity Today*, USA, February 2006.

sexual misconduct over a long period of time. Earl Paulk was forced to resign in October 2005 as archbishop of the International Communion of Charismatic Churches (ICCC). A member of his local church – the 6,000-member Cathedral at Chapel Hill in Decatur, Georgia, USA – filed a lawsuit on the 31st August charging him with using his position and spiritual role to manipulate women to have sex with himself, with members of his family, and with others, including visiting pastors.

The lawsuit sought monetary damages from Earl Paulk and his brother Don Paulk for engaging in illicit sex – and from the church's board of directors for acquiescing in and covering up their misdeeds.[3] This was not just one momentary moral lapse, but appears to have been a series of sexual misdemeanours over many decades. This example may come from the USA, but I could reluctantly list many more from the UK, and even some concerning overseas missionaries both male and female.

A publication of the King James Version of the Bible which was printed in 1632 became known as 'The Wicked Bible' because the seventh commandment erroneously read *'Thou shalt commit adultery'*! It would seem that many Christians have been just as casual about observing Exodus 20 today as those publishers were about printing it then.

SEXUAL PURITY ESSENTIAL TO A LIFE OF HOLINESS

In his delightful book *Pleasures for Evermore* Sam Storms writes a chapter on 'Sex and Integrity' in which he reminds us that sex was originally God's idea. 'God created us as

---

[3] *Christianity Today*, March 2006.

sexual beings, and *no one wants our sexual satisfaction more than God.'* Furthermore, for centuries the Christian mystical tradition has taken the erotic language of the Song of Songs as the means for describing the experience of union between the soul and God. St Bernard of Clairvaux in his sermons and commentary on the Song of Songs expounds on the spiritual aspects of this with enthusiasm. Sexual union and intimacy were given in creation to foreshadow the total union of God with the individual soul. Such intimacy results in ecstasy. There will be no place for marriage in heaven – the spiritual ecstasy between God and each individually redeemed human soul will be fully satisfying and perfectly sublime.

Yet the battles in this arena can be unrelenting. 'The power of sex can dismantle our life faster and with more fury than anything else. When it is unleashed it seems that normal, rational human beings will sacrifice anything to its insistence.' There, but for the grace of God, go many of us.

Storms was actually writing on this subject at the time of the then President Bill Clinton's unprecedented testimony before a grand jury, in which he 'confessed' to having misled his family and the American people about his relationship with a 21-year-old intern at the White House. Storms continues:

> [As] if that was not bad enough, one needed only to wait until today (18/8/1998) to hear the reactions of people around the nation. Amazingly, the majority of those interviewed by the media didn't seem to care that our (married) president had engaged in sexual activity with a young lady not much older than his own daughter. They were even less concerned that he had lied about it to everyone on national TV.

Would it be any different in Britain? Surely we live in an equally crooked and perverse generation?

But the kingdom of God is totally different – it is built on purity and righteousness. It lifts the mind essentially onto higher things – things above. And this works its way out into holiness of living, expressed in our relationship with God and in our relationships with everyone else, including our spouses and families. How a man relates to his wife will have a direct effect on his relationship with Christ and will significantly impact his work. Sam Storms puts it succinctly: 'The heart of purity is purity of the heart.'

PURITY HAS MANY 'FACES'

Clearly the word 'pure' (Greek *katharos*) has many 'faces' – cleanliness, walking in the light, single-heartedness, integrity, honesty ('as good as one's word'). It means ingenuous (transparent, open and above board), innocent (unsophisticated), trusting, with genuine motives. Believers are to be morally pure and sincere. The lifestyle of church members is to be utterly different from the corrupt and crooked generation around us.

PURITY HAS ONE SOURCE

I am the Lord your God; consecrate yourselves and be holy, <u>because I am holy</u>. (Leviticus 11:44)

Holiness was, is and ever will be intrinsic to the nature of God. *'Holy, holy, holy is the Lord God Almighty,'* cried the seraphs in Isaiah's vision. When confronted with such stark purity, it was no wonder that Isaiah realised his utter unworthiness in God's presence and cried out, *'Woe to me . . . I am ruined! For I am a man of unclean lips'* (Isaiah 6:3, 5).

The prophet Malachi wrote, *'Who can endure the day of his coming? Who can stand when he appears? For he will be like a refiner's fire'* *(3:2).* Habakkuk said to the Lord, *'Your eyes are too pure to look on evil; you cannot tolerate wrong'* *(1:13).* Theologians tell us that holiness is of the essence of God: it makes him the 'Wholly Other'. He is utterly untainted by evil. The Scriptures insist that we be holy, simply because he is holy *(1 Peter 1:16).*

THE HEART OF ETHICS

Holiness is a fundamental ethic of God's kingdom. It is foundational to the King's moral highway for his subjects: *'A highway will be there; it will be called the Way of Holiness'* *(Isaiah 35:8).* Holiness or purity can be no idle pursuit for God's people. It is a primary calling – not an option, but an obligation.

Earthly rulers, priests and prophets may have outwardly observed their holy rituals, but this has not precluded a secret indulgence in impurity.

One Episcopal Church diocese booked all its clergy for a midweek retreat with their bishop into a large hotel with all expenses paid. The organiser was shocked and surprised to receive a huge bill for late-night showings of pornographic films charged to most of the rooms. Corruption under such leadership easily spreads – like the rot of a bad apple in a storage barrel.

No wonder the church (the new Israel) is sternly bidden *'to be holy [or pure]; without holiness no one will see the Lord'* *(Hebrews 12:14).* Holy people are Christians who *'strive always to keep [their] conscience clear before God'* *(Acts 24:16).* *'Man looks at the outward appearance, but the Lord looks at the heart (1 Samuel 16:7c).* A. W. Tozer reckoned sadly that the average 'so-called' Bible Christian in our times is but a wretched parody of true sainthood.

STEPS TOWARDS HOLINESS

Question: 'How can I, a born-again Christian, become pure, holy or sanctified?' There are at least six positive steps to be considered, and these are examined below.

(1) FINDING THE WILL TO COMMITMENT

Holiness is two sided. On God's side, he sanctifies our sinful hearts through Christ's blood, shed on Calvary, and through the ongoing convicting and sanctifying work of the Holy Spirit. But on the human side we need to be seriously committed to holiness also, repenting of our sins, resisting temptation, and re-presenting ourselves to God as living sacrifices in his service. Oswald Chambers summarised the genuine attitude succinctly in a title for his 'Daily Readings' – *My Utmost for His Highest.*

'Growing in holiness is like riding a bike,' says Rob Warner. 'If you stop pedalling, you fall off.' We start by sanctifying ourselves in prayer, confession and repentance, and dedicating (or rededicating) ourselves to the Lord. We are to be separated from sin – separated unto him!

To walk with God means keeping a good relationship. Adam did not do this. He became alienated *(Genesis 3:23).* Enoch did. He was translated *(Genesis 5:23).*

A vital part of keeping a good relationship includes prayer. Our experience of prayer may be likened to the Jews' experience of manna *(Exodus 16).* Sheila Cassidy says,

It is strange stuff, prayer, not really the sort of thing you would expect to keep a happy permanent relationship going and sustain you on your life's journey, and yet it does. Like the Israelites, we must gather our 'manna' each morning: It can't be stored, but must be collected fresh every day. It's unlike anything else, but if we take it in faith, we will most surely find it really does sustain our relationship with the Lord, and gives us the strength to finish our long trek through the wilderness of life.[4]

The problem with prayer is the same as the problem with manna: it can be pretty tasteless and we get bored with it. The Israelites complained of their unvaried daily diet of manna, just as we might mutter, 'I can't be bothered to pray today. I don't seem to get anything out of it.'

We long for prayer to be tasty, comforting and even exciting, as the Israelites longed for the *'meat . . . [and] the fish we ate in Egypt at no cost – also the cucumbers, melons, leeks, onions and garlic. But now we have lost our appetite; we never see anything but this manna!' (Numbers 11:4–6)*. Prayer can seem dry and boring, but if we persist, it will keep our relationship going along life's journey.[5]

We can learn to develop a regular self-discipline in prayer. Richard Foster illustrates the importance of this from a real-life scenario during the Second World War. Writing of Dietrich Bonhoeffer, he says,

It is no accident that his lectures often returned to the *disciplina pietatis*. He was training for a life in which the powers of body

---

[4] See the CAFOD/LT Lent Book, *Your Kingdom Come* (Darton, Longman & Todd, 1997), pp. 70–71.

[5] Ibid.

and soul are placed entirely in the service of Christ . . . a life of uncompromising adherence to the Sermon on the Mount in imitation of Christ . . . Bonhoeffer's personal habits of daily meditation, prayer, and sacrament intensify his teaching on 'formation'.

This is what enabled him to make 'the heart-wrenching decision' to return from a brief escape to the USA back to his home in Nazi Germany under Hitler. This is what enabled him to live through that difficult period of national history with the Christian people of Germany, so that he might take part in his country's reconstruction after the war. This is what enabled him to describe (and truly experience) his imprisonment, suffering and loss as a 'wondrous transformation'. This is what enabled him to walk, still chained, out of his prison cell to a martyr's triumphant death by hanging.[6]

(2) FINDING THE PRICE TAG

Christians are faced with an ongoing and often intense spiritual battle. The one thing that the old nature in us hates is a commitment to purity. But where there is determination to wage this warfare, our God, who knows the heart, will also want to help us when he sees we really mean business. The flesh will soon be crying out that the cost is too high. But when most of us started out on our pilgrimage we were warned that although 'the entry fee was nothing, the annual subscription was everything'![7]

---

[6] Richard Foster, *Streams of Living Water* (HarperCollins, 1998), pp. 77–78.

[7] David Watson.

In *The Imitation of Christ*, Thomas à Kempis, the four-teenth-century Augustinian monk, stressed that the carnal appetites needed to be dealt with firmly in the *early stages*:

> It is hard to give up old habits and harder still to conquer our own wills. But if you cannot overcome in small and easy things, how will you succeed in greater? Resist your evil inclinations in the beginning and break off evil habits, lest they gradually involve you in greater difficulties. Oh, if you could only know how great a peace for yourself and how great a joy for your fellows your good endeavour would win, you would have greater care for your spiritual progress.[8]

A Young Man's Struggle

Selwyn Hughes, one of the best known Christian counsellors of our day, writes of his own youthful testing times in Wales when out with his born-again girlfriend.

> One of the things I struggled with during that courtship was the whole issue of sexual thoughts. It was not there strongly at first, but it arose one night about three months after our relationship began. One summer evening we were lying together on the mountain side when my girlfriend said, 'I think we ought to go now before we do something drastic.' I fought hard against lustful and licentious thoughts until one night, worn down by the conflict that was going on inside me, I shut myself in a room and prayed, 'Lord, inside me is a team of wild horses that are out of control. If You can't control them, no one can. And if they can't be controlled then I would rather die.' God understood my desperate state and met with me that night in an unforgettable way. After a long time of waiting before Him,

---

[8] Thomas à Kempis, *The Imitation of Christ* (Penguin, 1952), p.38.

I was given a vision of Christ upon the cross. I saw Him hanging there; saw the spittle of the soldiers on His cheek, the blood running down His naked body. Suddenly the vision vanished and all that remained was an empty cross. Then the impression came that the cross I was seeing was one on which I should be crucified. Not in a literal sense, of course, but in the way the apostle Paul refers to in his writing to the Galatians: 'I have been crucified with Christ and I no longer live, but Christ lives in me. The life I live in the body I live by faith in the Son of God, who loved me and gave himself for me' (Galatians 2:20).

The implication of this seemed to me at that time that, just as Christ had been crucified, I needed to be also, albeit in a very different sense. It was not that I had to atone for my sin – that had been accomplished once and for all by Christ's death for me – the invitation now being presented to me was to place myself symbolically in His hands so that a deathblow could be delivered to the ruling passions of my life.

In my vision I saw myself nailed to the cross. There was no pain, just a sense of absolute surrender. When the vision vanished I was filled with an incredible peace. I spent the whole night in prayer and the next day, even though I had gone without a night's sleep, I felt as if I was walking on air. Over the weeks that followed I became aware that, as my previous encounter with the Holy Spirit had given me a new sense of power, this had given me a new sense of purity. I do not wish to imply that the Holy Spirit comes only at such times into a Christian's life. He resides in a Christian's heart permanently. However, I believe there are crisis moments in our lives when a special work needs to be done and He undertakes that work in response to our willing prayers.[9]

---

[9] Selwyn Hughes, *My Story* (CWR, 2005), pp. 422–44.

(3) FINDING THE 'FAST' TRACK

There is always a shameful tendency to forget the Lord (even to get slack and rebel) once we are comfortable and well satisfied in his service. A commitment to fasting helps us to counter that constant temptation.

> But Jeshurun [The Upright One – Israel] grew fat and kicked;
>   filled with food, he became heavy and sleek.
> He abandoned the God who made him
>   and rejected the Rock his Saviour.
> They made him jealous with their foreign gods
>   and angered him with their detestable idols.
> (Deuteronomy 32:15–16)

> I supplied all their needs,
>   yet they committed adultery.
> (Jeremiah 5:7)

Paul insisted on the importance of disciplining the bodily appetites and not thinking about *'how to gratify the desires of the sinful nature' (Romans 13:14)*. The value of fasting as an aid to subduing the body and mastering the appetite has always been recognised. In an old homily of the Church of England (written in 1562), we are told that 'the first end of fasting is to chastise the flesh, that it be not too wanton, but tamed and brought into subjection to the spirit'. Jesus set us an example by his own fasting. After his baptism he was led by the Spirit into the wilderness for a period of 40 days – a period ending with some awful temptations. And that was not the only time he fasted.

He explained to his disciples how his Father sustained him at such times. Arriving in the heat of the day at

Sychar's well, he was counselling a sinful woman, while his disciples were still out searching for food. When they returned with their provisions they urged him to eat, certain that by then he must have been famished, as they were: *'Rabbi, eat something.'* But he said to them, *'I have food to eat that you know nothing about . . . My food . . . is to do the will of him who sent me and to finish his work'* (John 4:31–34).

(4) DEVELOPING A DISCIPLINED LIFESTYLE

'Everyone who competes in the games', said St Paul, writing to the converts at Corinth, *'goes into strict training . . . I beat my body and make it my slave so that after I have preached to others, I myself will not be disqualified for the prize'* (1 Corinthians 9:25–27).

The 'natural' man tends to rebel against discipline. Six chapters into *Tom Sawyer*, Mark Twain introduces us to the juvenile pariah of the village, Huckleberry Finn, son of the town layabout and drunkard. Huck was a natural man in the raw! Trying to avoid developing a respectable lifestyle while living with the good-willed but puritanical Widow Douglas, Huck protested to his friend Tom Sawyer, 'I've tried it but it don't work, Tom. It ain't for me . . . The widder eats by a bell; she goes to bed by a bell; she gets up by a bell – everything's so awful reg'lar a body can't stand it.'

Before discussing the need for self-control, we should remind ourselves afresh that God is actually on our side in this struggle. On the one hand holiness was first imparted to us by God, *'Sanctified in Christ Jesus and called to be holy'* (1 Corinthians 1:2). He gave us his Spirit to make us holy at the time of our new birth (people may not always be conscious of the exact date of this – it comes upon some like a creeping dawn and to others as a lightning flash). God is within us assisting us in our fallen, selfish, human nature, and causing his nine-fold fruit of the Spirit to be seeded in us *(Galatians 5)* for our co-operative cultivation. Thus he is transforming us (with ever increasing glory) into the image of God *(2 Corinthians 3:18).* But our 'sinful nature', which is still with us till the day of our resurrection when the *'perishable must clothe itself with the imperishable, and the mortal with immortality' (1 Corinthians 15:53)*, yet desires what is *'contrary to the Spirit' (Galatians 5:17).* So *'if we, or anyone among us, should ever claim to be without sin, we deceive ourselves and the truth is not in us' (1 John 1:8).*

Following Bible teaching we are being called into a vital role . . . we are being called to be holy and to put to death the old nature within us. *'By the Spirit you put to death the misdeeds of the body' (Romans 8:13).* Paul reckoned he needed to do this every day *(1 Corinthians 15:31).*

God's gracious work of sanctification in us is clearly conditional − it depends upon our willingness to co-operate with him in fulfilling this 'call to be holy' as we contend with the world, the flesh and the devil. We have been freely given a clean garment of righteousness but we are called faithfully to keep it clean and keep ourselves *'from being polluted by the world' (James 1:27).* We must watch the company we keep, the friendships we make, the literature we read, the films, videos and TV programmes we watch, the leisure pursuits we take up, and anything else which might engross our interest, absorb our energy or control our thinking.

When the mind is being filled with good things, it is much less preoccupied with bad things. There is an old but amusing story of an alchemist who used to advertise a patent medicine powder that he claimed would turn water into gold. 'But when you mix it,' he would say, 'you must never think of red monkeys, or it will not work.' No one could ever start this experiment, because no one could ever *not* think of those red monkeys! We cannot force ourselves *not* to think of something, but we can profitably train ourselves positively to think of something different – something higher, something better, something edifying.

I remember being greatly helped as a young man by a verse from the longest psalm. I underlined it heavily:

> *How can a young man keep his way pure?*
> *By living according to your word.*
> *(Psalm 119:9)*

Thinking good positive thoughts and constantly meditating on God's word is the best way to keep the heart and mind on the right track.

In our new life in Christ we are expected to be what we have been made to be through our new birth. This is not an area in which our fierce personal struggles are unique – on the contrary, they are universal, common to all. It is comforting to know that even Jesus was *'tempted in every way, just as we are – yet was without sin'* (Hebrews 4:15). There is no sin in being tempted, but there is sin in giving in to temptation.

This is where resolve and effort on our part are important. That is why Paul goes to some lengths to show how he too has to grapple with the same problems. He writes, *'I fight. . .'*, *'I run. . .'*, *'I beat my body. . .'*, *'I die daily. . .'*, and again he urges his readers to do what he is trying to do: *'Let us purify ourselves. . .'*, *'Let us make every effort. . .'*, *'Let us throw off everything that hinders. . .' (Galatians 2:20; 1 Corinthians 9:26; 15:31; 2 Corinthians 7:1; Hebrews 4:11; 12:1).*

> To war with oneself is the hardest war.
> To conquer oneself is the finest victory. (Anon.)

Being human, and still bearing our old nature, we so easily *'grieve' (Ephesians 4:30)*, *'quench' (1 Thessalonians 5:19)* and *'resist' (Acts 7:51)* the Holy Spirit of God. We can only keep going in a life of purity and holiness by God's help, constantly asking him to grant us true repentance, to cleanse our hearts through the blood of Christ, and to fill us anew with his sanctifying Spirit. We go on crying out to God for grace to help us in these times of need, and when he sees we really mean it, he quickly discerns the sincerity of such prayers and hears them.

> *The sacrifices of God are a broken spirit;*
> *a broken and a contrite heart,*
> *O God, you will not despise.*
> *(Psalm 51:17)*

So we need never give up, but press on towards the goal, being confident that *'he who began a good work in [us] will carry it on to completion until the day of Christ Jesus' (Philippians 3:12–14; 1:6)*.

And there is something more we need to know for our encouragement – something wonderful is going on behind the scenes as we determine to press on: *'we . . . are being transformed into his likeness with ever-increasing glory, which comes from the Lord, who is the Spirit' (2 Corinthians 3:18)*.

(5) FINDING THE ESCAPE ROUTE

Alternatively, we can find other things to do. God always provides us with a way of escape if we have a heart to look for it *(1 Corinthians 10:13)*. With every temptation there is always a way of escape. How often we will need to do what Joseph did when Potiphar's wife tried to seduce him – simply get away from that place or person fast *(Genesis 39:12)*. Paul passed on similar advice to Timothy: *'Flee the evil desires of youth' (2 Timothy 2:22)*.

Billy Graham used to say that a mouse, when it is being chased by the farmer's wife, is not looking at the menacing broom which she is thrashing about behind him, but for the nearest mousehole ahead of him, down which to escape.

(6) FINDING A NEW PERSPECTIVE

Evil things are usually good things in the wrong place, or used in the wrong way. Sand on the seashore is beautiful and clean, but, as I soon found out during inspections on parade during national service in the army, sand in the barrel of a rifle is classed as filthy and merited severe punishment. Firing a bullet through a 'filthy' fire-arm damages the barrel.

Impurity with regard to sex means it is viewed or experienced in ways that are contrary to the will of God as revealed in Scripture. This may seem a difficult commitment for some, who may find a comment made by Pastor Richard Wurmbrand helpful. It is taken from one of his sermons which he regularly communicated in secret code to other prisoners during his 14 years in a tiny underground cell in Romania, while incarcerated by the Communists.

The wardens rarely speak to us, everyone sits alone in his cell without any book, or writing material, and according to his preparation broods or meditates, loses himself in erotic imagination etc. There was a time when I was obsessed with erotic fantasy. My head was a merry-go-round of lustful images. At first I fought against them in vain. Then I said to myself that if marriage is a symbol of the union between Christ and His Church, erotic imagination and love-play, which are basic to marriage, might also have a holy sense. When I stopped worrying about these fancies they lost their importance.[10]

We read in Colossians 3:1: *'Set your hearts on things above, where Christ is seated at the right hand of God . . . not on earthly things.'*

AN IMPORTANT LESSON FROM HISTORY

Why is it so easy to lose sight of the priority of purity? Perhaps an illustration from history will help. After the Reformation period, from the fifteenth century to the middle of the seventeenth century, during which time 'England became the people of a book, and that book was the Bible',[11] there appeared to be a new spiritual mood for progress from the previous century: a yearning – a sincere hope, even – for a 'pure' church. Its watershed was the Cromwellian era. The intention was to implement a fully Calvinist reformation to purify the national church. This included such notions as the removal of prelacy, the restoration of purity in the church and personal piety as a

---

[10] Richard Wurmbrand, *Alone with God – Sermons from Solitary Confinement* (Hodder & Stoughton, 1988), pp. 17, 18, 23, 24.

[11] John Richard Green (historian).

way of life for the membership. When it became clear that prelacy was too difficult to dismantle, a large number, known as Separatists, left the established church to form their own congregational churches. But the pious hope for purity in individual hearts and lives had already taken root in both groups – in some of the remnant who stayed in, and in most of those who left. A lifestyle of purity was typically exemplified in such books as *Pilgrim's Progress*, written by John Bunyan during one of his two imprisonments between 1660 and 1677. The book emphasises a life's journey of personal regeneration, sanctification and morality.

This refocusing on purity began to produce the desired moral fruits, and many of the godly men and women among them became leading intellectual giants. They were the light, the salt and the yeast in the midst of a very corrupt world that reached its nadir in the court of Charles II (1660–85). The flagrant promiscuity of Charles appalled even the contemporary diarist Samuel Pepys (hardly known for such piety himself). But, of course, those who strove for such personal purity and publicly preached about the need for consecrated lifestyles were never without their critics – and like Bunyan himself many among the poorer ranks of society ended up in prison for making their principles public.

Later, once they became recognised for the goodness they modelled, for the godly influence they wielded, for the charitable projects they pioneered, for their honesty in business and their whole ethos of self-improvement, these godly people became secretly admired and respected in many parts of society, though some of the scorn and rejection still continued.

HOW DID THIS PROCESS GO SO WRONG?

In such circumstances there were plenty of people out there who were attracted to these pious characters, wanted to emulate them, to associate with them and their good causes, hoping that some of their reputation would wear off on them. There was growing evidence of the benefits to be gained in being associated with folk with such reputations – good, honourable and trustworthy men and women.

But, all that glistered was not gold. There was a downside. Many people wanted the benefit of being considered virtuous without the virtue itself. They went to church, but did not commit to Christ. They were seen to associate with the good, but did not amend their characters. It became easy to confuse those who were 'puritan' by name and those who were 'puritan' by nature, and often the godly were blamed for the evils of the ungodly. The word 'puritan' acquired various secondary and vaguely uncomplimentary connotations – usually associated with fanaticism, judgementalism and hypocrisy. H. L. Mencken sarcastically defined a 'puritan' as 'a person in constant dread that someone somewhere might be happy'.

An artist once sang *Rigoletto* poorly. People booed her. Indignant, she said to her colleagues, 'What an uneducated audience! They dare to jeer Verdi!' But, of course, they were not jeering the composer but the performer – not blaming the music but the singer. It may well have been too easy to confuse the genuine Puritan virtue of holiness with a current culture that called itself Puritan.

Hypocrisy

There were many who associated with the true Puritans, adopting their pious language and some of their external customs, who sadly continued in their old ways of conducting shady businesses, keeping up sordid liaisons and practising un-Christian behaviour at home. (We have only to read Pepys's diaries for a glimpse of this kind of lifestyle.) But it did not escape the notice of their closest acquaintances, those who knew of their pretences too well. Their own children observed it. And their acquaintances grew sick of their sham. Many such deceptions dragged on into the Victorian era. It was natural by then for the world to take a cynical view; to assume and then assert that all those who sought to have pure hearts and godly lifestyles must be pompous and sanctimonious humbugs. The 'real thing' had become badly tainted.

But there was another dimension for which sadly Puritanism really was to blame. This was legalism and judgementalism – *'Do not handle! Do not taste! Do not touch!' (Colossians 2:21)*. They forgot that salvation was by grace alone, and ignorantly overlooked the fact that it is impossible to legislate for either corporate or personal integrity.

Some who genuinely wanted to cultivate a Puritan lifestyle mistakenly resorted to legalism as a simple and compelling way of coping with the challenges of living. Not surprisingly they soon found themselves being spurned for becoming (or seeming to become) censorious and unloving with their 'holier than thou' attitudes. They became not-very-nice people to have around. They had become the type of Pharisee that Jesus had inveighed against so vehemently.

Initially the Puritan colonists in North America had brought a great good to New England with them, but sadly by the seventeenth century their hair-splitting interpretation of Scripture had become overwhelmingly legalistic. In the 'Code of Connecticut' we read:

> No one shall run on the Sabbath Day, or walk in his garden, or elsewhere, except reverently to and from meeting. No one shall travel, cook victuals, make beds, sweep house, cut hair, or shave on the Sabbath. If any man shall kiss his wife, or wife her husband on the Lord's Day, the party in fault shall be punished at the discretion of the court magistrates.

A further undermining of the Puritan lifestyle was brought about by those who professed to exemplify it but forgot the priority of love. Andrew Carnegie (1835–1919), the Pittsburgh steel magnate, was the world's most famous philanthropist, prior to today's Bill Gates and Warren Buffett. He was a 'rags to riches' man who did an immense amount of good and one hesitates to criticise such a wonderfully generous character. However, he apparently marred his godly reputation by being 'so convinced of his own rightness – in business and philanthropy – that he could not conceive of himself as being wrong'. A biographer, Peter Krass, described him as being 'intoxicated by his own holiness'.[12] He married rather late in life and had only one child, a daughter called Margaret, whom he never really got to know, and who considered him a hypocrite – appearing to be much more godly than he really was.

It was the shameful hypocrisy of some Puritan Christians

---

[12] Elizabeth Grice, article in the *Daily Telegraph*, 29th June 2006, p. 19.

that gradually undermined a movement which had brought so much good to society.

Marista Leishman, daughter of another famous man, has recently written a book entitled *My Father – Reith of the BBC*, which reveals the unappeasable side of her father who, ever courageous and energetic, saw prodigious achievements during his pioneering days as the first director of the BBC (retired 1938). But he was a man who found children distasteful, upset colleagues and employees constantly and bullied his faithful wife Muriel in both her company and behind her back, while flirting outrageously with his secretaries. He was a man who fought tirelessly for Victorian values at work (which she lauded), but failed miserably to practise Victorian values at home (which she lamented). His biography exemplifies the darker side of human nature.

Scrupulosity

Other genuine believers sadly became overscrupulous in their heart-searchings. They spent too much time concentrating on their inner feelings and failings. They gave long hours to examining their consciences and ended up losing all their joy in Christ, which should have been such a magnetic characteristic of their bearing towards outsiders.

So we can all understand the reason for the little girl's prayer, 'Dear Lord, please make the bad people good and the good people nice.' Or the litany of Teresa of Avila, who is supposed to have written, 'From . . . sour-faced saints, spare us, good Lord.' Both the hypocrites and the spoilsports are perversions of 'the genuine article', and this has been an abiding excuse for many neither to seek purity, nor to pursue holiness. But the will of God remains unchanged.

He still says, *'Be holy, because I am holy' (1 Peter 1:16)*. Our ideal must always be Jesus, who was ever pure and utterly holy. He lovingly exemplified this by his life. People were drawn to his godly nature and delighted in his simple, liberating teaching.

The Recoiling of the Old Nature

Here we leave the unhappy side of Puritanism to reflect on the natural condition of the human heart. The flesh recoils and rebels at perseverance in the cause of purity. Good resolutions can be abandoned quickly when the cost seems too high. How truly Scripture tells us, *'The heart is deceitful above all things and beyond cure' (Jeremiah 17:9)*. The heart is impatient, intolerant and indignant about what it naturally regards as interference or any imposition over its carnal desires, claiming it has the freedom to do just whatever it wants – tragically confusing liberty with licence. Slowly and surely the enemies of God have persuaded the world to compromise with an alternative godless culture. The real nature of this culture is revealing itself today as cynical, disrespectful, tasteless, rebellious, violent, cruel, gross and yobbish.[13]

Delaying the Decision

Perhaps we are saying 'yes' in our hearts: 'Purity of life is right, but this is not the time for getting it right; call me later, Lord!' The dissolute Augustine is on record as praying in just that mode: 'Lord, give me chastity – but not yet!'

---

[13] See Francis Gilbert, *Yob Nation: The Truth about Britain's Yob Culture* (Portrait, 2006).

Procrastination is my sin.
It brings me naught but sorrow.
I know that I should stop it.
In fact I will – tomorrow.

PROMISED REWARD

The promise to those who keep themselves pure is that they shall see God. Henry Miller began writing *The Tropic of Cancer* with the mocking boast that he had never feared God, and if ever he saw God's face he would spit on it. Miller died in the early 1980s. But of one thing we may be certain: he never spat on the face of God. Were there still opportunity to speak to God at such a time, there would be only one prayer to offer: 'Lord, have mercy on me, a sinner!'

SEEING GOD – THE VISIBLE ASPECT

Jesus, the Son, is the image of God the Father, *'the exact representation of his being' (Hebrews 1:3)*. Jesus sees God the Father and knows him intimately, because he is the only begotten Son who comes from the bosom of the Father *(John 1:18)*. *'For God was pleased to have all his fullness dwell in him' (Colossians 1:19)*. No one has ever seen God the Father, except, of course, his Son, who has made the Father known to us *(John 1:18)*. When his disciples begged Jesus to show them the Father, Jesus gave them some insight into the mystery: *'Anyone who has seen me has seen the Father . . . I am in the Father, and . . . the Father is in me.'* Yet he went on to say, *'I am going to the Father' (John 14:9–12)*. That is as near as we shall ever get to understanding the mystery, until the kingdom of glory has fully come with Christ's return.

The Jews accepted what they regarded as the invisibility of God. God had said to Moses, *'You cannot see my face, for no one may see me and live' (Exodus 33:20).* God is invisible and cannot be seen by mortals, so how shall we, or how can we ever, expect to see him?

SEEING GOD – THE INVISIBLE ASPECT

Paul prays that the Ephesian Christians may *'know this love that surpasses knowledge' (Ephesians 3:19).* Since we know God's face cannot be seen, we have to understand that 'seeing God' is seeing his face in a way that surpasses sight. Jesus talked about the eye being single. He meant being able to look at life without worldly, selfish or impure prejudices. This will enable us to see God's purposes in and through conflicting situations *(Matthew 6:21).* Purity of heart creates clarity of vision.[14]

Some seem to see God plainly – if not physically face to face. Those holy men who claimed to have seen him in the Bible saw him in the spirit by special revelations and visions, not face to face. On the other hand when the Bible says that God spoke to Moses *'face to face' (Numbers 12:8),* the implication is that Moses had a clarity of revelation not given so plainly to others. We have to assume that although Moses did not, in fact, see God's face, nevertheless the words which God spoke to him were as plain and clear as if he had been watching God's lips – the form of words communicated was unmistakable, although the face of God was invisible. Moses may not have been permitted actually to

---

[14] Chris Spicer, *Eight Characteristcs of Highly Effective Christians* (Monarch, 1996), p. 157.

see the face of God, but he was given a higher form of revelation than others. When it came to 'seeing' God, Moses still only saw his *'form' (Numbers 12:8)*.

WAYS OF 'SEEING' GOD

For the time being his face remains hidden, but his 'invisible qualities' may be clearly seen from his creation *(Romans 1:20)*; his presence may be sensed and his voice may be heard. God may be seen with 'the eyes of the heart', while veiled beyond the perception of the eyes of the head. But God remains always beyond full knowing (we see through *'a glass darkly'*, only a *'reflection as in a mirror' (1 Corinthians 13:12, KIV and NIV respectively)* until the kingdom has been fully established on earth, and the pure in heart will be the first to see him as he truly is, and to know him as he is known.

We May Sense His Presence

Jesus says, in the Sermon on the Mount, that the blessing on those who are pure in heart is that *'they will see God'*. To put it on a material level, just as we need to keep our spectacles clean to see others clearly, so we will need to keep our hearts clean to see God clearly – to trace his handiwork, to sense his presence, to feel his pleasure, or to hear his voice.

We See Life in a New Way through the Spirit of God

There is a verse in the hymn 'Loved with Everlasting Love' by George Robinson which describes how born-again believers see the world around them in a new way:

> Heaven above is softer blue,
> Earth around is sweeter green.

> Something lives in every hue,
> Christless eyes have never seen.

We Can See the Way God Is Leading

Job had been through many severe testing times and kept his faith in God. Finally, after all he had been through, and after all his complaints and questionings, the Lord *'answered Job out of the storm' (Job 38:1)*. God addressed a number of penetrating and profound questions to him. Job, who thought he had all the answers, was dumbfounded. He realised that, in fact, he had no answers. Finally Job opened his mouth (probably stammering):

> *You asked, 'Who is this that obscures my counsel without knowledge?'*
>   *Surely I spoke of things I did not understand,*
>   *things too wonderful for me to know. . .*
> *My ears had heard of you*
>   *but now my eyes have seen you.*
> *Therefore I despise myself*
>   *and repent in dust and ashes.*
> *(Job 42:3–6)*

God had revealed himself to Job. He will reveal himself to us also, even if not in the same way. We can have an assurance of God's revelation today through Scripture, but also apart from Scripture, though never in contradiction to it. We can hear his voice or see his way forward through such gifts as prophecy. We can sense how he leads, how he helps us to make good choices and take wise decisions. Somehow a Scripture passage prompts us, some 'light' shines on the way ahead to indicate his will, or a voice behind us directs us saying, *'This is the way; walk in it' (Isaiah 30:21)*. Our God is not like the lifeless wooden idols worshipped by the pagans, which had mouths and could not speak. Our living God speaks.

We May See God's Will in Our Dreams

An angel of the Lord appeared to Joseph in a dream. 'Get up,' he said, 'take the child and his mother and escape to Egypt. Stay there until I tell you, for Herod is going to search for the child to kill him.' (Matthew 2:13)

We May See God's Will in Our Visions

(i) A 'Commonplace' Vision

The Old Testament, prophets were called 'seers': they saw God in signs and situations, in dreams and visions, often through the simplest of images such as a plumb line, a basket of fruit, or a potter at work on his clay. And as they prayerfully meditated on what they were seeing, God would show them what he was seeing.

(ii) A 'Clear, Open Vision'

Isaiah could obviously see his vision very clearly: *'My eyes have seen the King, the Lord Almighty' (Isaiah 6:5).*

(iii) A 'Comatose' Vision

These may occur while lying on a bed between sleeping and waking *(Daniel 4:5).*

(iv) An 'Ongoing Internal' Vision

In Daniel's case *'visions . . . passed through [his] mind' (Daniel 7:15).*

(v) An 'External Supernatural' Vision

Daniel saw some mysterious 'writing on the wall' *(Daniel 5:5)*. After many doors had shut in Paul's face as he eagerly sought to press further into obvious key areas of Asia Minor, he had an unmistakable vision of a man from Macedonia begging him to *'come over to Macedonia and help us' (Acts 16:9)*. He obeyed and crossed the Aegean Sea to Greece, where God richly blessed his ministry – though not without the usual beatings, stonings and imprisonment along the way.

We May See Pictures When We Seek His Face in Prayer

> *My heart says of you, 'Seek his face!'*
> *Your face, Lord, I will seek.*
> *(Psalm 27:8)*

God loves it when we seek his face, even though he will never actually reveal it to us fully.

There is a short, inspiring book by Brother Lawrence (1605–91), a lay Carmelite monk who served his fellow monks as chief cook and bottle-washer in the kitchen of a Parisian monastery. The pages are full of his simple maxims and the book is aptly called *Practising the Presence of God*.[15] This humble monk learned to take it by faith that God was always beside him – even in the kitchen. He was as close to God when doing his chores in the scullery as he was when saying his prayers in the chapel. Brother Lawrence

---

[15] Brother Lawrence, *Practising the Presence of God* (Whitaker House, 1982).

explained, 'What I am doing now is what I will do for all eternity, I am blessing God, praising Him, adoring Him, loving Him with all my heart.' One cannot but sense the fragrance of God in the book.

Using poetic licence to express a mystery, a convenient contrivance for expressing the otherwise inexpressible, Brother Lawrence sensed the presence of God with such reality that it could be said he saw the face of God quite clearly. Readers will be inspired to emulate his practice – and especially his persistence – and will discover Brother Lawrence's secret for themselves.

The Russian Archimandrite Sophrony also writes of the 'Experience of Eternity through Prayer',[16] where he sees a centuries-old tree with branches reaching into the clouds but whose roots go deep down into the earth. The deeper the roots in prayer, the higher the branches seem to be spread. The deeper we go, the closer we get, and the clearer the vision of God.

SEEING GOD FACE TO FACE

But God's face still remains beyond our focus. This will not be granted us until the kingdom of God has been fully established on earth, and then *'we shall see face to face' (1 Corinthians 13:12).*

> *Look, he is coming with the clouds,*
> *and every eye will see him,*
> *even those who pierced him. . .*
> *(Revelation 1:7)*

---

[16] Archimandrite Sophrony, *His Life in Mine*, trans. R. Edmonds (A. R. Mowbray, 1977), p. 17.

For the unrepentant briefly in remorse and for the pure in heart eternally in rejoicing, all shall see him as he truly is – radiant in purity and glorious in holiness.

MEDITATION

I made a covenant with my eyes
not to look lustfully at a girl.
(Job 31:1)

* * *

Old John Newton, the converted slave trader, once said, 'I am not what I ought to be, I am not what I want to be, I am not what I hope to be, but, still, I am not what I once used to be, and by the grace of God I am what I am.[17]

* * *

Bless'd are the pure in heart,
For they shall see our God;
The secret of the Lord is theirs,
Their soul is Christ's abode.
(John Keble)[18]

* * *

Lord, we Thy Presence seek,
May ours this blessing be;
Give us a pure and lowly heart,
A temple meet for Thee.
(William Hall)

* * *

---

[17] J. C. Ryle, *Home Truths* (Charles Thynne, undated), pp. 94–5.
[18] *Hymns Ancient and Modern*, No. 261.

Almighty God,
To whom all hearts are open,
All desires known,
And from whom no secrets are hidden:
Cleanse the thoughts of our hearts
By the inspiration of your Holy Spirit,
That we may perfectly love you,
And worthily magnify your holy name;
Through Jesus Christ our Lord. Amen.[19]

---

[19] 'The Collect for Purity', *The Alternative Service Book* 1980.

7

Peace in Our Time

Blessed are the peacemakers,
for they will be called sons of God.
(Matthew 5:9)

INTRODUCTION

NO PEACEMAKER IN SIGHT

A Pacific South West aircraft crashed in California in 1987 with 48 people on board. Flight investigators found a gun in the wreckage, and from other evidence were able to piece together the tragedy that had destroyed the plane. The gun had been bought by David Burke, a former flight attendant who had lost his job with the airline for stealing. Unbeknown to others, Burke had kept his security pass, by which he managed to get on the plane carrying the gun. A voice recorder revealed that Burke had gone up to his former boss, Ray Thompson, who was also on the flight, saying, 'Hi, Ray. I think it's sort of ironical that we end up like this. I asked for leniency for my family: remember? Well, I got none, and you'll get none.' With that he shot Thompson, then killed the crew as well. The plane nosedived to the ground and all 48 passengers went to their death. A terrible tragedy. We are told never to take revenge: that is God's prerogative. *'Vengeance is mine,'* says the Lord.

VICTIM WAS THE PEACEMAKER

A photograph appeared in the press in 1972 showing a young girl, weeping profusely. Her clothes had been stripped off by American bombs that had just destroyed her village, still clouded over with black smoke. Armed soldiers around her appeared to be unmoved. John Plummer, one of the helicopter pilots who helped organise the attack, was shocked by the picture; it continued to haunt him for the next 24 years. He had longed to be able to find the girl, and tell her how sorry he was for his part in her tragedy. But how could he possibly find her, let alone identify her, after all those years? He had sought God's help, which had led him into the Christian ministry. When the photo was published he was a Methodist pastor in Virginia, USA. But still he did not even have a clue as to the girl's name.

Friends tried to convince him that there was no need to go on feeling guilty. After all, he had tried to ensure that there were no civilians in the village when the napalm bombs were dropped. But his conscience still tormented him, and his guilt broke up his marriage. He had driven himself to drink.

Finally, on Veterans' Day 1996, he went to the Vietnam memorial in Washington with a group of fellow pilots, also intent on burying their past. To his amazement, when he got there, he found himself speaking to a Vietnamese woman named Phan Thi Kim Phuc, the girl, now a grown woman, who had been in the picture! She had come there to tell them all that she was not bitter, and that even though she still suffered from the burns that she had received that day, she forgave the men who had bombed her village, *and wanted only peace*.

Plummer began to splutter over and over, 'I'm sorry, I'm sorry, I'm sorry.' She simply embraced him and said, 'It's all right. I forgive you.' John's nightmare was finally over. He had found peace at last.[1]

PEACEMAKING IS GOD'S NATURE

PEACEMAKING IS ON GOD'S HEART

God is one. The Father, the Son and the Holy Spirit are one God – three persons in one God. The three persons of our triune God live in perfect love and harmony together. And God desires this harmony between the various parts of his creation on earth. He loves the world so much that he sent his only begotten Son to make peace for us; to bring us back into harmony with himself and with our fellow beings. One of Jesus' titles is actually 'the Prince of Peace'. Jesus is the great reconciler and peacemaker. He made peace (becoming the peacemaker *par excellence*) between sinful humanity and our holy God. He made that peace through his own blood on the cross. He did not die for his own sin. He had no sin. He died for our sins. He died, the just for the unjust, to bring us to God *(1 Peter 3:18)*. Proof that his atoning death for our sin was accepted by the Father is the well-attested fact that Jesus was raised from the dead by the power of the Holy

---

[1] Adapted from *Renewal* magazine, May 1998.

Spirit – a sure sign of God's acceptance. And then he was seen by so many witnesses *(1 Corinthians 15:3–4)*. The loving peacemaking of God is at the heart of the gospel. The Father, the Son and the Holy Spirit live together in perfect love, peace and harmony. In his high-priestly prayer Jesus prayed to the Father for his followers *'that they [all his disciples] may be one as we [the Godhead] are One' (John 17:22)*. Peace *with* God is the state of affairs which God endorses and in which God rejoices. The peace of God, primarily and fundamentally, creates a new relationship of forgiveness and acceptance – and the source from which it flows is ever the cross: 'Jesus made peace by the blood of the cross'[2] *(Colossians 1:20)*.

Thomas à Kempis gave some 'useful admonitions for a spiritual life':

First keep thyself in peace, and thou shalt be able to pacify others.
A peaceable man doth more good than he that is well-learned. . .
A good peaceable man turneth all things to good. . .
And others there are that keep themselves in peace, and
study to bring others unto peace.[3]

PEACEMAKING IS OUR RESPONSIBILITY TOO

WE FOLLOW THE PATHS OF PEACE

We are bidden to keep the peace. *'Seek peace and pursue it' (1 Peter 3:11)*. *'If it is possible, as far as it depends on you, live at peace with everyone' (Romans 12:18)*.

---

[2] James I. Packer, *Knowing God* (Hodder & Stoughton, 2005).
[3] Thomas à Kempis, *Of the Imitation of Christ* (first published in Latin 1470, first translated 1677, reprinted Henry Frowde, OUP, 1906).

God's blessing is on the peacemakers, but not necessarily on the peace-lovers – the latter will do *anything* for the sake of keeping peace, for example giving in to their children and spoiling them for life. They want to make peace at all costs. This may work as a temporary measure, but the long-term problem remains unresolved, just smouldering beneath the surface. New crises may erupt at any time. 'Many a man thinks he loves peace by doing nothing when in fact he is piling up trouble for the future'[4] – for himself and for others.

PEACEMAKING INVOLVES ACTION

God Blesses True Peacemakers

(1) In the Church

The psalmist writes:

> How good and pleasant it is
> when brothers live together in unity!
> *(Psalm 133:1)*

God calls for unity in the church. *'Don't have anything to do with foolish and stupid arguments, because you know they produce quarrels. And the Lord's servant must not quarrel' (2 Timothy 2:23–24).* Quarrels undermine unity. Jesus, as our High Priest, prays *'for those who will believe in me . . . that all of them may be one' (John 17:20–21)* – not necessarily one in organisation, but one in the unity of the Spirit, positively wanting to meet up with one another to bless and encourage each other in the Lord. *'Let us not give up meeting together' (Hebrews 10:25).*

---

[4] Jo Frost, *Supernanny* (Channel 4).

Paul was distressed to hear of two ladies quarrelling in the church at Philippi and wrote:

I plead with Euodia and I plead with Syntyche to agree with each other in the Lord. Yes, and I ask you, loyal yokefellow, help these women who have contended at my side in the cause of the gospel. . . (Philippians 4:2–3)

Elsewhere he wrote, *'Brothers, if someone is caught in a sin, you who are spiritual should restore him gently' (Galatians 6:1; cf. Matthew 18:15).*

Peacemaking is not passive compliance, but positive constructive action. Peacemakers do more than just live peaceable lives; they pray for peace, they actively seek to 'make peace', to bring about reconciliation, to put an end to bitterness and strife. Such peace is not simply appeasement, but may sometimes involve grasping some prickly nettles. It can be costly. We remember how Moses attempted to make peace between his fellow Israelites and, like a dog with its tail between its legs, went running into self-imposed exile *(Exodus 2:13–14).*

(2) In the Home

God wants the hearts of the fathers drawn to their children and the hearts of the children drawn to their fathers *(Malachi 4:6). 'Fathers, do not exasperate your children' (Ephesians 6:4).* He wants husbands and wives to get on well together. *'Husbands, love your wives, just as Christ loved the church and gave himself up for her' (Ephesians 5:25). 'What God has joined together, let man not separate' (Matthew 19:6). ' "I hate divorce," says the Lord God' (Malachi 2:16),* because he knows how much pain it causes to all involved. Marcel Proust commented, 'It's seldom that one parts on good terms, because if one was on good terms one would not part.' God does accept that there are exceptions, for example as the sequence to unfaithfulness *(Matthew 9:9)*, and he understands when marriages sometimes break down, but he still hates it, and wants couples to make every effort to be reconciled, if possible, for their own sakes and for the sake of their children.

As a young minister I overlooked the biblical greeting of peace to a house as rather formal and old fashioned. But, as I grew a little more mature, I realised that there is spiritual reality in seeking to bless a home with such meaningful words: *'Peace to this house.'* As Jesus said, *'If a man of peace is there, your peace will rest on him; if not, it will return to you'* *(Luke 10:5–6)*.

(3) Between Friends

Friends are important to most of us. But friendship must be mutual if it is to be constructive. We appreciate all that our friends give us, but we need to ensure that the relationship is reciprocal, and that we play our part fully and care for our friends also. We read in Proverbs: *'A friend loves at all times'* *(17:17)* and, *'Wounds from a friend can be trusted'* *(27:6)*. Amos asked, *'Do two walk together unless they have agreed to do so?'* *(Amos 3:3)*. All friendships need to be kept in a good state of repair, and require as much communication as is reasonably possible. Actually friendship has to be the basis for every good marriage too. *'A friend . . . sticks closer than a brother'* *(Proverbs 18:24)*.

(4) Between Neighbours

'Love your neighbour as yourself' *(Matthew 19:19). 'As far as it depends on you, live at peace with everyone' (Romans 12:18).* Of course, there will always be sad cases where there is nothing more that you, or a mediator acting on your behalf, can possibly do to repair a broken relationship between friends or neighbours. Entreaties are ignored, peace-offerings are rejected, apologies are spurned, and doors are shut to any and every overture of peace. Nevertheless, Jesus told us to love our enemies *(Matthew 5:44). 'A gentle answer turns away wrath, but a harsh word stirs up anger' (Proverbs 15:1).*

(5) Between Rival Industries

Unless one moves in those circles, it is really surprising to learn how many businesses refuse to deal with each other because of some sense of past grievance or slight. One of the encouraging signs of the times is that in the last few years a number of professional Christians have been led to establish reconciliation agencies – and some of these are working at very high levels in the nation.[5]

(6) Within a Nation

'Every kingdom . . . city or household divided against itself will not stand' (Matthew 12:25). There are always tensions within any nation – between regions, for example, because those further

---

[5] e.g. Institute for Christian Conciliation – a division of Peacemaker Ministries, 1537 Avenue D, Suite 352, Billings MT 59102, USA. Also the Christian Mediation and Arbitration Service – contact Chris Smyth by email, office@christianmediation.org.uk. Recommended reading: Ken Sande, *The Peacemaker* (Baker Books, 2004).

from the centres of power are resentful of those who are nearer. Different regions are resentful of the position, industry or wealth of other regions. Different cultures and classes have their distinct issues. Peacemakers are watchful and can propose ameliorating measures to head off crises. 'A stitch in time saves nine.' A civil war is one of the most ugly and awful experiences for any nation on earth to undergo. Families and personal loyalties are divided and the resulting wounds and emotional traumas take decades, if not centuries, to heal. In the USA one can still discern residual prejudices in the south resulting from the civil war which occurred over 200 years ago.

Cesar Lopez is a young guitarist aged 32. When he was nine his older sister became a fatal victim of the interminable fighting that had been going on for over 40 years within the South American Republic of Colombia. Lopez has never known a time of peace during his whole life. No one dared to speak up, as no one knew who might be shot or blown up next. And no one knew who might do the shooting or the blowing up. In 2002 Lopez became a pacifist and decided to start a peace movement. He converted a disused machine-gun into a guitar and called it an *escopetarra* (a name made up from the first part of the Spanish word for 'firearm' and the ending of *guitarra*). He also gave some of these instruments away to his guitar-playing friends, which they now use to sing songs of peace. They also organise musical festivals. An instrument once intended to create destruction is now used for creating something beautiful. Lopez and his friends are standing up and using their voices for peace. It could be the beginning of a breakthrough. It has at least created hope.

(7) Between Nations

'We must take risks for peace, because the world is too dangerous unless we learn to listen and talk to each other.'[6]

Robert Oppenheimer supervised the making of the first atomic bomb. He appeared before an American congressional committee where he was asked if there was any defence against this awesome new weapon of war.

'Certainly,' replied the great physicist.

'And that is. . .?' someone retorted.

The committee awaited his reply in grave silence.

Dr Oppenheimer paused before finishing his answer softly. 'Peace,' he said.

Everyone can pray and work for peace, even if not everyone can be practically involved in a national or an international peacemaking process. Anyone can seek to pour oil on troubled waters and view problems constructively by trying to see difficulties from differing perspectives. Everyone should be able to learn to listen quietly and to try and understand both sides in any quarrel.

Attitudes to War

The teaching of Christ in the Sermon on the Mount rules out violence. However, this is not an ideal world, and Christians live in a world where evil rages aggressively. Confronted by this, the church has found it necessary to rationalise the use of force. Traditionally there have been three major attitudes to war, outlined below.

---

[6] Billy Graham, *The Secret of Happiness* (Word Publishing, 1985).

(1) A Just War

St Augustine taught that war could be justified if the objective was the establishment of justice and the restoration of peace. But then war should only be waged under the authority of one's ruler, and engaged in justly. Faith must be kept, and there must be no looting, massacres or profaning of places of worship. Also clergy, whether secular or regular, should not be permitted to take up arms.

(2) The Crusading Ideal

Crusades were regarded as holy wars fought under the auspices of the church with a mandate from the Pope (although there was very little that was Christian to be discerned in the manner in which the Crusades were conducted) for the sake of an ideal, for example the recapture of the Holy Land (1095) or Constantinople (1202), or some such 'holy' objective. The enemy (the Ottomans, Islam) was depicted as representing evil.

(3) Pacifism – the Only Way

In this view, Christians must quite simply never take up arms for making war.

After two world wars, it seems that all three of these positions came back on the table for reconsideration. Under the United Nations Charter many have come to believe that warfare between nations can no longer be justified. Too many innocent people get killed or wounded. With the introduction of rockets and nuclear weapons, many churchmen have reverted to a position of pacifism.

Reconsideration: a Doctrine of Deterrence

Since the events of 9/11 and the destruction of the Twin Towers in New York, some leaders have come to believe that this entirely new situation calls for a reconsideration of the traditional views outlined above. Most people believe that their rulers have an obligation to defend them against terrorist attacks and suicide bombers. Speaking pragmatically, no democratically elected leader could continue to hold office if he or she was not seen to be doing everything possible to defend his or her citizens.

A 'doctrine of deterrence' is regarded by some leaders as the only way to ensure protection from one's enemies. This means for them it is necessary to adopt a policy of 'first-strike capability' to achieve victory – to take out enemy rockets and nuclear arms before their enemy could use them, because afterwards it would be too late. This sounds sensible enough. But the presenting fallacy is that the home ruler would have to strike first to achieve victory and the enemy might never actually have been intending to strike; only threatening.

LET EVERY MAN BE FULLY PERSUADED IN HIS OWN MIND

Arguments are interminable. It seems from Christ's teaching that we are not to defend ourselves personally, nor to take revenge, but simply to turn the other cheek. OK . . . but what about my wife and children? Most Christians would feel they had a clear obligation to defend their kith and kin against an assailant. Paul writes to Timothy, *'If any one does not provide for . . . his immediate family, he has denied the faith and is worse than an unbeliever' (1 Timothy 5:8)*. Paul may actually have had family provision more than family protection in mind when he wrote that, but the principle would be the same.

Definitely Maybe

So often, however, the will of God is not immediately clear. The story of Dietrich Bonhoeffer would seem to demonstrate the dilemma. As he wrestled with the political developments under Hitler in Germany, Bonhoeffer saw that 'ethics' could never mean the enunciation of a system of principles by which one could be equipped to make correct moral decisions in every situation as required: 'Man does not always have the good fortune to choose between a right course and a wrong one; often he is faced with a decision in which every possible course has an element of evil in it.'

In pondering this dilemma I have been re-reading Bonhoeffer's biography. This godly one-time Lutheran chaplain in London returned to Germany before the Second World War. He was greatly concerned about the progressive Nazification of the German church. He became a leader of the new Confessing Church – a modern puritan movement created to counter the highly compromised traditional church. The Confessing Church was basically opposed to violence. But Bonhoeffer felt conscience-bound to resign from the movement he had co-founded when he came to believe that the only option left was a 'coup' and Hitler's violent removal from office. The resistance movement, with which he became increasingly involved, organised a plot to blow up Hitler which failed. Although he had no hand in the actual plot, Bonhoeffer was arrested by the Gestapo in

1943 on a charge of complicity and was finally hanged for treason in 1945.

In his book *Ethics* Bonhoeffer struggled with the enigmatic rights and wrongs of such action, and I include part of his rather tortuous reasoning here:

> But if someone sets out to fight his battles in the world in his own absolute freedom, if he values the necessary deed more highly than the spotlessness of his own conscience and reputation; if he is prepared to sacrifice a fruitless principle to a fruitful compromise, or for that matter the fruitless wisdom of the *via media* to a fruitful radicalism, then, for him, beware lest precisely his supposed freedom may ultimately prove his undoing. He will easily consent to the bad, knowing full well that it is bad, in order to ward off what is worse, and in doing so he will no longer be able to see that precisely the worse which he is trying to avoid may still be the better. This is one of the underlying themes of tragedy.[7]

It is well worth making a real effort to understand Bonhoeffer's reasoning here. *'With justice he judges and makes war' (Revelation 19:11).*

UNDERLYING OBSTACLES TO PEACEMAKING

(1) Ambition

This is the drive to succeed in the world, to make our mark and become 'top dog', and to stay at the top. Jesus, on the other hand, is directing our energies into the very opposite

---

[7] Mary Bosanquet, *Bonhoeffer – True Patriot* (reprinted A. R. Mowbray, 1978), p. 220.

direction – that of serving others and sitting in the lowest seats.

(2) Pride

This is at the heart of the old nature in man. But peace-making will hardly succeed unless we humble ourselves. It is much wiser to humble ourselves than to have to wait for God to bring us low.

(3) Vengeance

This again is an attitude of the natural man, but it leads to bitterness, resentment and constant fear of reprisal. The Bible is quite clear:

> *Do not repay anyone evil for evil. Be careful to do what is right in the eyes of everybody. If it is possible, as far as it depends on you, live at peace with everyone. Do not take revenge, my friends, but leave room for God's wrath, for it is written: 'It is mine to avenge; I will repay,' says the Lord . . . Do not be overcome by evil, but overcome evil with good. (Romans 12:17–19, 21)*

(4) Prejudice

Few of us can probably appreciate how much both our upbringing and our culture have created prejudices in our own minds. It often demands a complete paradigm shift to see things in another light and discover we could be wrong!

WHEN AND HOW DO WE WAGE PEACE?

There are six attributes that we need.

(1) The Conviction that the Task Is Worth Tackling

We need to engage in the process with hope and prayer. There is no point entering into a peacemaking enterprise if one does not sense that there is at least some desire for reconciliation and hope of reaching it.

(2) Love

Put yourself in the place of those in conflict. Do to others what you would have them do to you. It is obviously important to speak and behave respectfully and gently. *'He who guards his mouth and his tongue keeps himself from calamity' (Proverbs 21:23).* Any other approach is guaranteed to prove counterproductive.

(3) Sacrifice

The whole exercise is bound to be time consuming, even if both sides are co-operating fully, so it is vital to give plenty of space and not to rush things. Patience is always a virtue, and especially for peacemakers. The very fact that the parties have got into such an adverse situation is an indication that the issues have probably been mounting up over a considerable period. And aggrieved parties have a tendency to exaggerate their complaints. So be prepared to take good time.

(4) Patience

'Be patient and stand firm' (James 5:8). John Sherrill once wrote, 'For months we'd been meeting to discuss the basic question of the nuclear age. Ideas came slowly but I always

left the table with the feeling that we had not yet got to grips with the subject.'

(5) Listening

Wisdom always stops to listen to both sides. Consider a Christian hero, C. T. Studd, one of England's cricketing captains turned pioneer missionary. His missionary son-in-law, Alfred Buxton, came from peace-loving Quaker stock. Studd's daughter overhead Alfred once in dialogue with her father when the discussion terminated rather abruptly with the words, 'All very well for you, Alfred, but I can't afford to see the other side!' Even great missionaries can have their blind spots! Christians could be, and should be, the ideal people to be impartial in those situations where peace is called for.[6] Listening is vital. If either of the aggrieved parties should feel that he has not been properly heard, he will sense the peacemaker is not being fair, and may still find it hard to be reconciled on any basis being proposed. On the other hand, the mere fact that one has been fully heard is a healing factor in itself and often the speaker will see his own failures better as he talks it all over in the open.

(6) Diplomacy and Tact

'Let your conversation be always full of grace' (Colossians 4:6). One simply cannot be *too* diplomatic. One certainly must avoid being blunt. The manner and motive of the drill

---

[6] Edith Buxton, *Reluctant Missionary* (Lutterworth Press, 1968), p.60. This is written not to denigrate her father, whom she so greatly loved and admired, but just to reveal him as she reveals herself so intriguingly 'warts and all'.

sergeant is no model for a Christian who wants to build people up constructively and teach others how to cope with conflicting issues in a suitably Christian way. Remember,

> *A gentle answer turns away wrath,*
> *but a harsh word stirs up anger.*
> *The tongue of the wise commends knowledge,*
> *but the mouth of the fool gushes folly.*
> *(Proverbs 15:1–2)*

Problems usually need to be approached obliquely, as I found when working in South America. I discovered I needed to use subjunctives (the form of a verb used to express what is prayed, imagined, wished, or possible), saying 'it may be', or 'it might be', and leading by questions rather than directions. Be deferential and seek confirmation from each party when offering a point as a basis to work on. Smiles and humour often help to break the tensions and relax people, so long as neither side feels a joke is being used to get at them in particular. Think twice before speaking so that well-meaning words cannot be misinterpreted.

Pouring Oil on Troubled Waters

To sum up, peacemaking involves:

- Facing reality; seeking a fair and feasible resolution.
- Being constructive, not destructive.
- Sharing in God's mission of bringing wholeness (*shalom*) to the world.
- Respecting all parties.

Peacemaking is a divine work. Peacemaking means

reconciliation, and God is the author of peace and reconciliation. Keep praying!

WHAT SHOULD WE DO WHEN WE FEEL WE HAVE OFFENDED SOMEONE?

> *So if you are offering your gift at the altar, and there remember that your brother has something against you, leave your gift there in front of the altar. First go and be reconciled to your brother; then come and offer your gift. Settle matters quickly with your adversary who is taking you to court. Do it while you are still with him on the way, or he may hand you over to the judge, and the judge my hand you over to the officer, and you may be thrown into prison. (Matthew 5:23)*

As you become aware through reflection, prayer and hearsay that you have offended your brother, there are ten normal responses:

(1) Humble yourself quickly and determine to put things right. Delay can only worsen the situation and can harden an offended heart. *'Settle matters quickly' (Matthew 5:25).*

(2) Confess what you have done to God.

(3) Ask God for forgiveness. *'If we confess our sins, he is faithful and just and will forgive us our sins' (1 John 1:9).*

(4) Show your true repentance by making every effort to put things right.

(5) Ask the Lord to give you both the grace needed to fulfil your resolve satisfactorily. *'So that we may receive mercy and find grace to help us in our time of need' (Hebrews 4:16).*

(6) Go and speak face to face with the offended person if possible. Phone or write otherwise. Say what you have

to say with all the grace you can muster. *'Let your conversation always be full of grace' (Colossians 4:6).*

(7) As you greet the person it usually helps to take with you a small peace-offering. In your heart be praying, *'Peace be to this house' (Matthew 10:12 KJV).*

(8) Then confess your fault clearly. *'Confess your sins to each other and pray for each other' (James 5:16).* It's not enough to say 'I am sorry if I have done anything . . .' as it gives the impression you are not sure of what you have done wrong. This tends to aggravate the situation.

(9) Ask the person humbly if you may be forgiven for what you have said or done.

(10) Kiss (if appropriate) and make up. It could be good to make an arrangement to meet again socially as soon as possible.

WHAT SHOULD WE DO WHEN WE FEEL OFFENDED OURSELVES?

There are six possible human responses to an offence.[9]

(1) Overlook the offence. *'A man's wisdom gives him patience; it is to his glory to overlook an offence'(Proverbs 19:11).* See also *Proverbs 12:16; 17:14; Colossians 3:13; 1 Peter 4:8.* In Acts Paul said, *'God overlooked such ignorance' (Acts 17:30).*

(2) Seek reconciliation. This may be done through confession, loving correction and forgiveness. *'[If] your brother has something against you . . . go and be reconciled' (Matthew*

---

[9] See Sande, *The Peacemaker,* for the most thorough and helpful book on peacemaking that I have ever come across.

5:23–24). Paul wrote to the Colossians, *'Forgive as the Lord forgave you' (Colossians 3:13b).*

(3) Enter into negotiation. *'Each of you should look not only to your own interests, but also to the interests of others' (Philippians 2:4).*

(4) Find mediators. *'If he will not listen, take one or two others along' (Matthew 18:16).*

(5) Use arbitration. *'Is it possible that there is nobody among you wise enough to judge a dispute between believers?' (1 Corinthians 6:5).*

(6) Appeal to your church. *'If he refuses to listen . . . tell it to the church' (Matthew 18:17).* Direct church involvement is often viewed negatively among Christians today, but when it is done the 'Jesus way' – lovingly, redemptively and restoratively – it can be the key to healing rifts, saving relationships and bringing about justice and peace.

AIM AT CLARIFICATION

John Maxwell gives some very practical help in this area. He suggests using the term *clarification* in place of *confrontation* as a better approach all round.[10]

Steps towards Clarification

I find his 'commandments for clarification' very helpful, although I have adapted and abbreviated most of them as follows:

(1) Clarify personally and privately – not publicly.
(2) Clarify quickly (if possible).

---

[10] John Maxwell, *Developing the Leadership Within You* (Thomas Nelson, 1993).

(3) Clarify initially with thoughtful compliments and thankful appreciation of helpful services and personal sacrifices given hitherto (cf. *Proverbs 16:24*).

(4) Clarify by dealing with one issue at a time. Avoid harping back to that issue once the next point for clarification has been raised.

(5) Clarify only in cases of behaviour or situations where the person being confronted could be expected to change.

(6) Clarify without the use of sarcasm or exaggeration. Avoid such words as *never* and *always*. The person being confronted will immediately think of exceptions to any such charge, and it will put him or her on the defensive.

(7) Clarify, if possible, by presenting criticism as a positive suggestion, or present a problem and ask the person to think of some constructive way it might be resolved.

(8) Clarify without apologising, as that may distract from the seriousness of the problem being confronted. It could leave the person confronted with the impression that the leader is not really sure what he or she is about.

Plan Your Meeting

Prepare Your Attitude

Pray for wisdom and grace. You need to remember that people inherently want to do a good job – your aim is to encourage them with that attitude.

Richard Brown of Dallas says, 'I always apply a mental test before I go into these situations. I ask myself, "If I was on the receiving end of this message, would I think it was a fair thing to say to me?"'

Prepare Your Mind

Make a mental checklist:

- Identify the real issues involved, and avoid side issues.
- Be sure you are dealing with facts, and not guesses or hearsay.
- Determine how you will end if things turn out well, or if matters cannot be resolved.
- Following the advice above, make the initial meeting private – between you and the person involved.
- If this is unsuccessful, arrange for someone to accompany you the next time.
- If this is still unfruitful, then the person may need to be removed from the post if you are his leader. Find out first how you stand with the law about this. It may be possible to find a face-saving sideways move – assuming the mismanagement was in no way criminal.

> If we could only read the secret history of our enemies, we would find in each man's life sorrow and suffering enough to disarm all hostility. (Henry Wordsworth Longfellow)

> Seek first to understand, then to be understood. (Steven Covey)

FINDING THE PEACEMAKERS

Every church and every community needs plenty of peacemakers, and such people are there, if we know what we are looking for. We must seek out and learn to spot the peacemakers in the church and bless them. Paul challenges the Corinthian church to do this: *'Is it possible that there is nobody among you wise enough to judge a dispute between believers?' (1 Corinthians 6:5).*

Pray that God will anoint such peacemakers in your organisation, congregation or neighbourhood, while encouraging and involving those who clearly have that calling and anointing already – those with a gift from God for this Christ-like ministry. They are an invaluable element within any social group.

Discerning the Spirit of God in Potential Peacemakers

Sometimes, in praying over a man or a woman, I have sensed what I believed to be the leading of God to ask that person what they were experiencing at that moment. Quite often they would respond by saying they simply felt a very deep sense of peace. I would then ask if they had ever consciously attempted to be peacemakers in the church, their workplace or their neighbourhood. Quite often they would answer that they had in fact done so, or had a deep desire to do so. When that was the case, I would confirm this anointing with a prayer 'that peace would be multiplied to them' and then would openly bless and encourage the person actively to *'seek peace and pursue it' (1 Peter 3:11)*, making *'every effort to do what leads to peace' (Romans 14:19)*. I would explain also that it is not just a nice thought to bring peace in the name of Jesus, but a mandate from the Lord.

Happy are those who create right relationships between person and person, and blessed are they who know how to reconcile people with God – for they are doing God's work.

HOW PEACE CAN BE MADE

Be Humble

Two church members had quarrelled over an old line fence, and they had not spoken to each other for a long time. One of them, wanting to make peace, took his Bible and went to visit his neighbour. Handing his Bible to his 'old enemy', he said, 'John, you read, and I'll pray. We must be friends.'

But John, fumbling for his glasses, said, 'But I can't read. I haven't my spectacles.'

'Take mine,' said his neighbour.

After they had read the word and prayed together, they arose and embraced each other. John handed back the spectacles to his neighbour and said through his tears, 'Jim, that old line fence looks different through your glasses.'

As Billy Graham once said, when we have peace with God, we can see things through 'the other man's glasses' and do what we can to make peace.

Be Sensitive

I once had to remove someone from a role he had held in the church for five years. He was an older, faithful Christian, and he loved the challenge of what he was doing and put a lot into it. But it was quite obvious to me and to others that the time had come for a change, for reasons that are not necessary to mention here. I went to see him and, having first told him how I had appreciated his dedication to the task over the years, I then concluded by saying it was nevertheless time to begin thinking about a replacement for him, and I asked him to help me by keeping a lookout for a possible successor in the church, as, of course, I would too.

I advised him that I was hoping to make the change before the year was out. (I actually had a very suitable person in mind who could have taken over the role there and then, but by the end of the next year he was already getting involved in another ministry.) In fact it took me two years before, at last, I could find a suitable solution. When the time eventually came for the hand-over, the man was very upset and left me in high dudgeon. I was sorry that soon after he and his wife moved far away.

Three or four years later I was surprised and delighted to receive a note from him saying that he had seen I was booked to be speaking in his area, and he invited me to call in for lunch on the way. I was warmly welcomed. Not a word about the upset was mentioned. Clearly they had no wish to harp back to the old issue again. I felt they were making the best effort they could to patch things up, and I felt it right to accept it in the same wordless way. I am sure they were as grateful to God as I was to feel that we were truly reconciled once more. It might not have been quite the prescribed way one would expect as a mode of reconciliation, but I felt that their loving gesture came from the heart, and that was enough for me.

An Unexpected Gesture

Rich Nathan tells one of his favourite stories of peacemaking. The South African rugby team was playing in a World Cup tournament against New Zealand. The game was hosted in South Africa, which had been going through a very painful time of liberation from racial segregation. But the last rallying point of white racism was represented by the South African rugby team, which was totally white.

Nelson Mandela decided to lead a march of black South Africans to the stadium, which was filled completely with white fans on the first day of the World Cup tournament. The city of Johannesburg was on edge, because they thought a riot might ensue, but when Mandela got to the stadium he did something very unexpected. He did not make a speech on the steps of the stadium; he did not stand up before the television cameras and denounce the injustice represented by this game; nor did he threaten the remaining powers of the white regime as he led his black followers into the stadium. Instead he donned a white rugby team shirt and hat which he pulled out of his bag. Then he led his black marchers in a cheer for the white rugby team. This moved some of the white supporters to tears – they were receiving something they knew they did not deserve – and in response they joined in a cheer for Mandela and a cheer for their white South African team. Then they sang the national anthem and the black and white South Africans danced together. What a wonderful example of peacemaking – something radical and unexpected had a huge effect.

When Nelson Mandela became the first president of the new multicoloured 'Rainbow' nation of South Africa, he recognised that the future peace of his country would depend on forgiveness and reconciliation. He had spent well over 20 years in captivity as a political prisoner – 18 of them on Robben Island off the Cape. But he went more than 'the second mile' to conciliate his ex-enemies, visiting ex-president Botha, and inviting the former prison commander of Robben Island to a meal at his home.

Be Careful Not to Abuse the Ministry

Being a peacemaker does not mean going around deliberately looking for broken relationships to see if they need your ministry. Those who do that may soon be considered troublemakers rather than peacemakers.

Peacemaking or the Enactment of Revenge

The opposite of peacemaking is the avoidance of a divine duty, or simply a holding on to a grudge or a secret urge to get revenge.

PROMISED REWARD

CONSEQUENCES FOR PEACEMAKERS

> Wonderful news for the peacemakers! You'll be called God's children.[11]

> . . .they will be called sons of God. (Matthew 5:9)

> By peacemaking we share in God's nature – when we are making peace we are so like Him.[12]

As we enter by new birth into the kingdom of God we begin to enjoy the fruits of peace immediately, and we continue seeking to live in that peace – sharing it with others by our prayers for them and through our attitudes, words and deeds. The Anglican blessing, based on Philippians 4:7, says, 'Now may the peace of God, which passes all understanding,

---

[11] Bishop Tom Wright's paraphrase.

[12] Robert Warren and Sue Mayfield, *Life Attitudes* (Church House Publishing, 2004).

keep your hearts and minds in the knowledge and love of God.'

We shall be called sons, or children, of God. It will be in our nature, like God, to make peace. Ultimately we shall enter fully into God's peace. The Son of God himself, the 'Prince of Peace', made peace *through his blood, shed on the cross' (Colossians 1:20)*. Now *'he himself is our peace' (Ephesians 2:14)*, and so he shall be eternally. The *'God of peace'* will have sanctified us *'through and through' (1 Thessalonians 5:23a)*. We will be for ever under the reign of *'peace . . . from God the Father and the Lord Jesus Christ' (2 Thessalonians 1:2)*.

WHOEVER WOULD CALL US 'CHILDREN OF GOD'?

This is really a story about mercy, but the way such ministry is seen may apply equally to making peace.

One icy evening in New York, a little boy aged about six or seven was standing outside a large store. He had no shoes and his clothes were in rags. A young woman was passing by and saw him there shivering in the cold. Her heart was touched. She took his hand and led him into the store, where he stood meekly beside her as she bought him new shoes and fixed him up with a set of warm clothes. When they got outside again, she explained that she had to leave him now and told him to go home.

As they were parting the little boy looked up with a puzzled expression: ''Scuse me asking, ma'am, but are you God?'

'No,' she replied, smiling, 'I'm just one of his children.'

'I knew you had to be some sort of a relation!' he muttered, as he turned to go.

MEDITATION

The only safe and sure way to destroy your enemies is to make them your friends.

* * *

What causes fights and quarrels among you? Don't they come from your desires that battle within you? (James 4:1)

* * *

Lord, create in me a love for peace:
not peace that is the absence of struggle,
nor peace that is blind to injustice,
but peace that makes whole what is now broken.

(From *Further Everyday Prayers*)

* * *

Deep peace of the running wave to you,
Deep peace of the flowing air to you,
Deep peace of the quiet earth to you,
Deep peace of the shining stars to you,
Deep peace of the Son of Peace to you.[13]

* * *

Lord, make me an instrument of your peace.
Where there is hatred, let me sow love.
Where there is injury, pardon.
Where there is doubt, faith.
Where there is despair, hope.
Where there is darkness, light.
Where there is sadness, joy.

---

[13] Alan Wilkinson and Christopher Cocksworth, *An Anglican Companion* (CHP/SPCK, 1996), p. 33.

O Divine Master,
grant that I may not so much seek to be consoled, as to console,
not so much to be understood, as to understand,
not so much to be loved, as to love;
for it is in giving that we receive,
it is in pardoning that we are pardoned,
it is in dying that we awake to eternal life.[14]

---

[14] A prayer often associated with St Francis of Assisi.

8

Dying to Live

Blessed are those who are persecuted because of righteousness,
for theirs is the kingdom of heaven.
(Matthew 5:10)

The Lord is righteous.
(Psalm 11:7)

* * *

Lead me, O Lord, in your righteousness.
(Psalm 5:8)

* * *

He guides me in paths of righteousness
for his name's sake.
(Psalm 23:3)

* * *

May your priests be clothed with righteousness.
(Psalm 132:9)

* * *

Seek first his kingdom and his righteousness.
(Matthew 6:33)

* * *

I will show him [Paul] how much he must suffer for my name.
(Acts 9:16)

INTRODUCTION

This is a chapter that I did not look forward to writing. My heart was echoing the words of some disciples (after Jesus spoke to them about 'eating his flesh'): *'This is a hard teaching. Who can accept it?' (John 6:60).* I thought that I was going to have to end this book on a rather depressing note, but the more I have read and thought about it, the more I have sensed myself standing on holy ground. It has been both a challenging and an exhilarating exercise.

When we think of persecution, the mind almost instantly leaps to martyrdom. But of course not all persecution gets that far. It may amount simply to bullying. A recent survey of urban children (9–10 years) and of teenagers (13–15 years) carried out by the University of Wales reveals that those holding a religious conviction are much more likely to be bullied. Nearly 33 per cent of the Christians and 34 per cent of the Muslims feared being persecuted for their faith.

Persecution may take forms other than physical attack, such as hostile opposition, intimidation, slander or ostracism. There are many situations where families or friends have felt threatened by the possibility of one of their number breaking rank and becoming a Christian. There are also numerous cases where Christians speak out when something is wrong, and as a result find life very uncomfortable – even within their own families. We do not overlook the fact that 'it was the cleansing of the Temple which for Jesus led – within a few days – to Calvary'.[1]

---

[1] Mark Stibbe, *Revival* (Monarch, 1998), p. 81. See Luke 20:45–48 and Luke 23:1–49 and John, who places it at the beginning of his gospel (John 2:12–17).

THE RISKS OF RIGHTEOUSNESS

There are real risks for those who stand up for true righteousness whatever the opposition may be. Their faithfulness in this way might cause them any of the difficulties outlined below.

(1) LOSS OF LIVELIHOOD

I once preached on this subject in St Andrew's Church, Chorleywood, and the next week two of our members independently lost their jobs for making a stand for righteousness. One was an accountant who refused to sign a false document at his place of work, and the other was a nurse who objected to some unethical practice in the hospital where she worked.

(2) OSTRACISM

One can sense the fear of becoming social outcasts from the reply given by the parents of the man born blind whom Jesus had healed. The Pharisees questioned the parents, *'Is this your son? . . . Is this the one you say was born blind? How is it that now he can see?'* The parents replied,

> *'We know he is our son . . . and we know he was born blind. But how he can see now, or who opened his eyes, we don't know. Ask him. He is of age; he will speak for himself.' His parents said this because they were afraid of the Jews, for already the Jews had decided that anyone who acknowledged that Jesus was the Christ would be put out of the synagogue. (John 9:19–22)*

Seyran Ates, a Turkish Kurd who moved to Germany when she was six, had become a prominent Berlin lawyer who had repeatedly spoken out against forced marriages and honour killings. But she finally had to close her practice after receiving death threats from the families of many Turkish and Kurdish women whom she had represented in court over the last 20 years. She claims the police had refused to protect her despite threats against her life, including a shooting incident in which a colleague was killed and she was seriously injured.[2]

When Sherron Watkins, a vice president of Enron in the USA, finally felt conscience-bound to blow the whistle on the company – about the biggest and most successful business in the world – it threatened the future of the whole corporation. This certainly did not make her popular in the eyes of some of the corporation's 20,000 workers and their families, when so many of their jobs were threatened.

(3) BETRAYAL

By Their Families

Jesus pointed out that there would inevitably be such betrayals in times of persecution *(Matthew 10:21–33)*. He said:

> From now on there will be five in one family divided against each other, three against two and two against three. They will be divided, father against son and son against father, mother against daughter and daughter against mother, mother-in-law against daughter-in-law and daughter-in-law against mother-in-law. (Luke 12:52–53)

This was part of the tragedy in communist Russia, where children at school were encouraged to denounce their parents.

---

[2] Kate Connolly in *The Daily Telegraph*, 6th September 2006, p.16.

By Close Friends

This was the case with Jesus after he and his disciples had just shared the Passover together, and then had gone over to the Garden of Gethsemane to pray:

> *Judas, one of the Twelve, arrived. With him was a large crowd armed with swords and clubs, sent from the chief priests and the elders of the people. Now the betrayer had arranged a signal with them: 'The one I kiss is the man; arrest him.' Going at once to Jesus, Judas said, 'Greetings, Rabbi!' and kissed him.*
>
> *Jesus replied, 'Friend, do what you came for.'*
>
> *Then the men stepped forward, seized Jesus and arrested him.* (Matthew 26:47–50)

Scripture was being fulfilled.

> *Even my close friend, whom I trusted,*
> *he who shared my bread,*
> *has lifted up his heel against me.*
> (Psalm 41:9)

Or to drive the point home with a paraphrased version of another psalm (52:12–13):

> *If it were some enemy taunting me, I could have coped with it.*
> *If it were a rival taking the Mick, I could have just steered clear.*
> *But it was you, my great mate, my bosom buddy, my closest pal.*[3]

(4) PUNISHMENT FOR CONSCIENTIOUS OBJECTION

Many people in the past have been persecuted for being pacifists or conscientious objectors in times of war when it came to military service, or (in New Testament times) for

---

[3] Walter Brueggemann, *The Message of the Psalms* (Augsburg, 1984).

objecting to the paying of homage through some token sacrifice to 'Caesar as Lord'.

All sorts of difficult situations may occur when a state develops a persecuting paranoia.[4] Early Christians were frequently falsely accused of cannibalism and incendiarism. Paul could say, *'Rulers hold no terror for those who do right, but for those who do wrong' (Romans 13:3)*. True! They like their subjects to be honest, law abiding and hard working – but they do not like them when they refuse to deny their faith in God *(Daniel 3:4–22)*, or when they disobey a command which is immoral or plainly wrong. They become even less popular when and if their ruler does something unjust or unrighteous and they protest. John the Baptist was imprisoned for rebuking King Herod for living with *'his brother's wife, and all the other evil things he had done' (Luke 3:19)*.

Sometimes mere suspicion is enough to provoke a hostile response from those in authority. John Bunyan, a travelling tinker, was converted to Christ and became a Baptist preacher, speaking wherever he could. 'He seemed to the jittery authorities in Bedfordshire to be supplying the ideological back-up for the reinstatement of republicanism.'[5] Although he was not inciting any such thing, his preaching was regarded as fanning discontent against the restored regime of Charles II (notoriously corrupt) and the Church of England (notoriously compromised). He was warned in

---

[4] Readers are referred to Danyun's book, translated by Brother Dennis, *Lilies amongst Thorns* (Sovereign World, 1991). This reveals the frantically cruel methods of the state, even in our own times, to eradicate the house church movement in China.

[5] Christopher Hill, *John Bunyan and His Church* (OUP, 1989), p. 106.

1658 and imprisoned two years later, remaining in Bedford
jail for two periods covering a total of twelve years.

A WARNING

In spite of all Peter's encouragement to those who suffer for
the name of Christ, however, he still has to warn Christians
against developing a persecution complex. He reminds
them that not all suffering is the result of faithful service to
Christ. Some have certainly suffered persecution for righteousness' sake, but others have suffered for their own
ineptness and wrongdoing – even for meddling in other
people's affairs *(1 Peter 4:12–19)*.

SUFFERING IS A MYSTERY

This may seem to be a slight digression from the topic of
persecution, but persecution can certainly be, and usually
is, an acute form of suffering, even if not the only form. And
it raises the same question, 'Why?' Suffering is one of the
most profound dilemmas facing humankind in every generation in every society.

The story of Job, perhaps the oldest book in the Bible, is
built around the theme of his suffering. Job, like so many
people in life, is all along convinced that he has done nothing to deserve the suffering he has had to endure. Although
he cannot understand why he is going through such an
ordeal, he will not challenge God's right to let him suffer.
His friends think he must be wrong in saying he has done
nothing to deserve it and they mistakenly try to argue him
out of his stubborn conviction.

But there is a revealing 'behind the scenes' conversation

between God and Satan in the book. Thus we overhear the devil telling God that Job only serves him for what he can get out of it. God then allows Satan to test Job on those grounds: he may destroy Job's cattle, his crops and his family – all except his life. This will prove that Job is faithful. And the Lord says to Satan, *'Very well, then, everything he has is in your hands, but on the man himself do not lay a finger' (Job 1:12)*. In spite of the awful subsequent suffering, Job still maintains his integrity and trust in God. Then Satan says to the Lord, *'Skin for skin! . . . A man will give all he has for his own life. But stretch out your hand and strike his flesh and bones, and he will surely curse you to your face' (Job 2:4)*. Satan is then allowed to afflict Job with loathsome sores over the whole of his body. Even his wife, who has obviously lost her patience with God, says to him, *'Are you still holding on to your integrity? Curse God and die!' (Job 2:9)*. But Job endures it all patiently.

The book ends by demonstrating that they were all wrong; that we simply cannot presume to know the 'whys' of God. That part ever remains hidden in the mind of God – that is the mystery. Moses learned and taught very early on that *'The secret things belong to the Lord our God, but the things revealed belong to us and to our children for ever' (Deuteronomy 29:29)*. There are some things we will never be able to understand this side of glory.

Again, Jesus assured his faithful disciples of a place at his table in the coming kingdom, but then he warns them, *'Simon, Simon, Satan has asked to sift you [all] as wheat. But I have prayed for you, Simon, that your faith may not fail. And when you have turned back, strengthen your brothers' (Luke 22:31)*. We need to remind ourselves constantly that God will always be God. We can never fully understand the mystery of his thoughts and ways:

> 'For my thoughts are not your thoughts,
>   neither are your ways my ways,'
>   declares the Lord.
> (Isaiah 55:8)

If God allows us to go through suffering or persecution, so be it. His own Son endured the same processes.

Scripture tells us how much Jesus suffered on our behalf. It also tells us that Jesus, the author of our salvation, who was made to be sin for us though he actually knew no sin, had no sin and did no sin, was also made *'perfect [mature] through suffering' (Hebrews 2:10)*. And again, *'Although he was a son, he learned obedience from what he suffered' (Hebrews 5:8)*. There are certain virtues that can only be acquired through suffering.

THE POSITIVE SIDE

So we see there is a positive side to suffering. As gold needs purging through the hot flames of the furnace, and vines need pruning by the sharp knife of the vine-dresser, so Christians need suffering for their perfecting in maturity – in purity, in integrity and in fruitfulness *(John 15:1–2)*. Os Guinness sees suffering as something that can forge deeper character and arouse stronger compassion.

I remember, as a young man, reading the published diary of one of saintly Bishop Handley Moule's daughters. This 16-year-old bedridden girl was dying of tuberculosis. She wrote that she was trying to learn not to waste her suffering! I was staggered. This was a new insight for me. Such maturity was way ahead of her years – and certainly ahead of mine.

Suffering also enables God to get our attention, which is why C. S. Lewis called it 'God's megaphone'.

Alexander Solzhenitsyn, shut up for years in a Siberian gulag, admitted that 'it was only as I lay there on rotting straw that I sensed within myself the first stirrings of good'. He discovered truth there, deeper and more liberating.[6]

James wrote in his New Testament letter to Jews scattered abroad by persecutions:

> Consider it pure joy, my brothers, whenever you face trials of many kinds, because you know that the testing of your faith develops perseverance. Perseverance must finish its work so that you may be mature and complete. (James 1:2–3)

Brother Yun, when he was the young leader of a growing house church movement in northern China and once again put under excruciating torture by his Chinese prison guards, believed he was learning a fundamental lesson in those most extreme circumstances:

> In my proud heart I had been thinking that I was important to the Church, and that they needed me to lead them. Now I vividly understood that He is God and I am but a feeble man. I realised that God did not need me at all, and that if He ever chose to use me again it would be nothing more than a great privilege.[7]

WHEN PERSECUTION BEGINS TO RAGE

Persecution has been part of the armoury of bullies and tyrants since the beginning of time. It was manifested with

---

[6] Alexander Solzhenitsyn, *The Gulag Archipelago* (Harper and Row, 1978).

[7] Brother Yun, *The Heavenly Man* (Monarch, 2002).

the treatment of Christ himself, who was mocked and beaten and finally cruelly crucified. Great persecution arose after Pentecost against the church in Jerusalem, and they were all scattered about the region of Judea and Samaria *(Acts 8:1)*. Stephen, one of the earliest deacons, exercised a ministry of great power in Jerusalem. He was the first martyr *(cf. Acts 7)*.

When they heard this [Stephen's preaching] . . . they all rushed at him, dragged him out of the city and began to stone him. Meanwhile, the witnesses laid their clothes at the feet of a young man named Saul. (Acts 7:54–58)

This was Saul of Tarsus, who was laying waste the church, entering house after house, dragging off men and women and committing them to prison. Nevertheless, the church's witness under persecution and brave continuation in faithful preaching only increased. And the number of disciples grew.

Revival broke out in Samaria under Philip's ministry as he preached the good news about the kingdom of God there in the name of Jesus. In a futile effort to stop the spread of the gospel, Saul continued breathing out his *'murderous threats against the Lord's disciples'* and even went to the high priest asking *'for letters to the synagogues in Damascus, so that if he found any there who belonged to the Way . . . he might take them as prisoners to Jerusalem' (Acts 9:1–2)*.

It was while he was engaged in this very mission that Saul himself met the risen Christ, was converted, took the name of Paul, and became the great apostle for Christ to the Gentiles. In turn he fared no better at the hands of the authorities. He was not spared the kind of persecution being meted out to the other disciples – indeed, he often suffered worse. He described his imprisonments, with countless beatings, being *'exposed to death again and again. Five times I received from the Jews the forty lashes minus one. Three times I was beaten with rods, once I was stoned. . .' (2 Corinthians 11:23–25).* The way ahead was clear: *'We must go through many hardships to enter the kingdom of God' (Acts 14:22).* Paul also asserted, *'I consider that our present sufferings are not worth comparing with the glory that will be revealed in us' (Romans 8:18).* At the end of the same chapter Paul writes,

> *Who shall separate us from the love of Christ? Shall trouble or hardship or persecution or famine or nakedness or danger or sword? As it is written:*
>> *'For your sake we face death all day long;*
>> *we are considered as sheep to be slaughtered.'*
> *No, in all these things we are more than conquerors through him who loved us. For I am convinced that neither death nor life, neither angels nor demons, neither the present nor the future, nor any powers, neither height nor depth, nor anything else in all creation, will be able to separate us from the love of God that is in Christ Jesus our Lord. (Romans 8:35–39)*

Again Paul wrote with such confidence:

> *We are hard pressed on every side, but not crushed; perplexed, but not in despair; persecuted, but not abandoned; struck down, but not destroyed. We always carry around in our body the death of Jesus, so that the life of Jesus may also be revealed in our body. For we who are alive are always being given over to death for Jesus' sake, so that his life may be revealed in our mortal body . . . Therefore we do not lose heart . . . For our light and momentary troubles are achieving for us*

an eternal glory that far outweighs them all. *(2 Corinthians 4:7–11, 16–18)*

Paul unites the twin realities, the present suffering – which he now almost takes for granted – and the future glory. He reckons that our present suffering is just not worth comparing with the glory to be revealed. Suffering and glory are in completely different categories in Paul's book. Suffering is insignificant when placed alongside glory. He is not being insensitive about the human pain of persecution and other forms of suffering, as we know from his own experience of it.

The passage in 2 Corinthians compares the relative momentary affliction with the massive weight of eternal glory (fellowship with Christ that stretches into an endless future). My old tutor, Dr P. E. Hughes, understood Paul to be saying that suffering and persecution are literally 'weightless trifles' – but only when put on the scales alongside the *'eternal glory that far outweighs them all'* *(2 Corinthians 4:17).*

Paul could boast that he had been granted to suffer for the name of his Master: *'I bear on my body the marks of Jesus'* *(Galatians 6:17).* He shared his personal prayer and ambition with the Philippian believers, *'I want to know Christ and the power of his resurrection and the fellowship of sharing in his sufferings, becoming like him in his death'* *(Philippians 3:10).* Indeed Paul boasted of his church plants which endured suffering faithfully: *'Therefore, among God's churches we boast about your perseverance and faith in all the persecutions and trials you are enduring'* *(2 Thessalonians 1:4).*

We do not know exactly how and where Paul died, but we do know that Peter finally yielded up his life as a martyr. Indeed, tradition has it that sooner or later most of the other apostles found themselves martyred for their faith too. An exception was John the Beloved, who was persecuted and exiled to the island of Patmos, but as the story goes only escaped being cast into a cauldron of boiling oil in Rome by a miracle. He went on to Ephesus to fulfil the final commission of Jesus to look after his mother Mary, where, one tradition says, Mary eventually died.

WAVES OF PERSECUTION

Ten waves of persecution followed under the Roman emperors from AD 67 to 312. But all the while the church kept growing, and the Christian faith was taking firmer root. Tertullian once aptly observed, 'The blood of the martyrs is the seed of the church.' Many of the early church fathers also died as martyrs – the best known being the aged Polycarp, Bishop of Smyrna. He was told to sacrifice to Caesar or die, but boldly replied, 'Eighty and six years have I served Christ and he has done me no wrong. How can I blaspheme my King who saved me?' St Chrysostom, a prince of preachers, was also arrested for his faithfulness. While awaiting trial he said,

> What can I fear? Will it be death? But you know that Christ is my life and all that I shall gain by death. Will it be exile? But the earth is the Lord's. Will it be loss of wealth? But we brought nothing into the world, and can carry nothing out. Thus all the terrors of the world are contemptible in my eyes.

In the end he was exiled.

Tacitus, a Roman historian, writing of the early Christian martyrs, said,

Mockery of every sort was added to their deaths. Covered with the skins of beasts, they were torn by dogs and perished, or were nailed to crosses, or were doomed to the flames and burnt, to serve nightly illumination, when daylight had expired. Nero offered his gardens for the spectacle.

We are told that the martyrs went rejoicing to their deaths, as if they were going to a marriage feast. They bathed their hands in the blaze kindled for them, and shouted with gladness. One historian, witnessing their heroism, wrote, 'When the day of victory dawned, the Christians marched in procession from the prison to the arena as if they were marching to heaven, with joyous countenances, agitated by gladness rather than fear.'

When Ignatius was about to die for his faith in AD 110 he cried out, 'Nearer the sword, then nearer to God; in company with wild beasts, in company with God.' The biblical writer to the Hebrews had already reported what the secular historians were still observing:

> Others were tortured . . . Some faced jeers and flogging while still others were chained and put in prison. They were stoned; they were sawn in two; they were put to death by the sword. They went about in sheepskins and goatskins, destitute, persecuted and ill-treated – the world was not worthy of them. They wandered in deserts and mountains, and in caves and holes in the ground. (Hebrews 11:36–38)

Writing to his friend Donatus, St Cyprian, Bishop of Carthage, who was himself to suffer persecution and died in AD 258, comments:

> This seems a cheerful world, Donatus, when I view it from this fair garden . . . But if I climbed some great mountains and looked out . . . I would see brigands on the high road, pirates

on the seas, and in the amphitheatres men murdered to please applauding crowds . . . Yet in the midst of it I have found a quiet and holy people . . . they are despised and persecuted, but they care not. They have overcome the world. These people, Donatus, are Christians.

PERSECUTION IN BRITAIN

Bible Translators

In England we have two famous Bible translators who gave their lives for the cause of Christ. They were John Wycliffe, 'the Morning Star of the Reformation', and William Tyndale. Although the former died quietly in the parish of Lutterworth, his bones were later disinterred (in 1428) and, under orders from the Bishop of Lincoln, redressed in clerical garb so that he could then be publicly defrocked, and burned to ashes. The ashes were then scattered into the flowing water of the River Swift. I remind myself of it every time I travel up the M1, which bridges this river on the way to Nottingham.

A hundred years later (in 1536) Tyndale, as a refugee from the powers-that-be in England, was arrested in Antwerp. He had once said, 'I defy the pope and all his laws. If God spares me I will cause, ere many years, the boy that drives the plough to know more of the Scriptures than you do!' Tyndale's Bibles were printed and smuggled back to England, disguised as bales of wool. The Bishop of London, in order to show his disapproval, bought all the copies of the first edition and had them burned in public. With the bishop's money Tyndale succeeded in getting an improved second edition published and circulated back in England.

But then he was betrayed and burned to death in the square of Vilvoorde in Holland. His last prayer before he died was, 'Lord! Open the King of England's eyes!' Such were the men who prepared England for the Reformation spreading from Europe. There was still plenty of opposition to be faced by the faithful, as would be expected.

Leading Reformers in England

Leading Reformers included Bishop Latimer (along with Thomas Bilney, who led Latimer to Christ through his confession about what he had discovered while reading the New Testament). The elderly Latimer was joined by Nicholas Ridley, another Bishop of London, who, unlike his predecessors, supported the English Reformation. He was put under house arrest in the home of Mr and Mrs Irish, both of whom were won over by the Christlike example of his life. They became very saddened when they learned he had been sentenced to death. Ridley commented to Mrs Irish on his last morning that 'though my breakfast will be somewhat sharp my supper will be more pleasant and sweet'.

Bishop Latimer, being fastened to the other side of the stake to which Ridley was bound, was heard to call out as the burning faggots were laid at their feet: 'Be of good cheer Master Ridley, and play the man: we shall this day light such a candle, by God's grace, in England, as I trust shall never be put out!'

At the same time Archbishop Cranmer, who had at first recanted his reformed faith but then had reneged on his recantation, was also sentenced to death by burning at the stake. When the faggots were lit, he famously volunteered the hand which had signed the original recantation to be the first part of his body to be burned, while he remained bound to the stake in the midst of the mounting flames.

These deaths were terrible ordeals, and it took an agonisingly long time before their lives were finally terminated in the fires. The extent of the influence of these men in the promotion of the Protestant Reformation in England was immeasurable, and has been widely acclaimed in history.

During their ascendancy to positions of power the new Archbishop Cranmer had interceded for Catholics such as Thomas More, and also Archbishop Fisher, Anne Boleyn and Thomas Cromwell, who had all fallen from royal favour, but King Henry VIII remained adamant and had them all put to death. Then, when the Catholic Queen Mary ascended the throne, it was the turn of the Protestants to suffer again.

PERSECUTION CONTINUES

Those who follow the faith and example of the early church should not be surprised when they encounter persecution today. We, the servants, are not greater than our Master *(Matthew 10:29)*.

Dietrich Bonhoeffer seems never to have wavered in his Christian antagonism to the Nazi regime (he was even accused of involvement in a plot to rid the world of Hitler) – although it meant for him imprisonment, the threat of torture, danger to his own family and, finally, death. He was executed by the direct order of Heinrich Himmler in April 1945 in the Flossenburg concentration camp, only a few days before it was liberated. It was the fulfilment of what he had always believed and taught:

Suffering, then, is the badge of true discipleship. The disciple is not above his master. Following Christ means *passio passive*, suffering because we have to suffer. That is why Luther reckoned suffering among the marks of the true Church, and one of the memoranda drawn up in preparation for the Augsburg Confession similarly defined the Church as the community of those 'who are persecuted and martyred for the gospel's sake' . . . Discipleship means allegiance to the sufferings of Christ, and it is therefore not at all surprising that Christians should be called upon to suffer. In fact, it is a joy and a token of his grace.

GOD SUFFERS IN OUR SUFFERINGS

David Watson explains very vividly how God remains with us even in the midst of persecution.

God never promises to save us from adversity, only to be with us in the midst of it. Richard Wurmbrand is a Romanian pastor who endured fourteen years in various Communist prisons, where he was repeatedly tortured for his faith in Christ. 'They broke four vertebrae in my back and many other bones. They carved me in a dozen places. They burned me and cut eighteen holes in my body.' For three years he was in solitary confinement thirty feet below ground level, during which time the only persons he saw were his torturers. In despair he asked God to speak to him, to say something to him. At that moment he heard a terrible piercing cry. It was from another unfortunate victim who was being tortured. But Wurmbrand heard it as a cry from God's heart. God was revealing what he felt like when he saw his children in pain. 'In all their affliction he was afflicted' (Isaiah 63:9). God shares in our suffering. . . William Temple once put it like this: '"There cannot be a God of love," men say, "because if there was, and he looked upon the world, his heart would break." The Church points to the Cross and says, "It did break." "It is God who made the world," men say. "It is he who should bear the load." The Church points to the Cross and says, "He did bear it." Although Christ has suffered once-for-all on the cross for our sins, he still today weeps with those who weep, he feels our pain and enters into our sorrows with his compassionate love.[8]

PERSECUTION APPARENTLY ON THE INCREASE TODAY

Christians have not been alone. Jews, for example, have suffered outrageously. But Christians have certainly borne a large share of persecution, torture and martyrdom down the ages. And it is reckoned that there have been more people martyrd for their faith in Christ during this last decade than ever before, and that something like one Christian dies for his or her faith every minute of the day.[9]

I also have here on my desk a well-documented global review of the active persecution of Christians since the beginning of this third millennium. This is intended for submission to the parliamentarians of the UK, members of the European parliament, the United Nations and national and international religious leaders. It is entitled *Persecution of Christians Today – The Price of Faith*, and is published by the Maranatha Community.[10] It seeks justice for all, irrespec-

---

[8] David Watson, *Fear No Evil* (Hodder & Stoughton, 1984), p. 136.

[9] Readers can update themselves on the current occurrences of Christians being persecuted around the world by subscribing to the magazine *Response – a voice of the voiceless*, sponsored by Christian Solidarity Worldwide, which is dedicated to justice, freedom, peace and hope in the world today. Also by subscribing to *Witness – the Voice of the Persecuted Church*, founded by Richard Wurmbrand, obtainable from Release International, PO Box 54, Orpington, Kent, BRS 9RT, UK.

[10] UK Office, 102 Irlam Road, Manchester, M41 6JT.

tive of their religious or political convictions and practices. The evidence is carefully documented and each incident dated. Sadly the publication provides ample proof that persecution all round the world is by no means abating.

THE OTHER SIDE OF MARTYRDOM

The rabbi Joseph B. Soloveitchik writes, 'Suffering comes to ennoble man, to purge his thoughts of pride and superficiality, to expand his horizons. In sum the purpose of suffering is to repair that which is faulty in a man's personality.'[11]

'What is needed', writes Charlie Cleverly, 'is a resurrection of the spirit of the witnesses/martyrs. I believe God wants to call forth the truth of the martyrs and the courage of the martyrs and the sacrificial love of the martyrs.'[12]

Brother Yun, a one-time house church leader in China who was three times imprisoned and tortured for his faith, is much maligned and misrepresented even today. He welcomed persecution and imprisonment for Christ's sake. He said, 'Don't even pray for our release until we have completed what the Lord has put us in prison to do for him.'

William Booth appealed to his friends to consider those who had given up their lives for the faith:

What about these heroic spirits? What about those faces that look at you today through the blinding smoke and those devouring flames? Look again at those martyr-men. They

---

[11] Quoted in Harold S. Kushner, *When Bad Things Happen to Good People* (Pan, 2002), p. 28.

[12] Charlie Cleverly, *The Passion that Shapes Nations* (Kingsway, 2005), p. 17.

stood up before heaven and earth, and spoke in the loudest language that can be spoken for the truth and love and cause of Jesus Christ.

Dwight L. Moody was once asked if he had the grace to be martyred: 'No,' he replied. 'At the moment I am building a church in Chicago and I need the grace for that. If and when the time comes for martyrdom, then I trust and pray that God will give me the grace for that.'

A CONJECTURE

I have never heard this discussed, nor have I consciously read anything anywhere to back it up, which I am sure must reveal my ignorance as much as anything, but some of the sufferings appear so unbearable, and the martyrs' demeanour seems so calm and composed throughout the whole ordeal, that one is prompted to wonder if any of the martyred were granted the mercy of some divine alleviation from the awful pain. Could they have been granted some heavenly anaesthesia to deaden to some degree the most horrific sufferings endured in the cause of witnessing to God?

Three of Daniel's Jewish colleagues survived Nebuchadnezzar's fiery furnace when even the soldiers who threw them into it were burned up by the sheer heat. Their bodies were not harmed, nor was their hair singed. Their clothes were not scorched, nor was there even the smell of fire on them when they came out of the fire *(Daniel 3:19–27)*. There was certainly a divine intervention of some sort in those circumstances.

If Moody anticipated grace to help him in such a crisis, and if Scripture encourages us to ask for grace to help in time of need, then maybe sometimes God does grant a degree of numbness through the ordeal. How else could Archbishop Cranmer have offered his hand for the flames after he retracted his recantation, crying serenely, 'For as much as my hand offended, writing contrary to my heart, my hand shall be punished'? And as the fire around him began to lick up the faggots, he stretched out this offending member to the flames and held it steadily (except when he used it to wipe his face). Onlookers saw how his hand was burned before his body appeared to be touched. Burning one's flesh is acutely painful. His eyes were lifted up, and often he repeated 'This unworthy right hand!' and, so long as he was able, he repeated the words of the first martyr Stephen, 'Lord Jesus, receive my spirit . . . I see heaven open and Jesus standing at the right hand of God' *(cf. Acts 7:56)*.

Without trying to diminish his bravery in the least, this must be one of those times where God's promise through Isaiah had a literal fulfilment in some way: *'When you walk through the fire, you will not be burned' (Isaiah 43:2c)*.

In another account, a Chinese brother called Gui was horribly kicked and battered by a river's edge for his faithful preaching of the gospel.

Although brother Gui could hear them beating him, *he felt no pain whatsoever.* He was prostrated on the ground and he cried out, 'Lord, their feet have trodden on your head and their fists have beaten your body, for you have used your hands to protect me.' Without a doubt, if it were not for the Lord's protection, even if he [Gui] had a body of steel and bones of iron, he would have been beaten to pulp.[13]

---

[13] Danyun, *Lilies amongst Thorns*, p. 172.

When the first Ugandan martyrs were trussed and bound up in rush mats, and then fed onto the fire like so many logs, a godly guide heard them testify aloud to the 'coolness of the flames and to the waterfall that refreshed them as they died'.[14] It was not the same for all, however. Nicholas Ridley is said to have screamed to passers-by 'to pull off some of the wood' as he was burning at the stake.

I am not here suggesting that any form of alleviation was granted to Christ to diminish his suffering on the cross for our sins. Indeed, he deliberately refused anything to kill the pain. At one stage, as he was being crucified, the soldiers offered him wine to drink, mingled with gall – perhaps for that purpose; but when he had tasted it, he would not drink it (cf. Mark 15:23; Matthew 27:34). It was probably common practice for soldiers charged with the awful business of crucifixion to offer the victim something to deaden the pain, but Jesus refused. He knew he must drink the cup of divine wrath for our sins to the dregs. It is quite possible, however, that other Christian martyrs being crucified would have welcomed any painkilling drink on offer at such an awful moment.

Apart from the refining processes through any suffering for Christians, the process of excruciating martyrdom has been a unique way of reflecting the eternal glory of God in many places at unusual times. Any such triumphant martyrdoms must ever be a sign and a wonder to a world looking on.

---

[14] Cleverly, *The Passion that Shapes Nations*, p. 102.

PROMISED REWARD

. . .theirs is the kingdom of heaven. (Matthew 5:10)

'You have saved the best till now' . . . He thus revealed his glory.
(John 2:10–11)

Anton Chekhov has a scene in one of his plays where everyone has an apprehension that change may never come: 'You realise you're waiting for something to happen,' says one. 'Half the time you don't even know what it is. You're waiting for the next stage. Then in the end you realise there isn't a next stage. This is all there is.' I include this quote of hopelessness to contrast with the 'glory that shall be revealed'. Chekhov is by no means alone.

Lord Boothby once said that 'the idea of a spiritual Boothby sitting on a cloud, strumming a harp for ever and ever, had . . . limited appeal'. How tragic to conjure up a parody of glory and then discard it as of 'limited appeal'. But his picture is not one we ever see in the Bible. 'His Lordship' could have had no idea what the kingdom of heaven would be like. Had he listened to Paul, citing the Old Testament, he would have known that *'"No eye has seen, no ear has heard, no mind has conceived what God has prepared for those who love him" – but God has revealed it to us by his Spirit' (1 Corinthians 2:9–10).*

In concluding his biography, Selwyn Hughes, who had already lost his wife and only two sons, was waiting for advancing prostate cancer to claim his dying body. He wrote:

I find the thought that Christ has prepared a place for me tremendously moving (cf John 14:2–3). Some time ago I walked into a crowded meeting room and I was wondering whether I would find a seat, when someone said, 'Sit here, Selwyn. I have saved a place for you.' It was a wonderful feeling that someone had thought about me enough to keep a place for me. There is a place reserved for me in heaven. I won't have to scramble for it. It is waiting for me and I have no doubt I will be led to it by the Lord Himself.[15]

In C. S. Lewis's book *The Last Battle*, the children find themselves once again in Narnia. But when Aslan asks them why they look sad, they say it is because they always have to go back to their lives on earth. 'No fear of that,' says Aslan this time. And they realise that they have died in the train crash and they really are in Narnia to stay. C. S. Lewis goes on to say,

But for them it was only the beginning of the real story. All their life in this world and all their adventures in Narnia had only been the cover and the title page: now at last they were beginning Chapter One of the Great Story which no one on earth has read: which goes on for ever: in which every chapter is better than the one before.[16]

King David expressed his confidence and hope as an inheritor, by God's grace, of the kingdom of heaven, with the unforgettable words:

> *Surely goodness and love will follow me*
> *all the days of my life,*
> *and I will dwell in the house of the Lord*
> *for ever.*
> *(Psalm 23:6)*

---

[15] Selwyn Hughes, *My Story* (CWR, 2005), p.383.
[16] C. S. Lewis, *The Last Battle* (Bodley Head, 1956), pp. 183–4.

The reward for those who have remained faithful, in spite of their sufferings, has been confirmed to them by their inheritance in/of the kingdom of heaven.

This is the second time in these Beatitudes that Jesus has assured his disciples of their place in the kingdom of God. It is the same reward as that which was promised in the first beatitude, to the *'poor in spirit'* in Matthew 5:3. This glorious promise begins and ends the range of rewards promised by Christ in the Beatitudes.

> *Then I heard what sounded like a great multitude, like the roar of rushing waters and like loud peals of thunder, shouting:*
>
> > *'Hallelujah!*
> >
> > > *For our Lord God Almighty reigns.*
> >
> > *Let us rejoice and be glad*
> > > *and give him glory.*
> >
> > *For the wedding of the Lamb has come,*
> > > *and his bride has made herself ready.*
> >
> > *Fine linen, bright and clean,*
> > > *was given her to wear.'*
> >
> > *(Fine linen stands for the righteous acts of the saints.)*
>
> *Then the angel said to me, 'Write: "Blessed are those who are invited to the wedding supper of the Lamb!"' (Revelation 19:6–9)*

> *Then I saw a new heaven and a new earth, for the first heaven and the first earth had passed away, and there was no longer any sea. I saw the Holy City, the new Jerusalem, coming down out of heaven from God, prepared as a bride beautifully dressed for her husband. And I heard a loud voice from the throne saying, 'Now the dwelling of God is with men, and he will live with them. They will be his people, and God himself will be with them and be their God. He will wipe every tear from their eyes. There will be no more death or mourning or crying or pain, for the old order of things has passed away.'*

He who was seated on the throne said, 'I am making everything new!' Then he said, 'Write this down, for these words are trustworthy and true.'

He said to me: 'It is done. I am the Alpha and the Omega, the Beginning and the End. To him who is thirsty I will give to drink without cost from the spring of the water of life. He who overcomes will inherit all this, and I will be his God and he will be my son . . .' (Revelation 21:1–7)

MEDITATION

When I tried to understand all this,
it was oppressive to me
till I entered into the sanctuary of God;
then I understood.
(Psalm 73:16)

* * *

I . . . heard a voice say to me, 'Saul! Saul! Why do you persecute me?'
'Who are you, Lord?' I asked.
'I am Jesus of Nazareth, whom you are persecuting,' he replied.
(Acts 22:7–8)

* * *

Blessed are you when people insult you, persecute you and falsely say all kinds of evil against you because of me. Rejoice and be glad, because great is your reward in heaven, for in the same way they persecuted the prophets who were before you. (Matthew 5:11–12)

* * *

We are considered as sheep to be slaughtered. (Romans 8:36)

* * *

I consider that our present sufferings are not worth comparing with the glory that will be revealed in us. The creation waits in eager expectation for the sons of God to be revealed. (Romans 8:18)

* * *

We are hard pressed on every side, but not crushed; perplexed, but not in despair; persecuted, but not abandoned; struck down, but not destroyed. (2 Corinthians 4:8–9)

* * *

Who shall separate us from the love of Christ? Shall trouble or hardship or persecution or famine or nakedness or danger or sword? As it is written,
   'For your sake we face death all day long;
   we are considered as sheep to be slaughtered.'
No, in all these things we are more than conquerors through him who loved us. For I am convinced that neither death nor life, neither angels nor demons, neither the present nor the future, nor any powers, neither height nor depth, nor anything else in all creation, will be able to separate us from the love of God that is in Christ Jesus our Lord. (Romans 8:35–39)

* * *

He did not say, 'You will never have a rough passage, you will never be over-strained, you will never feel uncomfortable,' but he did say, 'You will overcome.' (Julian of Norwich, 1342–1416)

* * *

Our flesh will be the threshing floor
for the move of God we're praying for.
(Kevin Prosch)

* * *

Hast thou no scar?
No hidden scar on foot, or side, or hand?
I hear thee sung as mighty in the land;
I hear them hail thy bright ascendant star;
Hast thou no scar?

Hast thou no wound?
Yet I was wounded by the archers, spent;
Leaned me against a tree to die; and, rent
By ravening beasts that compassed Me, I swooned:
Hast *thou* no wound?

No wound? No scar?
Yet, as the master shall the servant be,
And pierced are the feet that follow Me;
But thine are whole: can he have followed far
Who has nor wound nor scar?
(Amy Carmichael)

* * *

Hard it is, very hard,
To travel up the slow and stony road
To Calvary, to redeem mankind; far better
To make one resplendent miracle,
Lean through the cloud, lift the right hand of power,
And with a sudden lightning smite the world perfect!
Yet this was not God's way, who had the power,
But set it by, choosing the cross, the thorn,
The sorrowing wounds. Something there is, perhaps,
That power destroys in passing, something supreme,
To whose great value in the eyes of God
That cross, that thorn, and those five wounds
bear witness.[17]

---

[17] Dorothy Sayers, quoted in Laurence Field, *Journey to Easter* (Augsburg Publishing House, 1958), p. 17.

* * *

Pastor Wurmbrand reckoned that the phrase 'Do not be afraid' occurred 366 times in the Bible. 'How like God,' he mused. 'That's one "Fear not" for every day of the year – including leap year!'

* * *

Jesus' Prayer in Gethsemane

> Father, if you are willing,
> Take this cup from me,
> Yet not my will, but yours be done.

Conclusion

As we have already seen, these Beatitudes represent the core teaching of Jesus with regard to character for his disciples. He indicates the basic attitudes to be cultivated by those who are entering his kingdom. They are attitudes that result in actions which serve to glorify God and bless the world. A recent programme on the biography channel reflected on the life of a famous film star, Audrey Hepburn, who spent her last years working for UNICEF – visiting war-stricken, drought-stricken, famine-stricken children across the world. After her death in the 1990s another actor, Harry Belafonte, drew attention to this wonderful sacrificial work and followed it with the remark, 'I think that a lot of people drew sustenance from that.' Indeed acts of goodness, kindness and mercy are always an inspiration and bring hope to others who experience them, see them or read about them.

EACH BEATITUDE BUILDS ON A PREVIOUS ONE

Taking a progressive view of each beatitude we see how *poverty of spirit* (a broken heart) is foundational. All the rest is built up on this. Then *mourning* brings empathy with God, which leads on naturally into *meekness*, and that changes completely the way we respond to life. From this standpoint seeking to keep *right* with God and seeing right being done to others becomes an increasing preoccupation.

This leads on to being forgiving and *merciful* to others as God has been merciful to us. We become increasingly aware of the need for self-control to enable us to keep close to God – to be *pure* and holy. Walking in purity and peace with God, we want to be like our Father in heaven, to keep the *peace* and to keep making peace.

Having travelled thus far along the Lord's highway (for highway it is) our faith becomes so emboldened and our love for God so expanded as to make us almost uncomfortably aware of an other-worldly authority about us. This can unwittingly become a disconcerting challenge to the world, especially for the powers-that-be. If the world could crucify the harmless and innocent Son of God, who personally exemplified the Beatitudes (and the world has done just that) then we should not be surprised if we too experience opposition, *persecution* and suffering for being on his side. Indeed being sent forth into the world by the Lord *'like lambs among wolves' (Luke 10:3)* inevitably spells out our vulnerability as witnesses for Christ. Wolves are not generally very kind to lambs! Yes, the risks are indeed great, but the rewards are greater.

No man can ever take from the blessing of the Beatitudes. 'It transforms the curses and troubles of this world into challenges and blessing. It becomes the heart of our faith.'[1] It is no wonder they are such a vital part of the teaching of Jesus.

---

[1] John Michael Talbot, *Blessings* (St Paul Publications, 1991), p.130.

These Beatitudes are among the literary and religious treasures of the human race. Along with the Ten Commandments, the twenty-third Psalm, the Lord's Prayer, and a very few other passages in the Bible, they are acknowledged by almost everyone to be among the highest expressions of religious insight and moral inspiration. We can savour them, affirm them, and engrave them on plaques to hang on our walls, but a major question remains: How are we to live in response to them?[2]

Simon Guillebaud has a comment which serves well to sum up why Jesus prioritised the Beatitudes:

People are not attracted by the hypocrisy of Sunday religion; they want the reality of a consistent and dynamic 24-7 relationship which transcends suffocating pressures and ambitions of day-to-day existence. Often our problem is not that we are living in the wrong place – rather we are not living out the reality of our faith where we are.[3]

God blesses us as we press on in life being shaped by these Beatitudes, and if we faithlessly and carelessly discard opportunity after opportunity, moment after moment, as not being the 'right' occasion or time to do this, we will have no other place or chance to receive the kingdom into our life. For those situations and those moments are our life.

Of course, these Beatitudes were very necessary for the leadership team Jesus was developing – his apostles – and indeed, are vital for all his church leaders of the future, so that they may each model them and pass them on to the newest converts.

---

[2] Dallas Willard, *The Divine Conspiracy* (Fount, 1998), p.112.
[3] Simon Guillebaud, *For What It's Worth* (Monarch, 2006), p.18.

(1) *Poverty of spirit* creates the true heart for *evangelism*, which has been defined as 'one poor beggar telling another poor beggar where to find bread'.

(2) *Mourning* is basic training for *prayer warriors*, or *intercessors*. Grief is the great enabler for sensing God's heart on a matter.

(3) *Meekness* is fundamental to *leadership*. Moses, about the best leader the world has ever known, was renowned for one thing – his meekness.

(4) A dedication to *righteousness* forms the heart of the *preacher* and the *prophet*.

(5) Learning to be *merciful* involves commitment to *love, forgiveness, stewardship* and *service* to others.

(6) The commitment of oneself to *purity* produces the hallmark of integrity and saintliness.

(7) A basic role in any community is *peacemaking*.

(8) *Suffering* has always been a basic element in the divine training programme for *character formation* – it was for Jesus (who was made perfect through suffering – Hebrews 2:10) and for his disciples. This often includes persecution, and sometimes ends in martyrdom – it did for Jesus, and for most of his apostles.

God's Priorities

Living the Lord's Prayer in the 21st Century

---

by J. John

Prayer shapes our lives. Through prayer we come to know the all-powerful God and who he is. Through prayer we allow God to direct our lives. The need to pray seems to be built into the heart of all human beings. So it was natural for Jesus' followers to ask him to teach them how to pray.

This book has been written for four groups of people:

- those who have just made a decision to follow Jesus
- those who have come back to faith after a time away from God
- those who know the Lord's Prayer but who feel they want to get to know and use it better
- those who are searching for God and feel that this prayer is a good way to start

Kingsway

Ten

Living the Ten Commandments in the 21st Century

---

by J. John

Imagine a world where people loved each other. What would it look like? How would people behave towards one another?

J. John explores an ancient code of behaviour that provides a window on life as it should be—life as it could be—where respect for others and for God determines everything we do.

The name that code normally goes by is the Ten Commandments. But be prepared for a few surprises.

'You will not be able to put it down . . .'

—ANDY REED
MP for Loughborough

'Christian teaching at its very best . . .'

—RABBI DR JEREMY ROSEN

 **Kingsway**

Surprised by the Voice of God

by Jack Deere

This book is written for ordinary Christians who want to hear God's voice above the clamour of everyday life. The still, small voice of God that spoke to Elijah in the cave is far more powerful than tradition or circumstance. But how do we tell when it is God speaking to us, and not our emotions, or the opinions of others, or even dark spiritual forces?

Jack Deere brings together inspiring stories from people who have learned to trust God's voice today, his own experiences in teaching and pastoral ministry, and mature biblical teaching—all of which can help us to understand the Bible and to hear from God both for ourselves and for those to whom we minister.

'Jack Deere has done it again. If anything, this volume is more compelling than the previous work, *Surprised by the Power of the Spirit.*'

—R T KENDALL

'Packed with gripping illustration, this classic has been written by a theologian to help the common man. It is full of practical wisdom and biblical insight. Those who "covet to prophesy", or to understand more about prophecy, will want to sell their beds to buy this book. Once started, the reader will be impelled to read right through.'

—DAVID PYTCHES

 Kingsway

Surprised by the Power of the Spirit

Jack Deere

'*Narrative theology at its best.*'
—GORDON D. FEE
Professor of New Testament,
Regent College

What caused a professor in a conservative evangelical theological college to change his mind about the Holy Spirit so radically that he had to leave?

Jack Deere explains how he came to believe in signs and wonders for today. In so doing he provides a profound biblical apologetic, arguing courteously for the view that the Holy Spirit's supernatural gifts did not cease in New Testament times. His careful work will serve Christians on both sides of the debate, as he marks out pitfalls which threaten to hinder the present-day supernatural ministry of the Holy Spirit.

'*Solidly anchored in the Bible.*'
—WAYNE GRUDEM
Professor of Biblical and
Systematic Theology,
Trinity Evangelical Divinity School

 **Kingsway**